THE NEW MIDDLE AGES

BONNIE WHEELER, *Series Editor*

The New Middle Ages is a series dedicated to transdisciplinary studies of medieval cultures, with particular emphasis on recuperating women's history and on feminist and gender analyses. This peer-reviewed series includes both scholarly monographs and essay collections.

PUBLISHED BY PALGRAVE:

CULTURAL DIVERSITY IN THE BRITISH MIDDLE AGES

ARCHIPELAGO, ISLAND, ENGLAND

Edited by
Jeffrey Jerome Cohen

CULTURAL DIVERSITY IN THE BRITISH MIDDLE AGES
Copyright © Jeffrey Jerome Cohen, 2008.

First published in 2008 by
PALGRAVE MACMILLAN®
in the US—a division of St. Martin's Press LLC,
175 Fifth Avenue, New York, NY 10010.

Where this book is distributed in the UK, Europe and the rest of the world,
this is by Palgrave Macmillan, a division of Macmillan Publishers Limited,
registered in England, company number 785998, of Houndmills,
Basingstoke, Hampshire RG21 6XS.

Palgrave Macmillan is the global academic imprint of the above companies
and has companies and representatives throughout the world.

Palgrave® and Macmillan® are registered trademarks in the United States,
the United Kingdom, Europe and other countries.

ISBN-13: 978–0–230–60326–4
ISBN-10: 0–230–60326–2

Library of Congress Cataloging-in-Publication Data is available from the
Library of Congress.

A catalogue record of the book is available from the British Library.

Design by Newgen Imaging Systems (P) Ltd., Chennai, India.

First edition: August 2008

10 9 8 7 6 5 4 3 2 1

Printed in the United States of America.

CONTENTS

ACKNOWLEDGMENTS

This book is the fourth I have published in the New Middle Ages series. I once again recognize that the volume would not have been possible without the enduring and indefatigable support of Bonnie Wheeler. She is truly a force of nature.

My thinking on this project has been influenced profoundly by my co-bloggers and our commentariat at In the Middle <jjcohen.blogspot.com>. I especially thank Eileen Joy, Karl Steel, Mary Kate Hurley, Liza Blake, Sylvia Huot, Holly Crocker, Michael O'Rourke, Dan Remein, and Sarah Rees Jones. My gratitude goes as well to the many students who sat through graduate seminars with names like "The Archipelago of England" and "Fantasies of the Aboriginal." This book owes much to our communal explorations. My colleagues in the English Department at the George Washington University have inspired me with their own transnational obsessions: Gayle Wald, Jim Miller, Holly Dugan, Lee Salamon, Jonathan Hsy, Antonio Lopez, Patty Chu, Robert McRuer, Jennifer James, Tara Wallace, Kavita Daiya, Lowell Duckert, Mike Smith, Judith Plotz, and (especially) the inimitable Gil Harris. Audiences at the following institutions welcomed and provoked me in ways that have left deep imprints on this project: American University, Hamilton College, Cornell University, Dartmouth College, the University of Rochester, and Harvard University. I'd especially like to thank Madhavi Menon, Michael Wenthe, Katherine Terrell, Alfred Siewers, George Edmundson, Peter Travis, Thomas Hahn, and Dan Donoghue. My deep gratitude to Lowell Duckert for creating this volume's index, and to Maran Elancheran for shepherding the book through production with characteristic charm. Finally, I am deeply grateful to the contributors to this volume for their passion, their patience, and their scholarship. It has been a joy to collaborate with them.

This volume is offered in memory of R.R. Davies, whose challenge to rethink Britain in non-Anglocentric terms has been inspirational to all of us.

INTRODUCTION: INFINITE REALMS

Jeffrey Jerome Cohen

An alium orbem somniat infinita regna habentem?

[Is he dreaming of another world containing kingdoms without number?]

—William of Newburgh, *History of English Affairs* (1.Prologue)

Other Worlds

Medieval Welsh and Irish texts offer stories of realms that exist in strange contiguity to everyday life, domains often entered through a hill or barrow that seem to be of two worlds at once. The Welsh otherworld of Annwn finds its gateway at Gorsedd Arberth, a mound atop which adventurers like Pwyll sit seeking wonders. In the account of Cú Chulainn's love for Fand, queen of the mysterious and aboriginal Irish people known as the *sídhe*, the hero enters a parallel universe through a nondescript tumulus. *The Wasting Sickness of Cú Chulainn and the Only Jealousy of Emer* [*Serglige Con Culainn ocus Óenét Emire*] describes the uncanny beings inhabiting this domain as differing from contemporary islanders in their customs, elder history, and potency in magic. Cú Chulainn is cured of self-destructive love for his Fairy Queen only through the intervention of an oblivion spell: he must forget the riches of her world to reinhabit his own. Like many Irish and Welsh stories involving hills as portals, the dominant narrative of *The Wasting Sickness of Cú Chulainn* seems to enfold within it an untold story about the belatedness of a people to the land they possess, figuring the territory's earlier inhabitants as an inhuman race whose traces are dwindling, whose presence lingers as if at dimming twilight.

Oddly enough, a gateway to such an Other World once opened in a mound in twelfth-century Yorkshire. The English historian William of Newburgh describes the circumstances. As an unnamed nocturnal traveler returned home, he found his journey interrupted when song resounded from what had until that moment been a familiar landmark:

> A countryman from this hamlet had gone to meet a friend staying in the next village. He was returning late at night a little drunk, when suddenly from a hillock close by…he heard voices singing, as though people were feasting in celebration.[1]

William assures us that this tumulus is quite near his own birthplace, that he has seen it numerous times himself. On this particular night a door into the mound has opened [in latere tumuli januam patentem] to reveal a celebration in progress:

> He approached and looked inside. Before his eyes was a large, well-lit dwelling crowded with men and women reclining at table as at a formal feast. One of the servants noticed him standing at the door, and offered him a cup.

Not the most polite guest, the man pours away the libation and flees to his village, clutching the empty goblet. The revelers pursue, eager to regain their stolen cup, but cannot overtake his horse.

The purloined vessel is described as mysterious in every way, "of unknown material, unusual color, and strange shape" [vasculum materiae incognitae, coloris insoliti, et formae inusitate]. The treasure is eventually bestowed upon King Henry as a gift, and then from the king of England passes to his brother-in-law, David King of Scots, and thence to Henry II. The goblet circulates from the enigmatic mound dwellers to an unnamed Englishman to a succession of regents (Anglo-Norman to Anglo-Scottish to Anglo-Angevin). Yet the vessel's path is determined not by some weighty history behind its fabrication (this is not the Grail, moving through a world it shapes), but via its inert status as mere curiosity. Through theft, the cup of unknown material becomes divorced from its history, becomes an object existing for an uncomprehending present. The goblet is transformed from the key to another world to a deracinated souvenir of some vaguely exotic elsewhere.[2] The feast once refused recedes from memory, taking with it the story of that community glimpsed within a now permanently inscrutable mound. A space unanticipated and entrancing, a space animated by a story that remains unspoken, dwindles once more into a lifeless curve of grass and dirt.

What would happen, though, if the tipsy English traveler had joined the celebration inside the tumulus rather than stolen its tableware and fled? Having stumbled across a queer intrusion into his accustomed ambit, could he have accepted its unlooked for invitation to conviviality? What would have come to pass had the man risked conversation with the subterranean congregants, if one of these amiable revelers had spoken the tale of who they were and what they honored at their elegant repast? Whose history would this mound-dweller narrate? Barely glimpsed by a passerby who preferred the security of his village over the incongruity of the enclosed feast, this history would likely be very different from the narrative William of Newburgh otherwise composes.

For William, too, refuses the invitation from the tumulus, discerning at the far side of the mound's open door a lost tale rather than a living one. A Yorkshire man for whom the earthwork had been a quotidian boyhood sight, William is an author proudly English. At the beginning of his work he states flatly that he composes "historiam gentis nostrae, id est Anglorum" [a history of our race, that is, the English] (1.Prologue). The Britons who had held the island long before "our race" arrived are, in his account, barbarians whose displacement was both necessary and just. The Irish, a people whose territories England was energetically annexing as William wrote, are likewise "uncivilized and barbarous."[3] For William of Newburgh insular history belongs exclusively to England. Anyone who insists otherwise—say, Geoffrey of Monmouth in his spectacular *History of the Kings of Britain,* a resolutely non-anglocentric account of the island's past—is ridiculously "dreaming of another world containing king-doms without number" [alium orbem somniat infinita regna habentem] (1.Prologue). Writing six decades after Geoffrey, William chronicles the story of a homogenized world containing precisely one realm, England.

Geoffrey had provocatively described a Britain possessed of so deep and so extensive a history that the Saxons, the progenitors of the con-temporary English, became parvenus, mere interlopers. Long before glorious monarchs like Alfred and Athelstan reigned, according to the *History of the Kings of Britain,* the Briton heroes Brutus, Brennius, and Arthur flourished, achieving in their centuries of insular rule martial feats unparalleled in what suddenly became a brief English history. Yet despite William's vitriol for Geoffrey's proliferative vision, despite his dismissal of Geoffrey's Arthurian history as mendacity, as a space oneiric rather than factual, William's *History of English Affairs* features a hillock that beckons with open doorway, the portal to another realm. The stately feast beheld within the tumulus transforms the mound from a local land-mark of no great significance to an alien interstice quite unlike the mun-dane expanses that surround its rise.

Had the celebrants of the mound's underground celebration been invited to speak their history, the narrative they would likely tell might reveal the difference between stories of England and stories of Britain, between the attenuated narrative of a kingdom that masqueraded as the entirety of an island and the histories of a tempestuous world too vast, too motley, too entangled within an archipelago of other realms to be so reduced.

Archipelago, Island, England

"British History has been much in the air of late," R.R. Davies observed two decades ago, "but it still seems strangely reluctant to come down."[4] Davies worried that embracing the label "British History" had enabled English historians to "confess their anglocentricity without performing practical penance," a state of affairs made no better by the fact that historians of Wales, Scotland, and Ireland often seemed "intent on cultivating their own corners" instead of adopting a more capacious, more gregarious mode. To move from England to Britain without sacrificing the diversity of the latter to an imagined uniformity in the former is, admittedly, not easy to accomplish—especially because medieval English writers had the infuriating habit of using *Britannia* or even *totius Britanniae* as a synonym for *Anglia*. Yet the difference between an analytical frame centered around medieval England and a wider, paninsular perspective has been well illustrated by Edward James in *Britain in the First Millennium*, a work that restores multiplicity to the island by examining its history over an exceptionally *longue durée*. James writes that his expanded temporal span ("the long first millennium") enables Britain to be studied "as the whole of Britain, from Cornwall to the Shetlands, rather than (usually) England or (sometimes) Wales or Scotland." A multifarious agent enmeshed within—indeed, inextricable from—a wide and volatile European context, Britain thereby becomes something more than "a self-sufficient island occasionally invaded or visited as if by aliens from another world."[5] Similarly, Barry Cunliffe assembles a vast sweep of cultures into a heterogeneous, enduring alliance he calls "the peoples of the long Atlantic façade of Europe." By resisting the impulse to linguistic segregation, Cunliffe is able to map how the shared experience of living between land and sea gathers seemingly disparate groups into a maritime network of unceasing interaction, shared experience, and cultural interchange, an Atlantic identity as evident in Norman conquistadors as in the Neolithic peoples of the southern British coast.[6] Both James and Cunliffe make clear the critical gains that accrue through the adoption of this transnational compass, especially when it takes as its point of departure a lively archipelago in constant and transformative contact with a far-extending world.

Most influential among medievalists attempting to emplace the insular Middle Ages within more capacious analytical frames has been the late R.R. Davies. His far-reaching work details how a restless expanse of islands contracted over time into the four well-delimited geopolitical entities we know today. In a vivid account of this long process of materialization and separation, Davies observes that countries do not descend fully formed from heaven but are

> shaped and reshaped here on earth by the stratagems of men and the victories of the fortuitous. But once they take root and are bolstered by the habits and mechanisms of unity and by a common mythology, they soon acquire an image, if not of immemoriality, at least of almost inevitable and organic development.[7]

"England," "Scotland," "Wales," and "Ireland" are not natural or even especially obvious partitions of the islands. Quadripartite division is the culmination of centuries of antagonism and alliance that could very well have produced a profoundly different configuration. The hard work of forging fate out of the vagaries of fortune, of creating circumscribed nations and discrete peoples from the sheer messiness of history, usually proceeds retroactively, positing in the past the unchanging solidities desired in the present. Patricia Ingham captures this process with eloquence when she writes:

> The nation is always an illusion, a fantasy of wholeness that threatens again and again to fragment from the inside out. Fantasies of national identity teach peoples to desire union; they help inculcate in a populace the apparent "truth" that unity, regulation, coordination, and wholeness are always better, more satisfying, and more fascinating, than the alternatives. Yet in order to promote desires for national unity, the nation, its core identity, must appear always to have been there, poised to fascinate its people, and ready to be desired.[8]

Whether within the parameters of nation, city, race, or some other solidarity, this desire for unity is frequently engendered through narrative. When examining or imagining the past, such discourses typically assume that when events take one of many possible turns, then that outcome was predestined, even providential. Colin Richmond, contemplating the expulsion of the Jews from England in 1290, writes of the "terrible and terrifying habit of viewing the past as inevitable."[9] When history is taken as a record of what *had* to happen, when texts record as inexorable the emergence of a nation and the abjection of other peoples, the composition of history and the fashioning of narrative can become exercises in justification and excuse-making rather than the opening up of the past to its fullest potentiality. To quote Davies once more, just because four well-bounded countries occupied Britain and Ireland by the end of the Middle Ages, "it need not, of course, have been so."[10]

A similar mixture of chance and strategy accounts for the genesis of the communal identities of the peoples dwelling on these islands in the Middle Ages. None had necessarily to recognize themselves as constituting a distinct community, as a people set solidly apart from other island dwellers. The fact that they did so should not obscure the contingencies behind the emergence of these separations, the ample potential that existed for history to have unfolded otherwise. Collective names can have profound historical effects, especially as categories humans deploy against each other or to delimit their own identities. Yet despite the stories such peoples tell themselves and announce to others, these groups typically possess limited internal homogeneity, and are never endowed with some core essence immune to historical change. Though nationalistic dreams posit enduring racial groups like the Romans, the English, the Welsh, or the Jews, intermingling and mutability are in fact human constants.[11] Collective identities and "distinct" cultures are the lively products of accreted and unstable hybridities. They are never as stable, enduring, or discrete as they make themselves out to be. When communal identities are built upon the embrace of a single language, culture, and history, then variation and diversity can be difficult to discern. Yet heterogeneity and excluded difference lurk, banished perhaps to dwell underground and out of sight, but surfacing irregularly and sometimes in surprising forms.

Britain had once been part of an island chain as enmeshed with Ireland and Scandinavia as with Europe and the Mediterranean. It was once an expanse that, as William of Newburgh feared, did consist of *infinita regna* [endless realms]. This multiplicity of dominions varied in size, stability, duration, and cultural composition. Though the island of Britain eventually came to be dominated by a single one of its kingdoms, this ascendant England never did fully absorb or anglicize the hybridity, the obdurate, and enduring differences out of which it had been formed.

The Infinite Realms Project

Though their authors invoke many recent critics for their inspiration, the chapters in *Cultural Diversity in the British Middle Ages* build upon a long scholarly tradition of employing commodious frames for the study of what otherwise might be seen as isolated national literatures. Working almost a century ago, Roger Sherman Loomis could be said to be the first modern postcolonial theorist of the British Isles, arguing that English romance had absorbed (none too graciously) much of its material from Irish, Scottish, and Welsh sources, and implicitly linking this incorporation to the kingdom's cultural conquest of its Celtic Fringe.[12] Over time medievalists have refined such study of cultural imperialism and commingling, stressing the uneven arrangements of power inherent in cultural contact. This volume is in fact something of a companion to *The Postcolonial Middle Ages*, a collection of essays that attempted to emplace medieval texts within the context of a heterogeneous and self-divided world stretching from Britain to the shores of the Mediterranean.[13] Our mission here is likewise that of provincializing England (to play upon the title of Dipesh Chakrabarty's *Provincializing Europe*), of viewing the kingdom and its capital city within a lens so wide that it is no longer the world's umbilicus, but one center among many, and not necessarily the actor of greatest importance.[14]

Like more traditional scholarship in medieval studies, much postcolonial medieval analysis has tended to be international in its focus, placing England within a European context. Such a perspective is invaluable, especially because through examination of the crusades (for example) its scope stretches geographically to the Levant, effectively challenging any tendency toward parochialism.[15] Yet this critical trajectory can sometimes lead too swiftly away from the archipelago where it commences. When England is tied more closely to distant nations and events than to the polities, peoples, and cultures with which the kingdom shared an island, and indeed a history, an understanding of the insular past in its full complexity can be constrained. Even in texts written within an England that might seem internally monolithic or homogenous, this book's authors find portals to strangely contiguous other worlds where recalcitrant differences, abiding possibilities, and alternative histories vivaciously endure. Francophone Normans and Jews, for example, inhabited the kingdom from the eleventh century—as did at various times Flemings, Italians, Danes, Welsh, Irish, and Scots. Though the Normans eventually assimilated into the population they had rendered subaltern in 1066, the Jews served as England's most contemplated minority population even after wholesale expulsion in 1290. Because of their religious, cultural, and (in the terms of the day) racial difference, the Jews appear in medieval English texts with an obsessive regularity out of all proportion to their actual numbers in the country. Jewish presence therefore figures large in the chapters that follow.

Since this volume undertakes to find truth in what William of Newburgh dismissed as a mere dream of an unbounded insular past, *Cultural Diversity in the British Middle Ages* could as easily have been entitled the Infinite Realms Project. Through close readings of medieval texts (some widely familiar, many less so), the contributors attempt to read England as a single—if singularly powerful—entity within a dispersive geopolitical network, within a capacious world. The contributors to this volume seek moments of cultural admixture and heterogeneity within texts that have often been assumed to belong to a single, national canon, discovering moments when familiar and bounded space erupts with *infinita regna*, kingdoms without number. This sudden door opening in a neighborhood tumulus invites those who would listen to the stories told by its subterranean congregants to hear narratives conjoining England, Britain, Sicily, Bohemia, Wales, Scotland, Normandy: other realms and other worlds.

Suzanne Conklin Akbari opens the volume with a chapter intimately connecting Anglo-Norman literature to a worldwide network of culture and power. "Between Diaspora and Conquest: Norman Assimilation in Petrus Alfonsi's *Disciplina Clericalis* and Marie de France's *Fables*" reexamines Anglo-Norman identity through the comparative study of Norman Sicily and England. Inspired by Horden and Purcell's comparative Mediterranean history, Akbari argues that peoples are best understood as participants in vast cultural flows that encompass major geographical structures. From Scandinavia in the north to the Mediterranean in the south, Norman culture of the Middle Ages was linked by sea routes that provided an economic and cultural continuity. Simultaneously, however, Norman identity evolved in dramatically different forms in France, England, Italy, and Sicily. In twelfth-century Sicily, Norman government sought to constitute a polity that sublimated ethnic and religious difference under the banner of the shared language of Arabic and a common administrative system. In twelfth-century England under Henry II, a heterogeneous collection of nations were also assimilated into a communal culture, but by very different means. Through a close reading of Petrus Alfonsi's *Disciplina Clericalis* and Marie de France's *Esope*, Akbari illustrates how the emergence of the frame tale narrative in twelfth-century Norman England mirrored forms of cultural assimilation that were simultaneously taking place. In a coda to the chapter, she considers the cultural resonance emerging from a Hebrew adaptation of Marie de France, "The Story of King Solomon's Daughter."

With "*Reliquia*: Writing Relics in Anglo-Norman Durham," Heather Blurton continues the focus upon the Normans, this time in a regional English context. Whether the poem known as *Durham* "represents the last gasp of Old English or the first breath of early Middle English" has been the central question of the text's analysis. Blurton considers this mediality from a different angle, reading the poem as a document produced in the midst of the power struggle in post-Conquest Durham: "Like an Old

English riddle that does not name its object of description, *Durham* omits mention of the city's most distinctive feature, the spectacular cathedral under construction at the moment of its composition." The poem instead describes the relics of saintly English kings, abbots, and bishops and enshrines them in a poem that is artfully crafted in Anglo-Saxon poetic form and language. The poem's single macaronism, "reliquia," is, in Blurton's reading, "the key to the work's meaning." *Durham* offers itself simultaneously as a reliquary for the past as well as a relic of that past. Its language and poetic form suggest that the poem is of much greater antiquity than it is—but not for purposes politically nostalgic. In the early twelfth century, "the monks of Durham were diligently engaged in creating textual evidence to buttress their community's claims specifically to Cuthbert's patrimony, and more generally to the power of the monastic community of the cathedral priory against that of the bishop and castle." Instead of understanding *Durham* as a transitional text, suspended between Old and Middle English, Blurton sees the poem as caught between two structures of power in early Anglo-Norman Durham, between castle and cathedral.

David Townsend deepens this emphasis on language, vernacularity, and corporate identity with "Cultural Difference and the Meaning of Latinity in Asser's *Life of King Alfred*." The Welsh priest Asser's text is often read as a principal site of ninth-century West Saxon hegemonic consolidation, the coming into being of Alfred's English nation. Townsend argues, however, that this biographical account of Alfred's rise to power contains in its rhetorical pragmatics an implicit, and often overlooked, assertion of enduring cultural diversity in Britain. Rather than obliterating differences among peoples in the service of a unitary, homogeneous, alienated perspective, Asser's Latinity deploys the metropolitan language of early medieval high culture to maintain a space for local difference. Such difference must exist in tension with the assimilative claims of the newly ascendant vernacular, but it need not be obliterated or abandoned by those for whom it holds definitional power. The possibility of local positionalities being refracted through the medium of Asser's Latinity suggests a far more complex model of the relationship of medieval Latin as a metropolitan language to the articulation of local subjectivities.

Cultural heterogeneity beneath what may appear to be monolithic sameness is also the theme of Jeffrey Jerome Cohen's "Green Children from Another World, or The Archipelago in England." Cohen turns to a late twelfth-century Latin text to study how tensions around colonization and assimilation found "subterranean" voice in the long wake of the Norman Conquest. The English historian William of Newburgh narrated a vivid tale of green children emerging from the ground in contemporary East Anglia. Seeming arrivals from a distant world, these strange siblings differed from their English discoverers in language, clothing, customs—differed, in the end, in their race. Yet, neither the boy nor the girl is as alien as they initially appeared. Once taught to eat local food, they lose their viridescence; once taught to speak English, they narrate their origin in a land that for all its distance touches England intimately. The account of the Green Children surfaces two stories that William of Newburgh cannot otherwise tell: how the Normans who had conquered the kingdom had vanished from the country without ever leaving, and how the contemporary nation had never come adequately to terms with the Britain that it pretended to have subsumed, with the archipelago of cultural difference and intractable hybridity dwelling still within.

Michael Wenthe likewise studies the difficulties of supposing discrete and enduring collective identities after the Norman Conquest. "Beyond British Boundaries in the *Historia Regum Britanniae*" argues that in Geoffrey of Monmouth's *History of the Kings of Britain*, Arthur's preeminence among the insular regents paradoxically depends upon his challenge to traditional understanding and preservation of British peoplehood. Arthur begins his reign as a champion who restores his people's fortunes within the island, but ends as the master of an international empire drawing allies drawn from diverse geographies. Arthur's federated approach to rule and his accommodation of foreigners among his counselors temper the force of British domination and ultimately color the sense of Britishness itself. The king's efforts to extend the British nation beyond Britain (and beyond Britons) challenge the conception of Britishness established by the nation-founder Brutus, rooted in ethnicity and place. Arthur's move toward hybridization and against traditional binarisms is thwarted by Mordred's rebellion, a rejection spurred by atavistic desire for a simpler expression of identity that depends on a purity imposed through exclusion. The limits of both Arthur's model of nationhood and Mordred's response can be seen in Arthur's failure to sustain his achievement and in Geoffrey's supersessionistic history, a history that repeatedly chronicles the replacement of one dominant group within Britain by another.

Kathleen Biddick extends this focus upon Geoffrey of Monmouth and island identities in "Arthur's Two Bodies and the Bare Life of the Archives." Biddick examines how the *History of the Kings of Britain* constitutes a formative moment in the medieval fabrication of what Ernst Kantorowicz called "the king's two bodies," the enduring body politic and the mortal body natural. Biddick demonstrates how archival practices were intrinsic to this invention, lodging themselves deep within

Geoffrey's text. The chapter observes how the accounts of the Pipe Rolls trace the bureaucratic involvement of archdiaconal circles (in which Geoffrey moved) with the Crown; it examines archdiaconal anxieties over petty geographical jurisdiction as expressed in the *Leges Edwardi Confessoris* (*Laws of Edward the Confessor*), and it traces their theological notions of sovereignty as echoed in *Norman Anonymous*. According to Biddick, Geoffrey stages the archival violence at stake in fabricating the king's second, divine body by bracketing his *History* with massacre, employing the Latin cognates of *caedes* [carnage, slaughter] to form these brackets. His use of massacre converges with contemporary Jewish concepts of the archive as the *porphyrion*, a vestment capable of transcribing every drop of blood of massacred Jews. The chapter reflects on the political theology of mundane bureaucratic archives and archives of trauma at the edges of Geoffrey's history.

As residents in a nation dissimilar in custom, ritual language, and religion, Jews in England found themselves objects of cultural fascination even after the Expulsion of 1290. Randy P. Schiff examines the role Jews played in a text composed after this forced departure. "The Instructive Other Within: Secularized Jews in *The Siege of Jerusalem*" argues that the alliterative romance should be read in the context of the contemporary collapse of the fantasy of English insular overlordship. Scholars have recoiled at the *Siege*'s endorsement of violence inflicted on Jews, reading the siege as Christ's vengeance upon the citizens of Jerusalem. Schiff warns, however, that given the poem's problematization of clear ethnic identification, critics should be hesitant to ascribe to the text a simple or reductive understanding of what the figure of the Jew means. Reflecting upon a Britain enmeshed in the painful, often violent process of border-formation, the author portrays the Jews as daunting insurgents rather than religious purists, undermining the theological pretensions of a Roman war machine—a machine motivated more by plunder than by its putative Christianity. By manipulating his sources to make a refusal of tribute trigger the Roman invasion, the *Siege*-poet links the Jews with the Arthurian rebels of romance, a genre ambivalently situated with respect to English empire. Apparently originating in western Yorkshire, the text speaks more to the bloody raids and sieges conducted by the Scots and English in the process of forming British borders—and perhaps also to the trauma of the 1190 massacre of Jews in Clifford's Tower in York—than it does to abstract theological interests. Much as the Jew, for Langland, acts as ethical instructor to English society, so does the *Siege of Jerusalem* secularize its narrative events so as to release the ambivalent energies of a Jewish Other who reveals the limits of an unchecked English expansionism.

Katherine Terrell brings us to the center of the Scotland at the edges of Schiff's chapter with "Subversive Histories: Strategies of Identity in Scottish Historiography." Terrell examines Scottish historiographical responses to Geoffrey of Monmouth's myth of Brutus, a myth that was repeatedly invoked in support of England's colonialist ambitions toward Scotland. Discussing responses to Geoffrey's myth in early fourteenth-century diplomatic texts and John of Fordun's *Chronica Gentis Scotorum*, the chapter argues that even as Scottish chroniclers established spatial and temporal boundaries to enforce the idea of a natural and autonomous Scottish identity, their persistently dialogic engagement with Geoffrey's text reveals the hybridity underlying their constructions of identity. These chroniclers' responses to Geoffrey cannot therefore be simply character-ized as either unambiguously hostile or as complicit in what R.R. Davies has called the "Anglicization of the British Isles." Rather, Terrell con-tends, the chroniclers resist English aggression as much by appropriating and adapting Geoffrey's highly effective narrative strategies as by directly challenging his authority.

Jon Kenneth Williams looks closely at the literature of another people who felt the force of English expansionism throughout the Middle Ages, the Welsh. "Sleeping with an Elephant: Wales and England in the *Mabinogion*" proposes that several pieces of Middle Welsh literature lay a theoretical groundwork that would enable the Welsh to perpetuate their language and culture in an age of seemingly inalterable foreign political and military occupation. "Culhwch and Olwen," the oldest Arthurian narrative, describes the island of Britain as a geography always and already marked by invasion and colonization, negating the Welsh myth of entitle-ment to the whole of the island. "The Dream of Macsen Wledig" in turn encourages its audience to be of service to the occupier, literarily Roman but historically English, so that the Welsh language might be preserved. Finally, the third branch of the Mabinogi, "Manawydan Son of Llyr," uses (in Williams' account) gentle satire to acknowledge the inescapable economic might of England. In so doing, the work playfully draws into sharp relief the twin worlds of the Wales of myth and the England of the medieval market economy, providing a vision of Welsh ability that is both strikingly optimistic and pragmatic.

Legendary histories, mythic foundations, and practical political con-siderations are likewise at the heart of John Ganim's "Chaucer and the War of the Maidens." Scholars have long puzzled why in the Knight's Tale Chaucer so severely shortens the spectacular battle against the Amazons as it was developed in his chief source, Boccaccio's *Teseide*, depending instead on the briefer account in Statius' *Thebeid*. Ganim speculates that the Amazonian materials acquired a new, unstable charge with the arrival of Anne of Bohemia and her marriage to Richard II. It is likely that the stories of the legendary founding of Prague by the prophetic female leader Libuše and through an associated battle against Amazon-like women (usually referred to as the "War of the Maidens") accompanied Anne and her courtiers to England. Recent scholarship on Queen Anne has provided a new window into our understanding of Chaucer and his culturally complex poetry. Ganim's contribution to this new emphasis is to suggest that traces of the legendary history of Bohemia can be located in the political unconscious of the Knight's Tale and perhaps in Chaucer's intricate deployment of gender as local topic and as political metaphor. Even it is impossible to prove that Chaucer was aware of the cultural freight of the female foundation of Queen Anne's homeland, Ganim provocatively points to striking analogues to the ways in which Chaucer deploys the powers of his Bohemianized women. In those works by Chaucer connected in some fashion to Anne and her native land, he finds an uncannily similar dispersal and division of female power.

Eileen Joy also details how gender functions in tales of violent masculine adventure and cultural colonization in her temporally intercut chapter "The Signs and Location of a Flight (or Return?) of Time: The Old English *Wonders of the East* and the Gujarat Massacre." Joy places the mass sexual mutilation, torture, and brutal murder of hundreds of Muslim women in Gujarat alongside the lines of the Old English *Wonders of the East* describing Alexander's murder of giant women "unworthy in their bodies." She argues that we can glimpse in both events a violence that can be understood to participate in what Dominick LaCapra, writing about the Holocaust, has described as a "deranged sacrificialism." Such violence is occasioned by the attempt to get rid of stranger-Others as "phobic or ritually impure objects" that are believed to pollute the *Volksgemeinschaft* [community of the people]. Both cases—one terrifyingly real, the other purely fictional— also reveal persistent social anxieties about the female body as formless contagion. Out of the horror and disgust that arises in the encounter with the female body perceived as monstrous, Joy traces an ancient and ritualized type of violence that is both morally condemnatory and ecstatic, and which can be seen, to a greater and more restrained degree, respectively, in the Gujarat genocide and the Old English text.

Eileen Joy's chapter leaves us in the very place we began: in a world that is culturally complicated, full of brutality based upon real and imagined differences, not much closer than medieval England was to realizing that the Other Worlds we banish to our undergrounds are in fact coextensive with our own.

Notes

1. *The History of English Affairs*, Book 1, ed. and trans. P.G. Walsh and M.J. Kennedy (Wiltshire: Aris and Phillips, 1988), 1.28.

2. Monika Otter analyzes the cup's diminution into ordinariness well in *Inventiones: Fiction and Referentiality in Twelfth-Century English Historical Writing* (Chapel Hill: University of North Carolina Press, 1996), 105.

3. I make this point at greater length in my chapter in this volume, stressing that despite his stridency agains the Welsh, Irish, and Scottish—William is fascinated with aboriginality, with stories of those who animated his landscapes long before the advent of the English. As Laurie A. Finke and Martin B. Shichtman have emphasized, this hybridity of cultures tended to produce "dialogically agitated sites of ideological conflict," such as texts in which one can discern both the voices of the dominant and the "fears and hopes of subordinated groups, as well as those who hope one day to be dominant": *King Arthur and the Myth of History* (Gainesville: University of Florida Press, 2004), 19.

4. "In Praise of British History," in *The British Isles 1100–1500: Comparisons, Contrasts and Connections*, ed. R.R. Davies (Edinburgh: John Donald Publishers, 1988), 9.

5. Edward James, *Britain in the First Millennium* (London: Arnold, 2001), 1. A nuanced archeological reading of insular material culture over a slightly less ambitious *longue durée* ("the whole of the Middle Ages" rather than James's "long first millennium") can be found in David A. Hinton, *Gold and Gilt, Pots and Pins: Possessions and People in Medieval Britain* (Oxford: Oxford University Press, 2005).

6. Barry Cunliffe, *Facing the Ocean: The Atlantic and Its Peoples, 8000 BC–AD 1500* (Oxford: Oxford University Press, 2001).

7. *The First English Empire: Power and Identity in the British Isles, 1093–1343* (Oxford: Oxford University Press, 2000), 54. Cf. p. 3, where Davies speaks of "the problem that is the British Isles." Davies makes a similar point specifically about the difficulty of defining medieval Wales in *Conquest, Coexistence and Change: Wales 1063–1415* (Oxford: Oxford University Press, 1987), 4. See also his words on the vanishing of Britain in *The Matter of Britain and the Matter of England* (Oxford: Clarendon Press, 1996), 15–16. Patrick Wormald offers some similar thoughts on the noninevitability of the emergence of England in "Bede, the *Bretwaldas*, and the Origins of the *Gens Anglorum*," in *Ideal and Reality in Frankish and Anglo-Saxon Society*, ed. Patrick Wormald, Donald Bullough, and Roger Collins (Oxford: Oxford University Press, 1983), 104 as does John Moreland, "Ethnicity, Power and the English," in *Social Identity in Early Medieval England*, ed. William O. Frazer and Andrew Tyrrell (London: Leicester University Press, 2000), 25. See also Benedict Anderson's influential conclusion in *Imagined Communities: Reflections on the Origin and Spread of Nationalism*, 2nd ed. (London: Verso, 1991), which likewise examines how historical chance comes to be figured as national destiny (12). Patrick Geary's work

is useful as well; for a general overview see *The Myth of Nations: The Medieval Origins of Europe* (Princeton: Princeton University Press, 2002). Further on writing insular history rather than English history, with an insightful meditation on the insufficiency of modern geographical terms, see Norman Davies' *The Isles: A History* (Oxford: Oxford University Press), esp. xxi–xlii and 10. For an exemplary literary treatment of such a geographically and epistemologically expanded world, see David Wallace, *Premodern Places: Calais to Surinam, Chaucer to Aphra Behn* (Oxford: Blackwell, 2004). Wallace writes: "To imagine English territory extending into continental Europe—with the Channel as a roadway rather than a defensive moat—immediately challenges received notions of 'insular' culture" (2).

8. *Sovereign Fantasies: Arthurian Romance and the Making of Britain* (Philadelphia: University of Pennsylvania Press, 2001), 17. Ingham specifically links this process with the mythic Arthur, through whom "an increasingly literate public can learn to desire a unified future by delighting in the imagined glories of a unified past." Ingham is especially good at recovering "alternative histories, alternative imaginings…the other dreams and desires sacrificed, often forcibly, to traumatic imperial, or national, unities" (2).

9. See Richmond's inspirational meditation on English national self-identity and the Jews in "Englishness and Medieval Anglo-Jewry," in *The Jewish Heritage in British History: Englishness and Jewishness*, ed. Tony Kushner (London: Frank Cass, 1992), 46.

10. *The First English Empire*, 54. Compare Lesley Johnson on the "teleological cast" of much thinking about medieval English history in "Imagining Communities: Medieval and Modern," in *Concepts of National Identity in the Middle Ages*, ed. Simon Forde, Lesley Johnson, and Alan V. Murray (Leeds: School of English, University of Leeds, 1995), 2. What Davies aims to do in restoring to these countries their contingency is to move away from anglocentric models of interpreting the isles and refrain from "compartmentalizing" the study of the four countries. See especially "In Praise of British History," 23.

11. The labor behind this process and the diversity it can obscure is well illustrated in the essays collected in *Imagining a Medieval English Nation*, ed. Kathy Lavezzo (Minneapolis: University of Minnesota Press, 2004). I have examined the topic at greater length in *Hybridity, Identity and Monstrosity in Medieval Britain: On Difficult Middles* (New York: Palgrave, 2006).

12. See, for example, *Celtic Myth and Arthurian Romance* (New York: Columbia University Press, 1927). Though his methodology is now discredited, his argument that England and France had been denying their own Celticism transformed the field. The desires propelling his scholarship are also not all that different from those of scholars who work on the materials today.

13. *The Postcolonial Middle Ages*, ed. Jeffrey Jerome Cohen (New York: Palgrave, 2000).

14. *Provincializing Europe: Postcolonial Thought and Historical Difference* (Princeton: Princeton University Press, 2000).

15. Important examples of this kind of emplacement of England within a vast world frame are Kofi Omoniyi Sylvanus Campbell, who locates late medieval depictions of race in temporal span that moves forward all the way to the contemporary Caribbean in his *Literature and Culture in the Black Atlantic: From Pre- to Postcolonial* (New York: Palgrave, 2006); and Geraldine Heng, whose *Empire of Magic: Medieval Romance and the Politics of Cultural Fantasy* (New York: Columbia University Press, 2003) is breathtaking in its geographical sweep. See also the essays collected by Ananya Jahanara Kabir and Deanne Williams in *Postcolonial Approaches to the European Middle Ages* (Cambridge: Cambridge University Press, 2005), in which the pieces by Nicholas Howe and Seth Lerer are especially good at situating Anglo-Saxon culture within a paninsular rather than (European) international context.

CHAPTER 1

BETWEEN DIASPORA AND CONQUEST: NORMAN ASSIMILATION IN PETRUS ALFONSI'S *DISCIPLINA CLERICALIS* AND MARIE DE FRANCE'S *FABLES*

Suzanne Conklin Akbari

This chapter examines Norman identity and diaspora comparatively, through texts composed in Sicily and England.

In 1760, an editor named Étienne Barbazan published a volume titled *Le Castoiement du pere a son fils*, a dialogue of father and son containing, in Barbazan's view, a compendium of learning to be devoutly absorbed by the attentive son. The editor presents the son's filial attention to his father's wisdom as a model for the reader, who should similarly embrace the paternal authority of eighteenth-century French civilization and government. In the brief remarks that immediately precede the text of the *Castoiement*, Barbazan states that this work is exemplary in that it "has as its object simply to inspire religion, good values, good conduct, submissiveness and respect for those persons of dignity who are installed by God to govern and protect us. Such are the sentiments of the anony-mous author, which I offer here to the public."[1] Barbazan prefaces his edition with three learned essays on philology, describing how the use of etymology to disentangle the French language from Celtic and Germanic interpolations enables a fuller knowledge of the foundations of French culture. In Barbazan's view, the filial learning enacted in the narrative of the *Castoiement* epitomizes the work of the philologist: "nothing instructs us better than the usages and the values of our fathers, and moreover nothing more fully clarifies for us both the origins and the variations of our language."[2]

It is enchantingly ironic that the text Barbazan chooses as an exemplar of essentially French national identity is an early vernacular rendition of the *Disciplina Clericalis*. Petrus Alfonsi, a Sephardic Jew educated in Muslim Spain and transplanted to Norman England, is the "Auteur anonyme" to whom Barbazan assigns this quintessentially French text. On two occasions in the text of the *Castoiement*, however, the heterogeneous cultural background of the *Disciplina Clericalis* emerges to challenge the philologist's assertion of the paternal authority of the French nation. On one occasion, Barbazan is puzzled by the allusion to the precious stone "jagonce" in the story of the bird who escapes from the farmer who traps him in a net.[3] Barbazan writes, in puzzlement, that this word "cannot be found in any dictionary." In the closing lines of the *Castoiement*, another philological obstacle presents itself with the phrase "Roi et Contor et Aumacor." Barbazan is mystified by the final word and writes in a footnote, "I have only seen this word here, and I can find no point of origin in Latin." He goes on to add that he has consulted one of the authors of the *Journal des Savants*, who tells him that the word is in fact Arabic.[4] Barbazan says no more; he does not draw out the implications of finding an Arabic word in the closing lines of this French text. Presumably, he would argue that this term has somehow strayed into a national literary tradition, that it is simply a foreign element that must be expunged in the search for the essential linguistic substrate of the French nation. As Barbazan puts it in one of his prefatory essays, "The art of etymology is that of stripping away that which is, so to speak, foreign [*étranger*], and by this means to recall [the words] to that simplicity which they all have at their origin."[5]

I have recounted this little fable of nationalist philology in order to illustrate the dangers of reading literature as a transparent reflection of culture. It is easy to see the pitfalls of Étienne Barbazan's effort to read the dialogue of the *Disciplina Clericalis* as a straightforward manifestation of the French nation in its infancy, and the paternal authority of the interlocutor as a virtual personification of the voice of that nation. We are perhaps somewhat less attentive to the potential pitfalls of reading the *Disciplina Clericalis* as a manifestation of an "Oriental" literary form: over the last few decades, several critics have described the *Disciplina Clericalis* in precisely these terms.[6] In the following pages, therefore, I will discuss some features of the *Disciplina Clericalis* in an effort to consider the ways that its frame-tale narrative is less an essentially Oriental form than a form that emerges from the phenomenon of cultural mediation. To put it another way, it may be useful to read the narrative structure of the *Disciplina Clericalis* within the framework of diasporic Norman culture rather than interpreting it as a straightforward importation of "Eastern" forms into a "Western" milieu. To this end, I will juxtapose the *Disciplina Clericalis* with the twelfth-century Anglo-Norman *Fables* of Marie de France, arguing that the cultural assimilation seen in Norman England can be fruitfully compared with that found in other medieval sites of Norman rule, such as Sicily. Descriptions of appetite and eating in the *Disciplina Clericalis* and the *Fables* reflect the culture of assimilation that is the matrix of twelfth-century frame-tale narratives, distinguishing them sharply from the later medieval frame-tale narratives with which they are often grouped, such as the *Decameron* and the *Canterbury Tales*.

Norman Diaspora

Norman culture of the Middle Ages spanned a wide geographical range, linked by sea routes that provided a source of economic and cultural continuity. This continuity has led some scholars to refer to the "Norman diaspora," that is, the fanning out of Norman communities across Europe and the Mediterranean, giving rise to a range of hybrid communities that share certain societal and cultural features. There are several reasons why we might want to hesitate in deploying the term Norman diaspora. It is first of all debatable whether the term "diaspora" can be appropriately used other than its original context, that is, with diaspora referring to the forced dispersion of Jews from Jerusalem in the first century, a usage popularized by Flavius Josephus in his Greek-language chronicle of Jewish history. Nonetheless, over the last two decades, the term diaspora has been extended to refer to a range of other manifestations of ethnic migration, perhaps most famously in the descriptions of the "African" or "black diaspora" described by Paul Gilroy.[7] We now find in the critical literature a range of diasporas: the "Irish diaspora," the "Italian diaspora," the "Indian diaspora," and—a rather ironic example—the "Israeli diaspora."

This generic use of the term to signify any dispersion of peoples is problematic. In the earliest adaptations, such as Gilroy's use of the term black diaspora, the analogy to the Jewish experience of oppression and violent removal from a homeland is paramount. Gilroy's account of the long-term effects of the Atlantic passage on African American slave communities takes pains to highlight the self-reflective identification of those peoples with Jewish communities living in exile or in captivity.[8] Other usages of the term diaspora, however, are far less scrupulous, neglecting what must surely be the most fundamental aspect of diaspora: like exile, diaspora is inexorably forced upon persons, not a state that one chooses freely.[9] In addition, the telos of diaspora as it is articulated within Rabbinic tradition (as a longed-for return to Jerusalem destined to be fulfilled in messianic time) is distinct from the way in which Jewish diaspora is understood within Christian theology: from a Christian perspective, the physical scattering of the Jewish people makes manifest in human terms the destruction of Jerusalem, as physical sign of the supersession of the Old Law by the New.[10]

For all these reasons, we might hesitate to employ the increasingly common term Norman diaspora. There is, however, a compelling argument for thinking through the implications of using the term, and for conceiving of it as a conceptual matrix for the study of premodern literary history. Medieval writers themselves invoke the model of diaspora in describing how Norman kingdoms come into being; they do so, however, not through reference to Norman diaspora, but through their characterization of Norman emigration and conquest in terms of the fictional Trojan history of emigration and the subsequent rise of European nations. Their characterization of Troy, in turn, draws upon a range of biblical models of the emigration of peoples, including not only the Genesis narrative of the population of the three known continents by the sons of Noah but also the narrative of Jewish diaspora known through the many retellings of Josephus. This latter model served particularly well as a template for the description of the role that cities play in the dissemination of peoples and nations, adding significantly to Noachid model (echoed in the dispersal of languages following the fall of the Tower of Babel) that lacked such a clearly defined point of origin. For an account of how nations arise from the ruins of a central, foundational city, the history of Jerusalem provided a vitally useful supplement.

The Trojan narrative is perhaps the most ubiquitous of all medieval historiography, used by a range of nations to describe their own ethnic origins. The account of the establishment of Rome by Aeneas after his flight from Troy served as the template for the narrations of the birth of numerous other nations in their own developing foundation myths. In addition, the history of Troy was readily enfolded within the overarching historiography of *translatio imperii* articulated by Paulus Orosius in the fifth century, perhaps in part because the trajectory of empire in both the *Aeneid* and Orosius's universal history passes from the eastern regions to Rome by way of Carthage.[11] In spite of the tendency of modern readers to emphasize the disjunction between Virgilian and Augustian modes of historiography, medieval readers seem to have eagerly integrated the two, adding Trojan genealogies and even entire narratives of the fall of Troy into late medieval adaptations of Orosius: in one extreme case, a fourteenth-century adaptation of the thirteenth-century *Histoire ancienne jusqu'á César* actually pops the whole of the *Roman de Troie* into the sequence of Orosian *translatio imperii*.[12]

The dispersal of peoples from Troy was clearly understood by medieval readers as being something like the diaspora described by Josephus. Medieval readers familiar with the popular fourth-century Latin rendition of Josephus's account attributed to Hegesippus read accounts of the forced dispersal of the inhabitants of Troy with a strong sense of the repetitious, cyclical nature of history, in which urban destruction is followed by the scattering of peoples to the four corners of the earth. It is consequently unsurprising that a whole series of medieval chronicles integrate the history of diaspora within the history of *translatio imperii*. This is evident not only in the many medieval redactions and continuations of Orosius's universal history, in which the account of the exile of Jews from Jerusalem in the first century serves as a template for the subsequent dispersal of peoples from cities after siege, most especially, Troy, but also in other histories of national origin. Both narratives of British descent (such as the eighth-century *Historia Brittonum* of pseudo-Nennius and the twelfth-century *Historia Regum Britanniae* of Geoffrey of Monmouth) and narratives of Norman descent (such as the tenth-century *De moribus et actis primorum Normanniae ducum* of Dudo of Saint-Quentin and its later iterations, as the *Gesta Normannorum ducum*, by Guillaume de Jumièges, Orderic Vitalis, and Robert de Torigny) recount the foundation of the nation in terms of the arrival and lineage arising from warriors escaping the ruins of Troy.[13] The fall of Troy and subsequent dispersal of its inhabitants follows the template of the fall of Jerusalem, in an implicit comparison that is only heightened through each city's supersessionist relationship to Rome: Troy gives rise to Rome in the national narrative first inscribed in the *Aeneid*, just as Jerusalem gives rise to Christian Rome in the ecclesiastical narrative recounted in the many redactions and adaptations of Josephus's *Bellum Iudaicum*.[14] The alignment of the fall of Troy with the fall of Jerusalem, and their common participation in the larger trajectory of Orosian *translatio imperii*, is perhaps most fully expressed in the *Flores historiarum* of Matthew Paris, in which the chronologies of Jewish and Trojan history are alternately recounted until both give way to the linear sequence of successive imperial powers as they devolve from Babylon, to Persia, to Greece, to Rome.[15]

It is through the model of Troy, then, that we can draw upon medieval historiographical models in order to conceive of Norman diaspora, a migration of peoples throughout the world that gave rise to a range of communities scattered across Europe and the Mediterranean. Unlike the simplistic narrative of nation implicit in the myth of Trojan descent, however, in which each exiled Trojan warrior serves as the father of a single, homogeneous people, the historical narrative of what we might choose to call Norman diaspora is far more heterogeneous. If there is a distinctive quality to be singled out in Norman culture, across Europe and the Mediterranean, it is precisely the quality of adaptability: that is, the chameleon-like ability to blend in, to assimilate, to take up numerous elements already present in a local culture, and to embed them within a layer of "Normannitas" that binds them all together. In making this argument, I want to stress the importance of not overlooking those qualities that serve to distinguish Norman culture in each of its various settings. One has only to look at recent scholarship illustrating how Norman identity evolved in dramatically different forms in France, England, Italy, and Sicily.[16] We can say, nonetheless, that the ability to assimilate local forms was part of a shared practice common to Norman societies, a practice that Karla Mallette has traced with remarkable eloquence in her recent study of medieval Sicily, and which has long been the object of study among scholars working on late eleventh- and twelfth-century England.[17]

It is in this framework—not in a nebulous Oriental context—that we might fruitfully place the *Disciplina Clericalis* of Petrus Alfonsi. Reading the *Disciplina Clericalis* in the context of Norman diaspora accomplishes three things. First, it allows us to stop reading literary forms as unproblematic cultural booty translated from one environment to another, and instead read them as the *products* of a rich history of cultural interaction. Second, it keeps constantly before the reader a memory of the migration of peoples—both imagined and actual—that lies behind the movement of stories, narrative forms, and modes of interpretation. Finally, it locates that memory of migration within the framework of diaspora, within the template of civic destruction and human dispersal that so powerfully informed the premodern imaginary. This final element is particularly apposite to the *Disciplina Clericalis*, which reflects a view of diaspora that is at once rooted in knowledge of Rabbinic tradition concerning Jewish exile, and embedded in a specifically Christian understanding of the role of the destruction of Jerusalem in sacred history. This latter understanding is painfully evident in the *Dialogi contra Iudaeos*, in which Alfonsi goes far beyond the Augustinian perspective on the continued Jewish presence in Christian culture, describing the diaspora not as a necessary reminder to medieval Christians of the supersession of the Old Law but rather as a violent collective punishment of the Jews for their knowing slaughter of the Son of God.[18]

Although some critics have suggested that the *Disciplina Clericalis* was composed by Alfonsi in Spain prior to his migration to England and France, there is no evidence for this assertion. The preponderance of surviving manuscripts are northern European, which is, if anything, evidence against this hypothesis.[19] Vernacular translations of the *Disciplina Clericalis*, beginning with the Anglo-Norman adaptions of the twelfth century such as that republished by Étienne Barbazan, are also evidence of northern circulation, if not—strictly speaking—of northern composition. It remains possible, of course, that Alfonsi assembled the *Disciplina Clericalis* in Spain and then disseminated it only after his journey to Norman England. The dialogic style of the treatise, however, links it with other productions linked to Norman England and northern France, such as the *De eodem et diverso* of Adelard of Bath and the *Dragmaticon* of William of Conches. The latter work is, like the *Disciplina Clericalis*, a dialogue of teacher and pupil: the *Dragmaticon* is a conversation between William himself ("Philosopher") and his student, the young Henry II ("Duke"). Like Petrus Alfonsi, Adelard of Bath and William of Conches were associated with the courts of Henry I and Henry II, both monarchs known for their patronage of science and philosophy as well as literature. Alfonsi's *Disciplina Clericalis*, therefore, can be appropriately read not just in the context of so-called Oriental wisdom literature, but in the context of the fusion of intellectual and cultural currents that characterized the twelfth-century Anglo-Norman court.

Court Literature and the Frame Tale

Of the many remarkable facets of the *Disciplina Clericalis*, perhaps one of the most remarkable is the way in which the text metaphorically describes its own narration in terms of appetite and food consumption. It is nothing remarkable to describe the acquisition of knowledge in terms of the consumption of food. Such analogies appear in the Bible, as well as in literature of biblical exegesis. Among twelfth-century expressions of this trope, perhaps the most famous appears in Bernard of Clairvaux's *Sermons on the Song of Songs*. There, Bernard describes the basic, literal understanding of scripture in terms of the milk that even an infant can consume, but characterizes the more substantial allegorical understanding of scripture as bread, or even as meat. These spiritual foods require a mature appetite and a more fully developed ability to assimilate such metaphorical foodstuffs. Even in Boethius's fifth-century *Consolation of Philosophy*, the teachings of philosophy are described as a kind of intellectual milk. Petrus Alfonsi repeats this trope in a passage early in the *Disciplina Clericalis*, in which the pupil asks his instructor: "If you have something in the recesses of your heart that the philosophers have said about this particular subject, tell it to me and I will retain it in my memory, which is very good, so that I can someday pass these tidbits on to my schoolmates, who have been brought up on the milk of philosophy."[20] Here, the metaphor is a rather standard one: that is, the intellectual milk of philosophy that nourishes the mind. There are two unusual features here, however. First, the pupil presents himself not just as the recipient of intellectual nourishment, but as a potential donor: give me these "tidbits," he says, so that I can pass them on. Second, he distinguishes between the "milk of philosophy" (which is, as noted above, a common trope), and the remarkably tantalizing morsels offered to him by his teacher ("delicatissimum alimentum," most delicate foodstuffs).

Metaphors pertaining to food—both the appetite for food and the consumption of food—appear throughout the *Disciplina Clericalis*. In some cases, the appetite for food (whether satisfied or frustrated) serves as the medium of instruction, as both the fable's protagonist and the attentive reader learn when body appetites must be controlled and when they must be obeyed. For example, in the story of "the two city dwellers and the country man," three men go on a pilgrimage to Mecca and try to outwit one another in order to secure the last scraps of bread in their communal store, and subsequently learn the following moral: "These two city men, when they decided to behave as animals, should have copied the nature of the gentlest animal. They deserved to lose their food." Here, the didactic end of the fable is conventional; what is unusual, however, is the narrative thread to which it gives rise. The moral of the fable, in this case, is uttered not by the teacher but by the pupil; and the narrative closes not with the usual appeal by the pupil to his teacher for yet another tantalizing tale, but rather an appeal by the teacher to the pupil. "Tell me, my boy," says the teacher, the story you have heard: "Such a story should be very amusing!"[21] Here, the conventional order of the fictional banquet is overturned, with the pupil begged by his teacher to recount an "amusing" tale.

The appetite for tales continues to be expressed throughout the narrative, with appeals for tales couched in terms of food and drink: "You have instructed me well," says the pupil, "and I have commended to my thirsting and eager mind all that you have told me about feminine tricks."[22] Another time, the teacher rebukes his overeager student, saying, "Are these not enough for you? I have already told you three parables." The student responds, "When you say three parables, you exaggerate the number, for they were short ones. Now tell me a long story which will fill my ears and will thus satisfy me."[23] Note that, in the first example, the acquisition of edifying knowledge is described in terms of the satisfaction of the appetite, while in the second, it is the delightful pleasure of the story itself that is said to satisfy the appetite. Among the many examples in the *Disciplina Clericalis*, however, nowhere is the nutritive metaphor more fully elaborated than in one of the most popular passages of the whole work: that is, the account of proper table manners. This passage was avidly adapted and even amplified in medieval redactions of the *Disciplina*; one fifteenth-century Latin version even inserts detailed information on how to eat an egg politely.[24]

The passage begins with practical information: you must wash first, and be careful to touch nothing but the food. You must wash after the meal, not just "because it is hygienic and well-mannered," but for reasons of health: "many people's eyes become infected because they wipe them without having washed their hands after eating." Here, courteous behavior and healthful behavior are perfectly aligned, and the observation of orderly progress at the table results in orderly progress both on the level of social interaction and individual self-regulation. The passage continues with an exposition of proper etiquette regarding invitations: just as there is a proper order in the manual taking up of the morsel of food, so there is a proper order in the acceptance of invitations. The careful exposition of the proper order of procedure, however, soon gives way to parody:

> The young man asked the old man, "What should I do when I am invited to eat? Should I eat very much or very little?"
>
> The old man said to him, "Eat very much. For if a friend invites you, he will rejoice in it, and if an enemy, he will be sad."
>
> The boy laughed when he heard this; and the old man asked, "Why are you laughing?"
>
> The boy: "I am reminded of the answer of Maimundus, the Negro slave: an old man asked him how much he could eat. He answered, 'Whose food, mine or some one else's?' The old man: 'Your own.' Maimundus: 'As little as possible.' The old man: 'Someone else's?' Maimundus: 'As much as possible.'"
>
> The old man said to the boy, "You only remember the words of the gluttonous, lazy, stupid, talkative, and trifling man, and whatever is said about a person of this type is found to an even greater extent in Maimundus."
>
> The boy said, "I like to hear about him because everything about him is funny, and if you remember anything about him, tell me, and I will consider it a great favor." (DC 22; ed. 334–40, trans. 98–100)[25]

What follows is the extremely comic "Anecdotes of Maimundus the Slave." In terms of the alimentary narrative traced in this essay, the most striking detail of the "Anecdotes of Maimundus" is the way that each tiny fragment of narrative is thrown, like a tasty morsel, into the waiting orifice of the pupil. After a few bits, the pupil says, "I have heard of his laziness; now I would like to hear of his talkativeness."[26] The give and take, the to and fro, of these anecdotes mimics the shallow appetite being satisfied by the short bursts of narrative. In short, hearing the "Anecdotes of Maimundus" is like eating a bag of potato chips: you are not satisfied by just one.

The pull of appetite, expressed in the insatiable desire to hear more, is countered in the *Disciplina Clericalis* by the discipline imposed in the social practices of eating. It is important to recall that the detailed exposition of table manners is the necessary precursor to the tasty anecdotes of

Maimundus. In the recounting of these anecdotes, the nested narrative of the pupil parodically reproduces the verbal exchange of the frame narrative within the exchange of Maimundus and his interlocutor. In this parodic repetition, the pupil plays the role of Maimundus, and his teacher—"the old man" or "senex"—is, precisely, "the old man." This momentary inversion of the authoritative role of the teacher, however, is soon restored: following the rapid-fire anecdotes of Maimundus, the narrative returns to its production of shimmering pearls of wisdom: "The philosopher says, 'All the good things of this world are mixed; you do not eat honey with poison.' Another: 'Everything in this world is changeable....' Another: 'The glory of the world ends in the twinkling of an eye.'"[27] In the *Disciplina Clericalis*, then, delicious morsels of narrative come in different forms: some are flavorful, nourishing foodstuffs; others are tasty but insubstantial, offering a fleeting burst of pleasure. Their value lies in their ability to prolong the attention of the pupil, to facilitate the transmission of knowledge not just to the individual, but to the larger cycle of learning, as the eager pupil stores up "tasty morsels" that he will be able to pass on to hungry learners of a future day. To put it another way, in the *Disciplina Clericalis*, auditory appetite is in the service of intellectual digestion.

At this point, it is fruitful to turn to the *Fables* of Marie de France, which make a strikingly useful foil to a reading of the nested narrative form of the *Disciplina Clericalis*. Composed sometime during the second half of the twelfth century, the *Fables* respond to the same readership that avidly took up the earliest vernacular translations of the *Disciplina*, that is, the *Castoiement du pere a son fils* discussed in the opening pages of this chapter. Marie's patronage by Henry II, to whom she dedicated her *Lais*, marks her as a thread in the tangled web of filiation that links several twelfth-century writers, philosophers, and scientists to the Anglo-Norman court of the Angevins. Marie's *Fable* 27 is, on the one hand, a quaint narrative typical of the vernacular texts related to the Latin *Romulus Nilantii*. It also expresses, on the other hand, the relatively sophisticated metaphor of the body politic articulated in detail in the late twelfth century by John of Salisbury in his *Polycraticus*. While John does not adduce a source for the metaphor, a version of it appears in the commentary on Macrobius composed by John of Salisbury's venerated teacher, William of Conches (who was also the teacher of the young Henry II). It is therefore possible that the metaphor of the body politic had a more local didactic currency before its popularization in the *Polycraticus*. In "De l'humme, de sun ventre, e de ses membres" [Of Man, His Belly, and His Limbs], Marie recounts the story "of a man." This story is not only a fable but also an "essample" worthy of remembering, for this single man is a microcosm of the social order. The hands and feet, believing themselves poorly served by the stomach, who simply "wastes" all that they have "gained," rebel. They refuse to procure nourishment for the belly and, as a result, the whole body is destroyed. Even though the members repent and "offer food and drink to the belly," the whole body becomes feeble and dies. The *exemplum* is this:

> Par ceste essample peot hum veer
> E chescun franc humme le deit saver:
> Nul ne peot aver honur
> Ki hunte fet a sun seignur;
> Ne li sire tute ensement,
> Pur qu'il voille hunir sa gent.
> Si l'un a l'autre est failliz,
> Ambur en erent maubailliz.
>
> [By this example one may see,
> And every wise man should know it,
> That no one can have honor
> Who does shame to his lord;
> Nor the lord, just the same,
> If he wishes to humiliate his people.
> If the one fails the other,
> Both of them will suffer for it.][28]

In the extended metaphor of the body, as in several of Marie's *Fables*, appetites of the individual get in the way of the smooth interweaving of the social fabric. Mutual trust and social interrelations disintegrate when the needs of the one take precedence over the needs of the community.

This dynamic can be seen, for example, in Marie's tale "Del lu e del chien" [Of the Wolf and the Dog]. A wolf and a dog meet. Seeing that the dog is well fed and healthy while he suffers, the wolf asks the dog how he has managed to become so prosperous. The dog generously offers to let the wolf in on his action: he says, "I eat well, and I have enough...Every day I sit at the feet of my master and gnaw on the bones, which is why I'm so fat and big."[29] Once the wolf discovers the price of this social contract, however—namely, the chain with which the dog is tied up—he beats a hasty retreat: "I'll never choose chain! I'd rather be a wolf, entirely free, than to live richly on a chain." The moral of the story is the parting of the ways: the wolf says, "'You go to the town, I'll go to the woods.' Thus by the chain is divided both their friendship and their companionship."[30] As in the earlier fable "De l'humme, de sun ventre, e de ses membres," the tale of the wolf and the dog concerns mutual trust and social interrelation. The delicious bones that have made the dog so fat are the catalyst for the story, but they are not in themselves enough to bring about the metamorphosis of the feral wolf into the domestic canine. In Marie's *Fables*, unlike the *Disciplina Clericalis*, food and appetite are not the medium of the social interaction, but rather the catalyst that precipitates the crisis.

A somewhat more intricate depiction of the way appetites serve as the catalyst for social change appears in Marie's fable "Del reclus e del vilein" [Of the Hermit and the Peasant]. In this story, the hermit is pestered by a peasant who demands to know "why Adam ate the fruit, which caused the people to be damned, and, when he ate the apple, why God did not forgive him."[31] The hermit comes up with a solution: he hides a mouse underneath a bowl and goes out, asking the peasant absolutely to stay away from the bowl. Unsurprisingly, the peasant, overcome by curiosity, lifts the bowl, and the mouse escapes. When the hermit returns, he expounds the moral: "You must not blame Adam anymore if he ate the fruit of the tree that had been forbidden to him by our Lord...He who thinks he can blame someone else should much better reproach himself."[32] Again, as so often in Marie's *Fables*, appetites are dangerous not so much insofar as they affect the life of the individual, but as they affect the life of the community. Adam should not have eaten the fruit, because humankind as a whole suffered for it; the peasant should not rebuke Adam—or anyone at fault—without first correcting himself.

Marie de France's *Fables* are a useful foil to the *Disciplina Clericalis* because their comparatively narrow focus serves to highlight some of the features that make the work of Petrus Alfonsi so extraordinary. On a narrative level in Marie's *Fables*, we find the vestiges of an interlocutory structure reminiscent of the *Disciplina*; in the *Fables*, however, the voice of the teacher is ubiquitous, with the voice of the pupil largely silent. Insofar as the voice of the pupil remains, it is in the implicit addressee to whom the narrator of the *Fables* addresses admonitions. The pupil is almost completely assimilated to the passive reader, who accepts the edifying tales of the *Fables* as they are spoon-fed to him in easily digested morsels. Marie's *Fables* resemble not so much Alfonsi's own version of the *Disciplina Clericalis* as the later redactions of the text made for preaching purposes, such as the work of Jacques de Vitry, in which the tantalizing fables of the *Disciplina* are retooled to make them serve more readily as sermon *exempla*.[33]

To find a responsive student who acts as an interlocutor as in the *Disciplina Clericalis*, it is necessary to turn to the scientific and philosophical dialogues of Alfonsi's contemporaries Adelard of Bath and William of Conches. Here, it is only possible to provide one brief example from William's *Dragmaticon* to illustrate this point. The *Dragmaticon* is a dialogue of a philosopher and a duke, that is, of a teacher—William of Conches—and his pupil—the young Henry of Anjou, soon to be Henry II, ruler of Norman England. Even in this most formal respect, the similarity to the dialogue format of the *Disciplina Clericalis* is evident, and the give-and-take of the interaction of teacher and student in the *Dragmaticon* makes this resemblance even more apparent. In a passage on sense perception and the faculty of hearing, the philosopher responds to the pupil with a playful allusion:

> *Duke*: There is one thing that still puzzles me about hearing. If I emit a sound in a cave or a high forest, someone repeats and returns my word to me.
>
> *Philosopher*: Do you not know, then, that this is performed by "Echo, the resounding nymph"?
>
> *Duke*: I am not Narcissus to be pursued by her. I ask for a physical explanation of the phenomenon, not for a fable.

After the philosopher provides a detailed account of the physics of sound in an echo, his pupil replies in terms that recall those of his counterpart in the *Disciplina Clericalis*:

> *Duke*: I do not know if what you are saying is true, but I do know that it pleases me a great deal. And so I am waiting all the more keenly for what remains to be said about the other senses.
>
> *Philosopher*: It pleases me that such explanations please you.[34]

Like Petrus Alfonsi, William of Conches highlights the philosophical authority of the educator. At the same time, however, the teacher has a playful side that manifests itself in poetic allusions. The eager anticipation expressed by the student finds its counterpart in the teacher's delight in offering these fascinating intellectual tidbits. Finally, it is striking that what is valued, in the dialogue of the *Dragmaticon*, is not simply the intellectual nourishment offered by the philosophical content of the dialogue, but the pleasure provided by the acquisition of that knowledge. "It pleases me," says the duke; "it pleases me that it pleases you," the philosopher responds.

In some respects, the literary qualities of the *Dragmaticon* cause it to resemble even more closely one of Petrus Alfonsi's other works, the "Epistola ad peripateticos." It is worth noting that the "Epistola" corresponds closely to the *Dragmaticon* in a number of other ways as well, especially in their common use of the recently disseminated translations of Constantinus Africanus. In Alfonsi's "Epistola," we find the familiar allusions to the "philosophical nectar" imbibed by those who love the pursuit of knowledge, as well as exempla reminiscent of the *Disciplina Clericalis*.[35] These exempla include the parable of the goat who fills his belly with grapevine leaves, and the marvellous story of the merchant who believes that the extravagantly priced, tiny white orbs sold in the market—actually pearls of great rarity—are actually simply overpriced onions. Following the latter story, Alfonsi describes how, elsewhere, he "took care to write a prologue on the truth of [astronomy] and on its most pleasant truth." In the present work, Alfonsi goes on to say, "part of this we transmit for your enjoyment, so that you may both see and know how desirable and how beautiful this art is."[36] Once again, the pleasure of receiving knowledge—and of imparting it—is the communicative glue that unites teacher and student into a perennial cycle of assimilating and redistributing knowledge.

Mediterranean Flow

We might think of this very cycle of the assimilation and redistribution of knowledge in contemplating the nature of medieval Norman culture, and the ways that it at once interacted with local cultures and produced a transnational culture stretching across Europe and the Mediterranean. On the one hand, each expression of medieval Norman culture must be understood as specific to the individual location, formed by the interaction of Norman elements with local features. On the other hand, Norman culture must be understood as a common, shared phenomenon precisely in terms of that process of assimilation: it is the methodology of interacting with local elements that produces the layer of culture that we can identify as "Norman." In thinking through this shared phenomenon, it might be helpful to study manifestations of Norman culture drawing upon the methodologies of Peregrine Horden and Nicholas Purcell, outlined in their very useful study of comparative Mediterranean history, *The Corrupting Sea*.[37] Horden and Purcell argue that cultures are best studied not as individual units that interact to a greater or lesser extent with surrounding units, but rather as participants in larger cultural flows that rest upon major geographical structures, such as the Mediterranean Sea. These cultural flows produced geographically and culturally contiguous societies that interacted to a variable degree, with periods of intensification alternating with periods of abatement. The twelfth century was certainly one such period of intensification, in which persons—and texts—circulated dynamically not just throughout the Mediterranean, but from the Iberian peninsula into Norman France and Norman England. Connections to Norman Sicily even further enriched the dynamic flow of ideas, the give-and-take that characterized this extraordinarily vibrant period in literary and cultural history. The dialogic structure of the *Disciplina Clericalis*, with the mutual relationship of teacher and pupil and its pervasive metaphorical linking of knowledge and delicious food, emblematizes precisely this dialectical relationship produced by the interaction of, on the one hand, the local hybrid culture of each Norman society and, on the other hand, the transnational

"Normannitas" that stretched seamlessly across borders. In the *Disciplina Clericalis*, assimilation of food mirrors assimilation of knowledge, and both of these mirror the assimilation of culture.

The approach to the *Disciplina Clericalis* that I have proposed here might serve as a helpful way of reading literary texts that are too often understood as privileged mediators of some kind of essential identity, whether that identity be defined in terms of ethnicity, national origin, or gender. Petrus Alfonsi has, in the past, been interpreted as just such a representative of "Oriental wisdom" or "Arabic literary tradition" or even, more recently, of Sephardic identity: Jacqueline-Lise Genot-Bismuth's recent edition of the *Disciplina Clericalis* makes a valiant effort to reconstruct the contours of "the postulated Hebrew of the original text," and repeatedly identifies its author not as "Petrus Alfonsi," but "Moses the Sefarad."[38] While some readers, such as Steven Kruger, have taken pains to understand the complex negotiations of a divided identity that underlies the *Disciplina Clericalis* and, even more prominently, the *Dialogi contra Iudaeos*, others seem too ready to locate some essential quality in the work, if not in the man himself.[39] In her brief yet perceptive discussion of Petrus Alfonsi, María Rosa Menocal describes him not in terms of "Oriental," Jewish, or Muslim identity, but in terms of Andalusi identity, as a representative of that heterogeneous, polylingual culture that was the crucible of a range of communities that interacted among and against one another. Even Menocal, however, characterizes the frame-tale form of the *Disciplina Clericalis* as an exotic import into European culture, a linguistic and cultural "translation" that imports the oral, vernacular modes of expression found in al-Andalus into the written, Latinate clerical culture of Europe. In her account, Alfonsi's work is "a translation from an oral to a written form, as much as from one language to another: from the vernacular...to a written Latin form with the veneer of learning."[40] What I have tried to offer here is a perspective on the *Disciplina Clericalis* in particular (and, I hope, on medieval literature in general) that makes room for a reading of literary form as the *product* of cultural interaction rather than simply its object. As an interpretive matrix, Norman diaspora allows a reading that is founded on the ebb and flow of cultural identity, rather than the fixed stability of national, ethnic, or geographical origin.

This chapter began with a little fable concerning the late eighteenth-century edition of the *Castoiement du pere a son fils*, in which Étienne Barbazan presents the French translation of the *Disciplina Clericalis* as the product of an "Auteur anonyme" who embodies the paternal authority of the French nation. For Barbazan, the paternal voice of chastisement is the voice of the past, ventriloquized by means of the philologist's task of etymological excavation. In responding to Barbazan's nationalist philology, we can do no better than to think of another late twelfth-century text produced in the rich literary and linguistic ferment of Norman culture, the Hebrew translation of Marie's *Fables* produced by Rabbi Berechiah ben Natronai ha-Nakhdan, who lived both in Normandy and in Norman England. In addition to his well known *Mishlei Shu'alim* (or *Fox Fables*), based largely on Marie's collection, ha-Nakhdan may have composed a Hebrew adaptation of one of Marie's *Lais*, "Guigemar," under the title "The Story of King Solomon's Daughter."[41] The frame-tale narrative, winding its way from the *Disciplina Clericalis* to the *Castoiement* to Marie's *Fables* to ha-Nakhdan's *Mishlei Shu'alim*, might thus be read not as an Oriental commodity but as the lingering trace of cultural flow, marking the movement of both literary form and narrative content across the rippling waves of nation, religion, language, and gender.[42]

Notes

1. "S'il y en a eu de trop libres dans leurs productions, il y en a eu qui n'avoient pour objet que d'inspirer la Religion, les bones moeurs, la bone conduite, la soumission et le respect pour les persones constituées en dignité, et placées par Dieu pour nous gouverner et nous proteger. Tel est l'Auteur anonime, dont je done l'Ouvrage au Public" (1). Étienne Barbazan, *Le Castoiement ou instruction du pere a son fils. Ouvrage Moral en vers, composé dans le treizieme siecle. Suivi de quelques piece historiques, et morales aussi en vers et du même siecle. Le tout précédé d'une Dissertation sur la Langue des Celtes. Avec quelques nouvelles observations sur les étimologies* (Lausanne and Paris: chez Chaubert and Claude Herissant, 1760).

2. Preface (vii–xi): "Il seroit à souhaiter que l'on pût doner les ouvrages de tous nos anciens Auteurs, rien ne nous instruiroit mieux des usages et des moeurs de nos peres, rien aussi ne nous eclairciroit davantage sur l'origine, et sur les variations de notre Langue" (vii).

3. The term corresponding to "jagonce" in the Latin text is "iacinthus" (jacinth or hyacinth; DC ed. 314). Quotations from the *Disciplina Clericalis* are taken from the Latin edition (with French translation) of Jacqueline-Lise Genot-Bismuth, *La Discipline de clergie/Disciplina clericalis* (St. Petersburg: Dom/Paris: Editions de Paris, 2001); English translations are taken from Joseph Ramon Jones and John Esten Keller, *The Scholar's Guide: A Translation of the Twelfth-Century* Disciplina Clericalis *of Petro Alfonso* (Toronto: Pontifical Institute of Mediaeval Studies, 1969). Both are subsequently cited by page number, with the abbreviation "DC."

4. "Aumacor. Je n'ai vu ce moit qu'ici. Et je n'en trouve point l'origine dans le Latin. M. de Guignes l'un des Auteurs du Journal des Sçavans, que j'ai consulté, m'a dit qu'en Arabe *Omara-Khor* signifoit *Principes Stabuli*. Aumacor peut fort bien répondre à notre mot connestable" (154n2, to line "Roi et Contor et Aumacor"). Note that in the Latin text, the line reads "Vbi sunt reges, vbi principes, vbi diuites qui thesauros congregauerunt

et inde superbi fuerunt?" (DC ed. 364). In his discussion of the French versions of the *Castoiement*, Tolan (following the observations found in the edition of Hilka and Söderhjelm) states that "the translator removes Arab and Muslim elements from Alfonsi's text"; John Tolan, *Petrus Alfonsi and his Medieval Readers* (Gainesville: University Press of Florida, 1993), 135. This is apparently not the case, as the text edited by Barbazan preserves all of those same features that Tolan notes as omitted in both the A and B versions of the *Castoiement*.

5. Étienne Barbazan, "Dissertation sur la langue des Celtes ou Gaulois" (*Castoiement* i–xlvi; here quoting Falconnet): "Il donne ensuite cette leçon: 'L'art étimologique est celui de débrouiller de ce qui pour ainsi dire leur est étranger, et par ce moien de les ramener à la simplicité qu'ils ont tous dans l'origine' " (xlvi).

6. For Hermes, the *Disciplina Clericalis* "occupies a very important position on the caravan route of the transference of oriental tales to the west" (8); Eberhard Hermes, ed. and trans., *The* Disciplina Clericalis *of Petrus Alfonsi* (1970. Trans. P.R. Quarrie. London: Routledge and Kegan Paul, 1977). In his extremely perceptive and foundational study of Petrus Alfonsi, Tolan identifies the *Disciplina Clericalis* as an example of "Oriental Wisdom literature" (*Petrus Alfonsi*, 82, 91). For Amer, the *Disciplina Clericalis* is not only a source of "fables arabes" (5) but a representative of a "tradition arabe" (20; cf. "la littérature didactique arabe" [129], "la tradition littéraire arabe" [169]) that participates in the transmission of "une théorie orientale de l'interprétation" typical of "fables arabes" (21); Sahar Amer, *Esope au féminin: Marie de France et la politique de l'interculturalité* (Amsterdam and Atlanta: Rodopi, 1999).

7. Paul Gilroy, *The Black Atlantic: Modernity and Double Consciousness* (Cambridge, MA: Harvard University Press, 1993).

8. It is important to note that there is a distinction to be made between the self-identification of African American slave communities with Jews living in captivity in Egypt before the Exodus and the state of diaspora. The former is in a state of anticipation, looking forward to the Promised Land and, ultimately, the Incarnation; the latter is (from the Christian perspective) in a state of despair, resulting from the Jewish rejection of the divinity of Jesus. For a thoughtful exploration of the distinction between these two states of being, see Brian Stock, "Exodus and Exile in Late Antiquity," in *La Estela de los Viajes: De la historia a la literatura*, ed. Francisco Jarauta [forthcoming].

9. For an exceptional argument concerning how diaspora might be conceived of as a chosen (rather than compelled) state, see the seminal article of Daniel Boyarin and Jonathan Boyarin, "Diaspora: Generation and the Ground of Jewish Identity," *Critical Inquiry* 19 (1993): 693–725.

10. On the distinct character of early Judaic and early Christian characterizations of the nature of Jewish exile from Jerusalem, their subsequent interrelation, see Israel J. Yuval, "The Myth of the Jewish Exile from the Land of Israel: A Demonstration of Irenic Scholarship," *Common*

Knowledge 12 (2006): 16–33, esp. 20–26. On the reciprocal nature of early articulations of Rabbinic and Christian theology and community formation, see Daniel Boyarin, *Border Lines: The Partition of Judaeo-Christianity* (Philadelphia: University of Pennsylvania Press, 2004).

11. On the four-part trajectory of Orosian *translatio imperii*, from east (Babylon) to north (Macedonia) to south (Carthage) to west (Rome), see Suzanne Conklin Akbari, "Alexander in the Orient: Bodies and Boundaries in the *Roman de toute chevalerie*," in *Postcolonial Approaches to the European Middle Ages*, ed. Ananya Jahanara Kabir and Deanne Williams (Cambridge: Cambridge University Press, 2005), 105–26, esp. 106–8.

12. Mommsen's argument that Augustine and his follower Orosius participated in a deliberate effort to displace Virgilian historiography has been extremely influential, leading to some blindness on the part of more recent scholars to the extent to which these were integrated in medieval historiography; see, for example, Ingledew's emphasis on the "Augustinian-Orosian displacement of Virgil" and subsequent "return" of Virgilianism (674). Mommsen, "Orosius and Augustine," Theodor E. Mommsen, *Medieval and Renaissance Studies*, ed. Eugene F. Rice, Jr. (Ithaca: Cornell University Press, 1959); Francis Ingledew, "The Book of Troy and the Genealogical Construction of History: The Case of Geoffrey of Monmouth's *Historia Regum Britanniae*," *Speculum* 69 (1994): 665–704.

13. For a synthetic overview of the many chronicles that collectively make up the medieval history of Troy, see Ingledew, "The Book of Troy," esp. 682–88. On pseudo-Nennius and Geoffrey of Monmouth, see Robert W. Hanning, *The Vision of History in Early Britain: From Gildas to Geoffrey of Monmouth* (New York: Columbia University Press, 1966). On Dudo of Saint-Quentin and later adaptations of the *De moribus*, see Eleanor Searle, "Fact and Pattern in Heroic History: Dudo of Saint-Quentin," *Viator* 15 (1984): 119–37 as well as her *Predatory Kingship and the Creation of Norman Power, 840–1066* (Berkeley: University of California Press, 1988).

14. On medieval views of Jewish diaspora and Christian Rome, see Suzanne Yeager, "The *Siege of Jerusalem* and Biblical Exegesis: Writing about Romans in Fourteenth-Century England," *Chaucer Review* 39 (2004): 70–102.

15. Matthew Paris, *The Flowers of History*, trans. C.D. Yonge, 2 vols. (London, 1853), 1:3–32. Ingledew suggests that this "strategy of parallelism between Jewish and British history attempts to adapt the latter to the biblical paradigm of the chosen nation" (699). The four empires of Orosius are Babylon, Macedonia, Carthage, and Rome; later adaptors of Orosius, such as Otto of Freising and Matthew Paris, redefine the empires as Babylon, Persia, Greece, and Rome. This move has three important effects: it flattens out Orosian *translatio imperii* from a schema that encompasses the four cardinal directions (see n11, above) into a simple east-west trajectory; it erases Africa from the history of empire; and it elevates Greece into the role of cultural and imperial precursor to Rome.

16. Most recently, see Nick Webber, *The Evolution of Norman Identity, 911–1154* (Woodbridge: Boydell, 2005) and Pierre Bauduin, ed. *Les fondations scandinaves en Occident et les debuts du duche de Normandie: Colloque de Cerisy-la-Salle (25–29 septembre 2002)* (Caen: Publications du CRAHM, 2005).

17. Karla Mallette, *The Kingdom of Sicily, 1100–1250: A Literary History* (Philadelphia: University of Pennsylvania Press, 2005), 17–46. For an overview and selection of primary sources, see Elisabeth M.C. Van Houts, *The Normans in Europe* (Manchester: Manchester University Press, 2000). Still useful is Charles Homer Haskins, *The Normans in European History* (Boston: Houghton Mifflin, 1915).

18. On Augustinian toleration and its adaptation in later medieval culture, see Jeremy Cohen, *Living Letters of the Law: Ideas of the Jew in Medieval Christianity* (Berkeley: University of California Press, 1999). For a perceptive reading of the *Dialogi contra Iudaeos*, see Tolan, *Petrus Alfonsi* 12–41, esp. 19–22.

19. In their foundational study, Hilka and Söderhjelm described sixty-three manuscripts of the *Disciplina Clericalis*, while Tolan, *Petrus Alfonsi*, Appendix 3 provides descriptions of thirteen additional manuscripts. Alfons Hilka and Werner Söderhjelm, eds., *Disciplina clericalis I: Lateinischer Text* (Acta Societatis Scientiarum Fennicae 39.4. Helsinki, 1911), i–xxix; Tolan, *Petrus Alfonsi*, 199–204.

20. "Sed si aliquid philosophorum huiusmodi reposuisti in cordis armariolo, largire michi discipulo, et ego fideli memorie commendabo, ut quandoque condiscupulis lacte philosophico educatis delicatissimum largiri possim alimentum" (DC 15; ed. 276, trans. 70).

21. *Disciplina Clericalis* 19, "De duobus burgensibus et rustico": "Et isti burgenses postquam uolebant animalis naturam sibi assumere, mitissimi animalis naturam sibi debuissent uendicare; et merito cibum amiserunt" (ed. 298, trans. 80). "Pater ad hec: Dic michi, fili, quid audisti? Quomodo contigit discipulo, quoniam tali narracio animi erit recreacio?" (ed. 300, trans. 80).

22. "Bene me instruxisti, et quod de illarum artibus retulisti siticuloso et desideranti animo commendaui" (DC 9; ed. 246, trans. 57).

23. "Magister: Nonne tibi sufficiunt ista? Tria tibi narraui, et tu nondum desinis instigare? Discipulus: Tria dicendo nimium auges recitando numerum, sed pauca sonuerunt uerba. Dic ergo unum quod longa uerbositate meas repleat aures, et sic michi sufficiet" (DC 11; ed. 252, trans. 59).

24. On the egg passage of the fifteenth-century Latin manuscript W2 (inserted just before the Epilogue), see the edition of the *Disciplina Clericalis* edited by Alfons Hilka and Werner Söderhjelm (Helsinki, 1911): the text containing the passage appears in Anhang II, 77, and the manuscript is described at pp. vi–vii, xxv. Noted in Tolan, *Petrus Alfonsi* 155 and 259n99.

25. "Filius: Dic ergo quomodo ubique debeam comedere. Pater: Cum ablueris manus ut comedas, nichil tangas nisi prandium donec comendas....Post prandium manus ablue, quia phisicum est et curiale; ob hoc enim multorum oculi deteriorantus, quoniam post prandia manibus non ablutis terguntur. Filius: Si quis inuitauerit me ad prandium, quomodo respondebo? Concedam statim an non Pater: Fac sicut auctoritas Iudeorum precipit! Dicit enim: Si quis inuitauerit te, uideas personam inuitantis. Si enim magna persona fuerit, statim concede; sin autem, secundum quod erit uel secunda uel tercia uice....Iuuenis senem interrogauit: Cum inuitatus fuero ad prandium, quid faciam? Parum uel nimis comedam? Cui senex: Nimis! Quoniam si amicus tuus fuerit qui te inuitauit, multum gaudeit; si autem inimicus, dolebit. Hoc audito risit puer. Ad quem senex: Quid rides? Puer: Recordatus sum uerbi quod audiui de Maimundo nigro. Quidam enim senex quesiuit ab eo quantum posset comedere. Cui ipse: De cuius prandio, de meo uel de alterius? At ille: De tuo. Maimundus: Quanto minus possum. Senex: De alterius quantum? Maimundus: Quanto magis possum. Senex: Tu modo recordaris uerborum cuiusdam gulosi, pigri, stulti, garruli et nigigeruli et quicquid tale de illo dicitur uel eo amplius in eo inuenitur. Iuuenis: Multum placet michi de eo audire, quia quicquid de eo est derisorium est. Et si quid de eius dictis uel factis mente retenes, eloquere, et habebo pro munere" (DC 22; ed. 334–40, trans. 98–100).

26. "Pigriciam audiui; modo garrulitatem eius audire cupio" (DC 27; ed. 340, trans. 101).

27. "Philosophus ait: Huius seculi bona sunt commixta; non enim comedes mel sine ueneno. Alius: Quecunque in seculo sunt commutabilia sunt....Alius: Quasi in ictu oculi finitur gloria mundi" (DC 27; ed. 346, trans. 103; cf. DC 28, ed. 350, trans. 105–6).

28. Fable 27; ed. Spiegel 96–98. All citations of the *Fables* are from Marie de France, *Fables*, ed. and trans. Harriet Spiegel (1987. Medieval Academy Reprints for Teaching. Toronto: University of Toronto Press, 1994). Translations are my own, as Spiegel's are often idiomatic.

29. "Jeo manguz bien, si ai asez...Devant les piez mun seignur / Puis chescun jur runger les os, / Dunt jeo me faz gras e gros" (Fable 26; ed. 94).

30. "'Ja chaëne ne choiserai! / Meuz voil estre lus a delivre / Que en cheine richement vivre...Va a la vile, jeo vois al bois!' / Par la chaëne est departie / Lur amur e lur cumpainie" (Fable 26; ed. 96).

31. "Pur quei Adam manga le fruit, / Par quei le people aveit destruit— / E, quant il la pume manga, / Pur quei Deu ne li parduna" (Fable 53; ed. 156).

32. "Ne voilez mes Adam blamer, / Si le fruit de l'arbre manga, / Que nostre sire le devea....Tel quide blamer le fet d'autrui, / Que meuz devereit reprendre lui" (Fable 53; ed. and trans. 158).

33. On Jacques de Vitry and sermon exempla, see Tolan, *Petrus Alfonsi* 140–46.

34. William of Conches, *Dragmaticon* 6.2.22; trans. Italo Ronca 164–54.

35. Petrus Alfonsi, "Epistola ad peripateticos," ed. and trans. John Tolan in *Petrus Alfonsi* (Gainesville: University Press of Florida, 1993), 163–81 (Appendix 1); quotation from 172.

36. Petrus Alfonsi, "Epistola," 175–76; quotation from 176.

37. Peregrine Horden and Nicholas Purcell, *The Corrupting Sea: A Study of Mediterranean History* (Oxford: Blackwell, 2000).

38. Genot-Bismuth describes her effort to reconstruct "l'hébreu postulé du texte original" of "Moïse le Séfarade" (87) in the introduction to her edition of the Latin text (with French translation) of the *Disciplina Clericalis*; see esp. 74–87.

39. Steven F. Kruger, "Conversion and Medieval Sexual, Religious, and Racial Categories," in *Constructing Medieval Sexuality*, ed. Karma Lochrie, Peggy McCracken, and James A. Schultz (Minneapolis: University of Minnesota Press, 1997), 158–79; Kruger, *The Spectral Jew: Conversion and Embodiment in Medieval Europe* (Minneapolis: University of Minnesota Press, 2006).

40. María Rosa Menocal, "An Andalusian in London," in *The Ornament of the World: How Muslims, Jews, and Christians Created a Culture of Tolerance in Medieval Spain* (Boston: Little, Brown, 2002), 147–57; quotation from 153. See also Menocal, *The Arabic Role in Medieval Literary History: A Forgotten Heritage* (1987. Philadelphia: University of Pennsylvania Press, 2004), 141.

41. The *Mishlei Shu'alim* are translated by Moses Hadas in *Fables of a Jewish Aesop* (New York: Columbia University Press, 1967). On the possible authorship of "The Story of King Solomon's Daughter," see Michael Chernick, "Marie de France in the Synagogue," *Exemplaria* (Fall 2006, online preprint).

42. An earlier version of this chapter was delivered at a conference on "The Persistence of Philology: Rethinking Comparative Literary History," March 15–17, 2007. Thanks to the workshop participants for their provocative comments.

CHAPTER 2

RELIQUIA: WRITING RELICS IN ANGLO-NORMAN DURHAM

Heather Blurton

*T*his *chapter revisits the scholarly consensus that the Old English poem*
Durham *is both formally and politically nostalgic by reading it as a political
gambit in the power struggles between the monks of Durham Cathedral against the
neighboring castle and its powerful bishops in post-Conquest Durham.*

In the early eleventh century, a monk named Elfred had a vision that
inspired him to seek out the relics of Bede and other northern saints and
reunite them with those of St. Cuthbert. In support of Elfred's contention
that he had deposited these relics inside St. Cuthbert's coffin for safekeep-
ing, Symeon of Durham offers the evidence of a certain poem written
in English:

> Cuius de Beda sententie concordat etiam illud Anglico sermone composi-
> tum carmen, ubi cum de statu huius loci et de sanctorum reliquiis que in
> eo continentur agitur, etiam reliquiarum Bede una cum ceteris ibidem
> mentio habetur.

> [His account of Bede agrees also with that poem in the English language
> which, when it speaks of the condition of this church and the relics of
> saints which are contained in it, mentions the relics of Bede there together
> with those of other saints.][1]

Scholars agree that this passage refers to the poem known as *Durham*.
Despite this fascinating evidence for at least one twelfth-century reader
of the poem, scholarship on *Durham* has largely focused on the linguistic

question of whether this poem represents the last gasp of Old English or the first breath of Middle English. Christopher Cannon, in an article that focuses on the implications of thinking about vernacular literacy in this way in twelfth-century England, writes that *Durham*:

> sits so conveniently on the customary divide between Old and Middle English (it is datable, by internal evidence, to 1104–9) that the line can be drawn right down the middle of the poem. Because of its "regular alliterative metre," it can be described as "the latest of the extant Anglo-Saxon poems," but because its language has changed substantially from the Anglo-Saxon standard…its language can also be placed firmly in the early Middle English (or "transition") period.[2]

This approach to the language of the poem translates into the ways the poem has been read as a literary artifact. Seth Lerer summarizes the critical orthodoxy in his survey of "The Afterlife of Old English":

> While it has, in fact, been included in the *Anglo-Saxon Poetic Records* (as the "latest of the extant Anglo-Saxon poems in the regular alliterative meter"), it has been appreciated in two contrasting and mutually exclusive ways. On the one hand, it has been studied as an eloquent survival of traditional techniques of verse-making two generations after the Norman Conquest—a way-station in the history of English metrics from *Beowulf* to Layamon. On the other hand, it has been understood as an antiquarian *tour de force* re-creating for a literate audience the older forms of poetry for purposes politically and culturally nostalgic, an act of artificial eloquence conjured out of the remains of a nearly lost tradition.[3]

The poem itself is a brief (only twenty-one line) description of Durham. It describes first the topographical setting of Durham in terms of lush abundance, then itemizes the equal abundance of its relics:

Is ðeos burch breome	geond Breotenricc,
steppa gestaðolad,	stanas ymbutan
wundrum gewæxen.	Weor ymbeornad,
ea yðum stronge,	and ðer inne wunað
feola fisca kyn	on floda gemonge.
And ðær gewexen is	wudafæstern micel;
wuniad in ðem wycum	wilda deor monige,
in deope dalum	deora ungerim.
Is in ðere byri eac	bearnum gecyðed
ðe arfesta	eadig Cudberch
and ðes clene	cyninges heafud,
Osuualdes, Engle leo,	and Aidan biscop,

Eadberch and Eadfrið   æðele geferes.
Is ðer inne midd heom   Æðelwold biscop
and breoma bocera Beda,   and Boisil abbot,
ðe clene Cudberte   on gecheðe
lerde lustum,   and he his lara wel genom.
Eardiæð æt ðem eadige   in in ðem minstre
unarimede   reliquia,
ðær monia wundrum gewurðað   ðes ðe writ seggeð,
midd ðene drihnes wer   domes bideð.

[This city is famous throughout Britain,
steeply founded, the stones around it
wondrously grown. The Wear runs around it,
the river strong in waves, and there in it dwell
many kinds of fish in the mingling of the water.
And there has also grown up a secure enclosing woods;
in that place dwell many wild animals,
countless animals in deep dales.
There is also in the city, as it is known to men,
the righteous blessed Cuthbert
and the head of the pure king—
Oswald, lion of the English—and Bishop Aidan,
Eadbert and Eadfrith, the noble companions.
Inside with them is Bishop Æthelwold
and the famous scholar Bede, and Abbot Boisil,
who vigorously taught the pure Cuthbert in his youth,
and he (i.e., Cuthbert) learned his lessons well.
Along with the blessed one, there remain in the minster
countless relics
where many miracles occur, as it is said in writing,
awaiting the Judgment with the man of God.][4]

The Latin rubric that precedes the poem in its only extant medieval manuscript, Cambridge, University Library, MS Ff.i.27, notes this thematic division, naming the poem: *De situ Dunelmi et de sanctorum reliquiis quae ibidem continentur carmen compositum*—on the site of Durham and on its relics.[5] There is, however, a missing third term that haunts this formulation—Durham Cathedral.

Durham Cathedral dominates the skyline of Durham, perched as it is on a bluff in a hairpin bend of the River Wear. The poem's refusal to describe the cathedral is even more striking if the critical consensus that the poem was composed for the translation of Cuthbert's relics into the cathedral in 1104 is correct.[6] The reason Cuthbert's remains were moved, of course, is that the Anglo-Saxon church into which they were painstakingly reunited with the relics of Bede and other northern saints was torn down by the second Norman bishop of Durham, William of St. Calais. In its place, the now famously Romanesque Durham Cathedral was in the process of being built in the Norman style and to Norman tastes.

This transformation of Durham's most notable landmark from Anglo-Saxon to Anglo-Norman is profoundly symbolic of the political situation of post-Conquest Durham. This chapter will seek to resituate *Durham* in the postcolonial climate of Anglo-Norman Durham. It will consider *Durham*'s engagement with the absent presence of the cathedral at the heart of the poem by suggesting in the first instance a new interpretation of the poem's meaning: that the poem may be read as having the form of a riddle whose solution is "reliquary." In this reading, the poem's odd use of the word "reliquia" becomes the key to its meaning. The poem offers itself in place of "ðem minstre" as a reliquary for the past, while simultaneously punning on the way it, through its use of Old English language and poetic forms, is itself also a relic of the past.

Second, this chapter will suggest one way in which this interpretation of *Durham* might help us to better understand the cultural work that the poem performed in its early twelfth-century context. The identification of *Durham* as either Old English or early Middle English is based on linguistic rather than political considerations. Nevertheless, to identify the poem as "Old English" is to make unavoidably political associations and inevitably to evoke the nostalgia about which Lerer speaks. As an Old English poem, *Durham* can only ever be "last," an afterthought in the "afterlife" of Old English. *Durham*, however, may be read not simply as a commemoration of the translation of the relics of Cuthbert in 1104, but as a self-conscious political intervention into that occasion. Considering the poem as a deliciously contrived piece of propaganda in Durham's post-Conquest struggle for legitimacy and power invites us to set aside the debate as to whether the poem is written in Old English or early Middle English and to consider the poem rather to be quintessentially Anglo-Norman in its aims and aesthetic. As an Anglo-Norman poem, *Durham* does not appear at all nostalgic, but rather fresh, lively, and stubbornly politically engaged.

Margaret Schlauch, in an influential article on *Durham*, has interpreted the structure of the poem as an example of the classical genre of *encomium urbis*, the praise of a city, making it the only extant Old English poem of its kind.[7] She writes:

> It is the existence of the first part [the description of Durham] which establishes this piece within a group of city laudations of the early Middle

Ages having precisely the same structure. All of them conclude with a celebration of the saints, martyrs, and relics associated with the town. The other poems are in Latin.[8]

Schlauch describes similar *encomia* of the cities of Milan, Verona, Monte Cassino, and, more locally for the *Durham* poet, York—all of which describe the physical aspect of the city as well as its saints. The description of Durham begins by announcing its fame throughout Britain ("Is ðeos burch breome/geond Breotenrice"), it then telescopes to the spectacular site of Durham itself, high on a cliff, encircled both by the River Wear and forest land ("Weor ymbeornad" and "wudafæstern micel"). This description of Durham, however, is not very descriptive at all. In so far as it echoes Bede's description of England in the first book of the *Ecclesiastical History*, which finds Britain teeming with wildlife and natural features, it may intend to inscribe Durham's quintessential Englishness at the same time as it pays homage to an important Durham saint.[9] On the other hand, however, the description offered of Durham is so general as to describe absolutely nothing. Rivers are generally full of fish and forests of animals, and the copiousness of landscapes is itself a poetic *topos*. More specifically, *Durham* here follows the description of York in Alcuin's *De pontificibus et sanctis Ecclesiae Eboracensis*:

> Hanc piscosa suis undis interluit Usa
> Florigeros ripis praethendens undique campos;
> Collibus et silvis tellus hinc inde decora.

> [Through York flows the Ouse, its waters teeming with fish,
> Along its banks stretch fields laden with flowers
> All about the countryside is lovely with hills and woods.][10]

If *Durham* is indeed an *encomium urbis*, it departs crucially from its genre: the other *encomia* discussed by Schlauch do describe their *urbi* in detail. Thus for example, to take the model closest to home, Alcuin describes a new church built in addition to York Minster by bishop Ælberht:

> Haec nimis alta domus solidis suffulta columnis,
> Suppositae quae stant curvatis arcubus, intus
> Emicat egregiis laquearibus atque fenestris.
> Pulchraque porticibus fulget circumdata multis,
> Plurima diversis retinens solaria tectis,
> Quae triginta tenet variis ornatibus aras.

> [This lofty building, supported by strong columns,
> Themselves bolstering curving arches, gleams
> Inside with fine inlaid ceilings and windows.

It shines in it beauty, surrounded by many a chapel
With many galleries in its various quarters,
And thirty altars decorated with different finery.] [11]

What these descriptions of York highlight is the fact that, if not for the naming of the River Wear, the distinctive topographical setting of the city of Durham would be unrecognizable from the evidence of these poetic lines. Nevertheless, *Durham*'s engagement with the tropes of *encomium urbis* highlights the referentiality of Durham as a real political space; a space that is, at the turn of the twelfth century, highly contested.

In any case, the poem's not naming Durham would be explained if it were not an *encomium,* but rather a riddle. Calvin Kendall has drawn attention to the riddling aspect of the poem:

> In one respect *Durham* differs from the models Schlauch cites. Unlike them, it does not name the city it celebrates. This seems a curious omission in an *encomium urbis.* There is no doubt that Durham is meant: the references to the River Wear and the Durham saints are conclusive.[12]

Kendall argues that *Durham* borrows aspects of the popular Old English literary form of the riddle, and he proposes that the key to the riddle of *Durham* lies in the puns on Cuthbert's name: both "Cuthbert," the patron saint of the community of monks (l. 10) and *cuð burch* the famous city ("burch breome") of the opening line.[13] I would like to pursue Kendall's suggestion that *Durham* has riddling elements and read it precisely as a riddle, although I would like to propose a different—or perhaps simply an additional—solution to its meaning. The punning structure that Kendall uncovers is implicated in the solution, although it is not the answer to this riddle. The poem, after all, names Cuthbert, a move that would be unusual if "Cuthbert" were its solution. It likewise names the River Wear, which means, if it is a riddle for either "Cuthbert" or for "Durham," it is not a very difficult one.

Like an Old English riddle that does not name its object of description, the poem does not describe Durham's most distinctive feature, the Anglo-Norman cathedral that was under construction at the moment of the poem's composition. Instead of the anticipated description of Durham—or, more specifically, of the cathedral towering over the bluff—the poem iterates the saintly rulers, both bishops, abbots, and kings, of Durham's past, relegating the building that houses them to a single half-line: "in ðem minstre." The emphasis is not exclusively on the important figure of Cuthbert, but on the sheer number of the relics—the "unarimede reliquia." This line, and the ones that follow, pose problems of interpretation.[14] But the Latin word *reliquia* calls attention to this line.[15] It gestures to the solution to the riddle: like Durham Cathedral, the poem itself is a reliquary for the "countless relics" it holds.

Durham, in other words, encodes its answer in Latin, even as it folds around the description of English saints and kings at its center. The construction of the poem as reliquary is surely the function of the envelope structure and metaphors of enclosure that Lerer has identified in the poem:

> Like the iterations at the close of *Daniel* and the envelope structure of Riddle 42, these many repetitions verbally enact the theme of *Durham*. Tracing their patterns we may find a poem that, in its concern with closure and enclosure, closes in upon itself. In the center of the poem, just as in the center of the church, are the remains of the great teachers. Cuthbert's name brackets the list of bishops, kings, and scholars, much as the coffin that contains his bones stands as a symbol for the whole tradition of monastic learning which his *clene* example set for later followers. Around the edges of the city flows the river Wear; around the *burch* itself ring stone walls. *Wundrum* and *wundrum* set off the entire text, much like the river or the wall that encircle the foundation.[16]

In its role as a reliquary, *Durham* pushes aside the claims of the new Anglo-Norman cathedral and offers itself as the more appropriate shrine. With its opening description of the topography of Durham, the poem becomes a reliquary not only for Durham's famous relics, but also for the site of Durham itself. Like a cathedral, it enshrines the space of Durham as well as its relics. In its closing lines, the poem gestures to the centrality of texts to the cult of relics and to the authenticating power of writing—"ðes ðe writ seggeð." Here, the text replaces the reliquary as witness—the poem is itself the reliquary. In this reading *Durham* becomes a struggle for the topography of Durham, as the poem reclaims the space on the bluff overlooking the River Wear from its new Anglo-Norman bishops and Anglo-Norman cathedral and substitutes itself for the cathedral as a final resting place for Anglo-Saxon kings and saints.

The use of English, then, is a form of political affiliation: it asserts old forms against new ones. Indeed, *Durham*'s use of double alliteration suggests a sort of overdetermined Englishness built into the very form of the poem. The use of English language and poetic form may suggest that the poem is of much greater antiquity than it actually is: that it, like the uncorrupted body of St. Cuthbert or the head of King Oswald, is a relic of the Anglo-Saxon past. But not necessarily, I would argue, for purposes that are "politically and culturally nostalgic." After all, what was there to be nostalgic about? Although the poem was composed at

least fifty years after the Battle of Hastings, a date of 1066 is premature
for understanding the Conquest north of the Humber. The situation in
the North was characterized by at least another half-century of political
turmoil, right up to the turn of the twelfth century. The first Norman-
appointed Earl of Northumbria was murdered in 1069. In the same year,
the community of Cuthbert once again fled with the saint, this time
from Durham to the safety of Lindisfarne. Æthelwine, the last Anglo-
Saxon bishop of Durham, was implicated in Hereward's revolt against
William the Conquerer, and died in prison in 1071 after the rebellion
was subdued. His successor—and the first bishop of Durham imposed
under the Norman regime—the Lotharingian Walcher, was murdered
in 1080 by the citizens of Durham. These events do not, however, form
a straightforward story of regional rebellion and the subsequent assertion
of centralized Norman power. In 1088, for example, the second Norman
bishop of Durham, William of St. Calais, was sent into exile for his role
in a rebellion against William Rufus. In its historical context, therefore,
Durham looks less like the remnant of a dead tradition and more like the
product of a situation that was constantly shifting at a moment when no
one could yet have known the final outcome.[17]

The internal politics of the cathedral monastery were likewise characterized by upheaval. The monastic community that had settled in
Durham with the body of St. Cuthbert was composed of married clerks
who were deemed insufficiently reformed by the bishops Walcher and
William of Calais. They were offered the opportunity of giving up
their families and accepting Benedictine monasticism, but, according to
Durham legend, only one monk accepted. So in 1083 the former monks
of St. Cuthbert were replaced by a community of reformed Benedictine
monks. Although the ejection of the Anglo-Saxon community coincides
with the Conquest, it is not necessarily a function of it, but may be rather
part of the general movement of Benedictine reform.[18] Indeed, the new
monks were not Norman like their bishop, but reformed English monks
from the South, who, according to Symeon of Durham, had read about
the glory days of Northumbrian monasticism in the works of Bede.[19]
After the reform, Symeon describes William of St. Calais appointing
offices for these new monks—among them the office of prior to govern
the community—and separating his estates from those of the monks:

> Denique terrarium possessiones illorum ita a suis possessionibus segre-
> gauit, ut suas omnino abepiscopi seruitio et ab omni consuetudine liberas
> et quietas ad suum uictum et uestitum terras monachi possiderent.
>
> [Then he segregated his own landed possessions from theirs, so that the
> monks should possess their lands for the purpose of their maintenance and

clothing, entirely free and quit of episcopal service and of all customary exactions.][20]

Although the clarity with which he describes the separation may have been partly wishful thinking on Symeon's part, E.U. Crosby describes a "gradual separation of the two endowments and the emergence of the chapter as a largely independent community of clergy."[21] Thus the monks began to think of themselves as a community somewhat separate from their bishop.

While this sense of community and the shared, and international, interests of reformed Benedictine monasticism may have prevailed over national or ethnic differences, they did little to smooth over the rift that widened throughout the twelfth century between the monks of St. Cuthbert and their powerful bishop. The position of the bishop of Durham was unique in terms of the temporal authority he exercised. In 1072 Earl Waltheof of Northumbria had begun to fortify Durham, building a castle practically alongside the cathedral on the top of the bluff. After Waltheof's execution for treason, however, William the Conqueror, in an unprecedented move, made Bishop Walcher Earl of Northumbria. After the subsequent murder of Walcher, the Bishops of Durham lost the title of Earl of Northumbria but retained temporal jurisdiction over County Durham as what later historians would call "Prince-Bishops." Throughout the twelfth century the processes by which the Bishop of Durham detached his jurisdiction from the king, and the monks of Durham detached their jurisdiction from that of the bishop, were ongoing and contested.[22]

At the beginning of the twelfth century, the monks of Durham are new—replacing the unreformed clerks who had so heroically (according to tradition) kept St. Cuthbert's body one step ahead of the Vikings. Durham, too, was a new town, without a long Anglo-Saxon past, consolidated in response to the Danish conquests. The monks of St. Cuthbert were left with divided loyalties and with a pressing need to assert their position against the consolidation of Norman power in the North, against the encroachments of the neighboring bishop and castle, and against those who might suggest that these newcomers had no true claim to the custody of Cuthbert.

In the early twelfth century, therefore—in response to conquest, both Danish and Norman, in response, as well, to the post-Conquest reform of the cathedral community and wholesale replacement of its clerks with monks, and finally in response to the imposition of new, and recognizably Norman, political, and architectural forms on the landscape—the monks of Durham were diligently engaged in producing a past for their cathedral.

They began by literally reclaiming Durham's past by reassembling the lands that had been lost during the years that the community was on the move.[23] Simultaneously, the monks were producing a mass of textual evidence to buttress their community's claims specifically to Cuthbert's patrimony and more generally to the power of the monastic community of the cathedral priory against that of the bishop and castle through an aggressive program of history writing. These texts included several manuscripts of Bede's life of St. Cuthbert, the *Historia de Sancto Cuthberto*, the eleventh-century chronicle now interpolated into the Red Book of Durham, and the historiography traditionally attributed to Symeon of Durham, as well as the poem *Durham*, which follows the *Libellus de exordio* (the *History of the Church of Durham*) in the Cambridge manuscript.[24]

It has long been recognized that the events of 1066 and the following decades inspired an upsurge in the writing of history in Britain, a wholesale recording and revision as monks attempted to reconcile the past with the present. Richard Southern describes

> a continuous process of collecting and arranging charters, transcribing documents, and carrying out minute investigations into chronology, topography, studying monastic buildings and inscriptions, assembling the texts of ancient learning, writing estate-histories, chronicles and biographies.[25]

If some, as H.S. Offler did, see an "atmosphere of calculated fraud" in much of this monastic production,[26] this was nothing new: monastic chronicling had always contained a large element of legitimizing claims to property and revenue. Texts are powerful weapons in the battle for legitimacy, and medieval monks recognized and manipulated this fact to their full ability: the new Benedictine monks of Durham were no exception.[27]

At the time of the 1104 translation of Cuthbert's relics into the new cathedral, the monks must have been feeling the necessity of buttressing their legal and moral rights more than ever. After the death of Bishop William of St. Calais, under whom the community had been reformed and the cathedral-building project inaugurated, the king appointed no other than the infamous Ranulph Flambard as the new bishop of Durham, a figure who Barbara Abou-El-Haj aptly characterizes as "a notorious plunderer, embezzler, and extortionist."[28] Alan Piper proposes that the *Libellus de exordio* was just such a response to the threat of Flambard.[29]

In response to these pressures, the texts that the monks were producing emphasized shared themes: they emphasize property and ownership, they emphasize the importance of Bede and of continuity with the Northumbrian past, they emphasize the miracle-working power of St. Cuthbert. The late tenth- or eleventh-century *Historia de Sancto Cuthberto*, for example, is more of a narrative cartulary than a history: in it the history of the community of St. Cuthbert is framed as a series of donations, and borders are noted punctiliously. In the *Libellus de exordio*, for example, Cuthbert appears in a vision to Abbot Eadred announcing:

> Dicito...regi ut totam inter Weor et Tyne terram michi et in mea ecclesia ministrantibus perpetue possessionis iure largiatur, ex qua illis ne inopia laborent.

> [Tell the king that he should give rights of perpetual possession to me and to those who minister in my church all the land between the Wear and the Tyne, so that they many not struggle in want.][30]

And the text frequently itemizes the property of the church of Durham: for example, Snaculf, son of Cytel, gave "Brydbyrig, Mordun, Socceburg, Grisebi cum saca et socne" [Bradbury, Mordon, Sockburn, and Girsby, with sake and soke].[31] The same is true of the short tract *De obsessione Dunelmi,* which follows Symeon of Durham's *Historia Regum* in the unique manuscript of both. Composed probably after the rebellion of Earl Waltheof in 1075, *De obsessione*, while it describes the eleventh-century history of the earls of Bamborough, their feuds, and their negotiations with Æthelred, Swein, and Cnut, intervenes in a property dispute regarding lands that had been alienated from the control of the church through the marriage of the daughter of one of its bishops.[32] The monks added further miracles to Bede's *Life of Cuthbert* that emphasized control of property and rebuke of secular authority.[33] One such example of St. Cuthbert's miraculous intervention comes when the Earl of Northumberland removes the church of Tynemouth from Durham's jurisdiction and gives it instead to St. Albans. Both the Earl and the Abbot of St. Albans subsequently suffer disasters at Tynemouth.[34] The plan worked: as William Aird indicates, there is every evidence that the monks of the cathedral successfully negotiated post-Conquest politics. He points out:

> As three of the bishops appointed to the church of St Cuthbert in the period 1071–1153 were formidable royal officials, the degree of freedom which the convent was able to obtain provides comment on the nature of, and resistance to, post-Conquest ecclesiastical and political domination.[35]

Many scholars have elucidated this sociopolitical context for hagiography and chronicle in Anglo-Norman Durham, and they have indicated the ways in which eleventh- and twelfth-century monks at Durham sought to invent a past for their community that would protect it into the future.[36] It simply remains to imagine *Durham* as part of this context. *Durham* participates fully in the context of eleventh- and twelfth-century Durham historiography. The trinity of saints, Cuthbert, Aidan, and Oswald, embedded at the center of the poem, are likewise featured in the *Libellus de exordio* and in manuscript collections of Bede's *Life of Cuthbert*.[37] Their miracle-working power is emphasized, as is the connection to the Northumbrian past, and the importance of the topography of Durham.[38]

Indeed, in addition to these shared themes, the manuscript context of the poem supports the claim that *Durham* was received, if not composed, as an item in Durham's evidentiary brief. Cambridge, University Library MS Ff.i.27 begins at the beginning with Gildas, Nennius, and Bede before bringing history up to date and locality with the *Libellus de exordio* and the *Historia de Sancto Cuthberto*. In addition to this historical overview, the manuscript offers supporting evidence of Durham's claims: a list of Æthelstan's donations to St. Cuthbert, a list of Durham's relics, and the poem *Durham*.[39] The manuscript presents a united front and a persuasive argument: it is not merely a collection of texts about Durham, it is the basis of the legitimacy and authority of the monks of Durham Cathedral.[40]

The poem *Durham* is particularly interesting, however, in its use of the English language and English literary forms. This suggests that if we are willing to think about English literature taking place in French in Anglo-Norman England, perhaps we might also consider the possibility that Anglo-Norman literature might take place in English. When used to describe a poem in the English language, "Anglo-Norman" emphasizes the dominant cultural and material conditions of production that enabled the articulation of literary texts in any language in Anglo-Norman England. Thus, instead of understanding *Durham* as a transitional text linguistically caught between Old and early Middle English, it is perhaps more helpful to understand it as caught between two structures of power in early Anglo-Norman Durham, between cathedral and castle.

The most important question to ask about *Durham* is not whether it is written in Old English or early Middle English but why it is written in English at all. Old English, we know, continued to be widely copied during the twelfth century.[41] In the second half of the eleventh century, the rule of St. Benedict was copied in English at Durham.[42] In manuscripts it was enough of a presence in twelfth-century Durham that a cathedral booklist has a separate section for books in English.[43] English was not only copied in the twelfth century it was also composed, and if these compositions appear with hindsight to us as nostalgic, it is important to remember that such a tone is in fact characteristic of most Old English-language poetry, in which the good old days are always/already gone.[44] As Seth Lerer demonstrates in his readings of *The Rime of King William* and *The First Worcester Fragment*, they often are engaged with quite contemporary political affairs.[45]

Read in this context, it is not surprising that a short poem about Durham should be composed at the very beginning of the twelfth century. From its manuscript context, it is nevertheless quite clear that *Durham* participates in and bolsters the claims to legitimacy of the monks of Durham cathedral. Someone in twelfth-century Durham thought that an English-language text was necessary to that case, or at least, would lend it credence. The use of English here suggests antiquity, but English is of no greater antiquity, and certainly of no greater authority, than the Latin that is the language of the rest of the Cambridge manuscript, and, indeed, of reformed Benedictine monasticism.[46] An English-language text may have been deemed necessary in this context partly because English continued to be considered a viable legal language of documentation.[47] Perhaps, moreover, an English-language text was considered to be especially authenticating because in the political climate of early twelfth-century Northumbria it may not have been entirely clear that the Normans were there to stay.[48]

Although *Durham* closely shares common themes and motifs with the other literature produced in post-Conquest Durham, it also stands alone as a short poem, a riddling poem. The riddle as a literary form is predicated on the absence of meaning. Riddling is a mode of irony that relies on a common understanding between the text and its interlocutor about what has not been articulated. If a riddle depends on the play of absences, this riddle does so more than most since not only the answer to the riddle—"reliquary"—is absent, but in this poem that lingers over the topography of Durham, so too is the most distinctive aspect of this topography, the cathedral on its cliff. Through its use of a riddling format, through its substitution of itself for the cathedral as a more appropriate reliquary for Northumbrian saints and kings, and through its use of the English language, *Durham* situates itself provocatively among the texts collected, copied, and composed in Durham in the eleventh and twelfth centuries. As an early twelfth-century, Anglo-Norman text *Durham* plays a role in the effort of the monks of Durham to assert the legitimacy of their custodianship of St. Cuthbert. We might read it likewise as playing a role in their negotiations for power against bishop and castle, as well as in the monks' manipulation of the past available to be co-opted by episcopal, secular, and indeed ultimately monastic, power. That an English-language text would be included in this program suggests ways of thinking about late Anglo-Saxon texts as politically expedient and politically powerful rather than politically nostalgic. In other words, it suggests that we might think of them as Anglo-Norman. In any case, with the composition of the poem *Durham*, the monks provided Durham cathedral with a powerful relic in the most fully medieval sense of the word—not a solitary remnant of a lost past, but a cult object capable of powerfully linking together past, present, and future.

Notes

1. Symeon of Durham, *Libellus de exordio atque procursu istius, hoc est Dunhelmensis, Ecclesie. Tract on the origins and progress of this the Church of Durham*, ed. and trans. David Rollason (Oxford: Oxford University Press, 2000), 166, 167.
2. Christopher Cannon, "Between the Old and the Middle of English," *New Medieval Literatures* 7 (2005): 214 [203–21]. Cannon's argument points out the difficulties inherent in maintaining the categories of "old" and "early Middle" when poems are considered in their manuscript context.
3. Seth Lerer, "Old English and Its Afterlife," in *The Cambridge History of Medieval Literature*, ed. David Wallace (Cambridge, UK: Cambridge University Press, 1999), 8 [7–34].
4. Elliott van Kirk Dobbie, ed, *The Anglo-Saxon Minor Poems*, ASPR 6 (London, 1942), 27; Lerer, "Old English and Its Afterlife," 21.
5. The poem is also attested by a transcription of Cotton Vitellius D xx, a manuscript that was destroyed in the Cottonian fire (Dobbie, *Anglo-Saxon Minor Poems*, xliii) and a transcription in Stanford University Libraries, Department of Special Collections, Misc. 010 [J1]. For the question of whether this last represents a new witness, see Daniel O'Donnell, "Junius's Knowledge of the Old English Poem *Durham*," *Anglo-Saxon England* 30 (2001): 231–45.
6. For the consensus, see Dobbie, *Anglo-Saxon Minor Poems*; Cannon, "Between the Old and Middle of English"; Kendall, Lerer, "Old English and Its Afterlife"; and Margaret Schlauch, "An Old English *Encomium Urbis*," *Journal of English and Germanic Philology* 40 (1941): 17 [14–28]. A dissenting voice is H.S. Offler, "The Date of Durham (*Carmen de Situ Dunelmi*)," *Journal of English and Germanic Philology* 61 (1962): 591–94.
7. With the possible exception of *The Ruin*. See D.R. Howlett, "Two Old English Encomia," *English Studies* 57 (1976): 289–93.
8. Schlauch, "An Old English *Encomium Urbis*," 17.
9. A very similar description, paying special attention to forests and rivers full of fish, is to be found at the beginning of Geoffrey of Monmouth's *History of the Kings of Britain*. Although *Durham* clearly follows Gildas and Bede with its use of the term "Breotenrice," its self-positioning as within "Britain" rather than "England" may be interesting to think about in the larger context of this volume.

10. Alcuin, *Versus de patribus regibus et sanctis euboricensis ecclesiae*, ed. and trans. Peter Godman (Oxford: Clarendon Press, 1982), 6, 7.

11. Alcuin, *Versus*, 118, 119.

12. Calvin Kendall, "Now Let Us Praise a Famous City: Wordplay in the OE *Durham* and the Cult of St. Cuthbert," *Journal of English and Germanic Philology* 87 (1988), 507–21, 511.

13. Kendall argues that the poem is not, strictly speaking, a riddle, but that it contains "riddling elements" (Kendall, "Now Let Us Praise a Famous City," 511).

14. See the discussion by Dobbie, *Anglo-Saxon Minor Poems*, 152–53.

15. It may be more correct to refer to *reliquia* as a loan word rather than a macaronism—it existed alongside the Old English "haligdom," "halignes," and "liclaf," but it was used just as often as well as in compounds such as "relicgang." I think, nevertheless, that the usage calls attention to itself in this context: "reliquium" is not common in poetry, and the meter of the poem seems to draw attention by stressing the first syllable.

16. Seth Lerer, *Literacy and Power in Anglo-Saxon Literature* (Lincoln: University of Nebraska Press, 1991), 202.

17. For a fuller account of post-Conquest politics in the north, see W.E. Kapelle, *The Norman Conquest of the North: The Region and Its Transformation, 1000–1135* (Chapel Hill: University of North Carolina Press, 1979). For the textual manipulation of ethnicity in these struggles, see Chapter Two of Robert M. Stein, *Reality Fictions: Romance, History and Governmental Authority, 1025–1180* (Notre Dame: University of Notre Dame Press, 2006), titled "Narrating the English Nation After 1066," and also Hugh M. Thomas, *The English and The Normans: Ethnic Hostility, Assimilation, and Identity 1066–c. 1220* (Oxford: Oxford University Press, 2003). For a discussion of post-Conquest cathedrals as contested spaces, see Jeffrey Jerome Cohen, *Hybridity, Identity and Monstrosity in Medieval Britain* (New York: Palgrave Macmillan, 2006).

18. Julia Barrow, "English Cathedral Communities and Reform in the Late Tenth and Eleventh Centuries," in *Anglo-Norman Durham, 1093–1193*, ed. David Rollason, Margaret Harvey, and Michael Prestwich (Woodbridge: Boydell Press, 1994), 25–39. Aird suggests that the pre-Conquest bishoprics of the reformed Peterborough monks Æthelric and Æthelwine may represent a similar pre-Conquest attempt to reform Durham (William M. Aird, *St. Cuthbert and the Normans: The Church of Durham, 1071–1153* [Woodbridge: Boydell Press, 1998]). Malcolm Baker cites C.R. Dodwell's observation that "among the first forty-six post-Conquest monks listed in the Durham *Liber Vitae* only a few Norman names occur, which indicates that under William of Saint Calais Durham was 'a predominantly Anglo-Saxon house.'" (Malcom Baker, "Medieval Illustrations of Bede's *Life of St. Cuthbert*," *Journal of the Warburg and Courtauld Institutes* 41 [1978]: 19 n21 [16–49]).

19. See the discussion of the "northern revival" in David Knowles, *The Monastic Order in England: A History of Its Development from the Time of St. Dunstan to*

the *Fourth Lateran Council, 943–1216*, (Cambridge: Cambridge University Press, 1941), 163–171.

20. Symeon, *Libellus de exordio*, 232, 233.

21. Everett Crosby, *Bishop and Chapter in Twelfth-Century England: A Study of the "mensa episcopalis"* (Cambridge: Cambridge University Press, 1994), 1.

22. For the development of the County Palatine of Durham see Gaillard Lapsey, *The County Palatine of Durham: A Study in Constitutional History* (Cambridge, MA: Harvard University Press, 1924). For the separation of the estates of the cathedral monastery from those of the bishop, see Everett Crosby, *Bishop and Chapter in Twelfth-Century England*.

23. Barbara Abou-El-Haj, "Saint Cuthbert: The Post Conquest Appropriation of an Anglo-Saxon Cult," in *Holy Men and Holy Women: Old English Prose Saints' Lives and Their Contexts*, ed. Paul E. Szarmach (Albany: State University of New York Press, 1996), 180 [177–206]; Bernard Meehan, "Insiders, Outsiders, and Property in Durham around 1100," *Studies in Church History* 12 (1975): 45–58.

24. In his recent edition, Rollason has pointed out that the title of the text formerly known as the *History of the Church of Durham* is more properly *Libellus de exordio atque procursu istius, hoc est dunhelmensis, ecclesie*. On the question of the attributions to Symeon of Durham see Antonia Gransden, *Historical Writing in England, c. 550–1307* (London: Routledge, 1974), 115–16; and Rollason, "Introduction," in Symeon of Durham, *Libellus de exordio atque procursu istius, hoc est Dunhelmensis, Ecclesie. Tract on the Origins and Progress of this the Church of Durham*, ed. and trans. David Rollason (Oxford: Oxford University Press, 2000), xliii–xliv. For the *Historia de Sancto Cuthberto* see *Historia de Sancto-Cuthberto: A History of Saint Cuthbert and a Record of His Patrimony*, ed. and trans., Ted Johnson-South (Woodbridge: D.S. Brewer, 2002); for the Red Book of Durham, see H.H.E. Craster, "The Red Book of Durham," *English Historical Review* 40 (1925): 504–32.

25. R.W. Southern, "Aspects of the European Tradition of Historical Writing: 4. The Sense of the Past," *Transactions of the Royal Historical Society*, 5th Series, 23 (1973): 249 [243–63].

26. H.S. Offler, "Bishop William of Saint-Calais, First Norman Bishop of Durham," *TAASDN* 10 (1950): 259 [258–79].

27. On this point, see especially Abou-El-Haj, "St. Cuthbert," Meehan, "Insiders and Outsiders," and Rollason, "Introduction," lxxxv–lxxxvi.

28. Barbara Abou-El-Haj, *The Medieval Cult of Saints: Formations and Transformations* (Cambridge: Cambridge University Press, 1994), 52.

29. Alan Piper, "The First Generation of Durham Monks and the Cult of St. Cuthbert," in *St. Cuthbert, His Cult and His Community to AD 1200*, ed. G. Bonner, D. Rollason, and Clare Stancliffe (Woodbridge: Boydell Press, 1989), 442 [437–46].

30. Symeon, *Libellus de exordio*, 124, 125. See also the discussion in Meehan, "Insiders and Outsiders."

31. Symeon, *Libellus de exordio*, 154, 155.

32. *De obsessione Dunelmi et de probitate Uchtredi comitis et de comitibus qui ei successerunt* (Of the siege of Durham and the honesty of Earl Uhtred and of the earls who succeeded him). *The Early Charters of Northern England and the North Midlands*, ed. C.R. Hart (Leicester: Leicester University Press, 1975).

33. See S.J. Ridyard, "*Condigna Veneratio*: Post-Conquest Attitudes to the Saints of the Anglo-Saxons," *Anglo-Norman Studies* 9 (1986): 196–97 [179–205] and Baker, "Medieval Illustrations of Bede's *Life of St. Cuthbert*," 16–17.

34. Bertram Colgrave, "Post-Bedan Miracles and Translations of St. Cuthbert," in *The Early Cultures of North West Europe*, ed. C. Fox and B. Dickens (Cambridge: Cambridge University Press, 1950), 315.

35. Aird, *St. Cuthbert and the Normans*, 7.

36. See especially Abou-El-Haj, "St. Cuthbert"; Baker, "Medieval Illustrations"; the essays collected in *Anglo-Norman Durham, 1093–1193*; Aird, *St. Cuthbert and the Normans*; and Rollason, "Introduction."

37. "At the start of his *libellus* Symeon set a triptych of saints: Oswald, Aidan and Cuthbert. This is not the only context in which the three are brought together in this way in the twelfth century. Among the fourteen twelfth century copies of Bede's prose *Life of Saint Cuthbert* that belong to the textual group associated with the cathedral priory, there are five manuscripts, among them the most closely connected with the cathedral priory, that also contain passages drawn from the *Ecclesiastical History* to form lives of Oswald and Aidan." (Piper, "The First Generation of Durham Monks and the Cult of St. Cuthbert," 443).

38. The deployment in particular of St. Cuthbert as the centerpiece of the project fits into a larger, national context of the appropriation of the Anglo-Saxon past, and, in particular, of Anglo-Saxon saints, on the part of Normans anxious to both consolidate and to legitimize their rule. Susan Ridyard has argued persuasively that the old view of Norman churchmen sweeping out English cults after the Norman Conquest is outdated (Ridyard, "*Condigna Veneratio*"). The Normans were, she argues, in fact far more concerned to profit where they could by appropriating powerful local cults. Durham had one of the most popular and powerful Anglo-Saxon cults, but it was a cult dislocated from its own past. Therefore the monks of Durham had to scramble to produce one. But if the cult of St. Cuthbert might be useful to the consolidation of Anglo-Norman power in the north then it could also be useful for the consolidation of the monks' control over St. Cuthbert in their struggle against their Norman bishops. Perhaps rather than reading into this movement Norman co-option of the English saints and thus of the English past, we might wonder whether, considering the durability of the Anglo-Saxon cults, the monks of Durham were involved in shaping the past that was available to be co-opted, of writing a version of the past that suited their view of the future.

39. Neil Ker, *A Catalogue of the Manuscripts Preserved in the Library of the University of Cambridge* II (Cambridge, UK: Cambridge University Press, 1857), 318–29.

Christopher Norton, in the most comprehensive analysis of this manuscript, points out that it is extremely unlikely that the shorter texts copied
at the end of the *Libellus de exordio* were space fillers. (Christopher Norton,
"History, Wisdom and Illumination," in *Symeon of Durham: Historian of
Durham and of the North*, ed. David Rollason [Stamford: Shaun Tyas, 1998]
66 [61–105]).

40. CUL MS F.f.1.27 is only the second half of the original twelfth-century
manuscript. What was the first half is now Corpus Christi College,
Cambridge MS 66, which opens with the famous Sawley World Map.
Christopher Norton has suggested that the book was originally compiled
as a gift for Bishop Hugh le Puiset (1153–1195) to remind him of his
obligations to the monastery. Norton notes: "the focus of the whole
volume is not on the bishops, but on the church of Durham, its relics,
properties, privileges and possessions" (Norton, "History, Wisdom and
Illumination," 98).

41. See Lerer, "The Afterlife of Old English," 8–9; Also Mary Swan
and Elaine Treharne, eds. *Rewriting Old English in the Twelfth Century*
(Cambridge, UK: Cambridge University Press, 2000).

42. Aird, *St. Cuthbert and the Normans*, 128. This is the bilingual Latin/Old
English text of Durham Cathedral MS B.iv.24.

43. Donald Matthew, "Durham and the Anglo-Norman World," in *Anglo-
Norman Durham, 1093–1193*, ed. David Rollason, Margaret Harvey, and
Michael Prestwich (Woodbridge: Boydell Press, 1994), 15 [1–22].

44. Andrew Galloway, for example, remarks that "Nostalgia is, to be sure,
an identifying marker of pre-Conquest English poetry; 'Durham' ends
with a list of deceased English spiritual heroes resting along with Saint
Cuthbert, who patiently awaits the Last Judgment...with no sign that
the Norman Conquest has interrupted that wait" (Andrew Galloway,
"La3amon's Gift," *PMLA* 121.3 (2006): 718 [717–34].

45. Lerer, "The Afterlife of Old English," 11–25.

46. CUL MS F.f.1.27 does have one other short Old English piece: this is the
version of Bede's "Death-Song" copied into the *Libellus de exordio*.

47. See, for example, Thomas Hahn, "Early Middle English," in *The
Cambridge History of Medieval Literature*, ed. David Wallace (Cambridge,
UK: Cambridge University Press, 1999), 63n6 [61–91].

48. As Aird points out, Durham's proximity to Scotland may also have made
it even more unclear as to whether Durham's political future lay to the
north or to the south (Aird, *St. Cuthbert and the Normans*, 8).

CHAPTER 3

CULTURAL DIFFERENCE AND THE MEANING OF LATINITY IN ASSER'S *LIFE OF KING ALFRED*

David Townsend

Asser's biography of Alfred the Great of Wessex *is often read as a principal site of ninth-century West Saxon hegemonic consolidation. Yet at the same time, this essay argues, its rhetorical pragmatics encode an implicit, and often overlooked, assertion of continued cultural diversity in Britain.*

If this collection takes as one of its sustained themes the contested subsumption of cultural and linguistic diversity into an unquestionable (which is to say ideological) wholeness, then I find it hard not to adduce the trinitarian career of Alfred the Great of Wessex—as ninth-century warrior, statesman, and scholar—as both beginning and origin.[1] As beginning, because Alfred's activity and its contemporary representation imparts powerful impetus to the ongoing process by which a welter of local cultures, dialects, languages, and ethnicities are elided into England. As origin, because modern scholarship has so often embodied a powerful desire to read Alfredian beginnings teleologically. By that process, Alfredian values come to be seen as finding ultimate fulfilment in modern scholarship's own values as an end. So, by way of notable example, the prestigious annual *Anglo-Saxon England* has for over three decades taken as its epigraph a brief quotation from Alfred's preface to his translation of Gregory the Great's *Pastoral Care*: "her mon mæg giet gesion hiora swæð"—"here may one still see the trace" of previous generations' learning, now putatively lost, with the clear implication that contributors have emulated Alfred in running such tracks to their source. But (as Allen J. Frantzen has pointed out) modern scholarship has by such a process of identification also often run the risk of recapitulating within itself occlusions of difference and contestation commensurate with those enacted in the original sources.[2]

Central to our direct knowledge of Alfred's career, as to its ideological representation, is the biography by Asser, Welsh churchman in the service of a Saxon king. It thus should afford little surprise that Asser's text has itself proven such a site of contention. The last century saw the text scrupulously edited from the vexed surviving postmedieval witnesses (by Stevenson); denounced repeatedly as forgery (by Galbraith at mid-century, more recently by Smyth); defended repeatedly as genuine (by Whitelock in answer to Galbraith, by Keynes in answer to Smyth); described condescendingly as an imperfect draft and minimally competent pastiche (by many of its students); and read as a cohesive embodiment of the Alfredian conflation of literacy and power (by Lerer).[3] The secondary scholarship has tended to treat cultural difference in Asser's text as inadvertently revelatory of the author's circumstances, rather than as central to the cultural work the *Life of Alfred* performs. The Welshness of the text's narratorial persona thus generally figures in modern scholarship either as transparent, ingenuously presented evidence for the historical truth of its author's biography; or else as the camouflage thrown up by a clever (but not too clever) later Anglo-Saxon bent on imitation of the historical Asser's voice. The often-adduced topoi of the debate include the presence of trilingual glossing of place names, in which Latin toponyms are accompanied by their English and Welsh equivalents; the accuracy of the Welsh historical events narrated in Chapters 79–80; and usages in the Latin that seem to suggest the idioms of a native speaker of Welsh.

Marginalized under the terms of such debate, however, are the rhetorical pragmatics that might allow us to think about such indices of linguistic and cultural difference as signifying something more nuanced than, on the one hand, an unselfconscious witness to the real circumstances of the text's production, or else, on the other, a falsified screen by which a forger intentionally impersonates the historical Asser. The recurrent debate over the genuineness of Asserian attribution, and the ways in which the signs of linguistic difference within the text have figured in that debate, have tended to obscure another question that bespeaks a different sort of cultural agency we might well otherwise attribute to the text. To wit: if we accept that the genuine Asser wrote the biography attributed to him, what then is the meaning of the text's Latinity? How might we see the Latinity of the *Life of Alfred* as positioned within a multiligual habitus, at a moment that the text itself celebrates as cultural consolidation but that simultaneously threatens a vastly accelerated subsumption of local subjectivity? We might reframe the question, in other words, not as that of the authenticity as opposed to the fictionality of the text's signs of linguistic difference, but rather as that of the effects in a specific milieu of the necessary fictionality of these (as of all) textual signs of linguistic difference. In the remainder of this chapter, I want to argue that Asser, architect of Alfredian authority, simultaneously deploys the Latinity of his text as a brake on that same linguistically consolidated hegemony—thus circumscribing the cultural capital, even as he builds it, of what will soon become, as Nicole Guenther Discenza proleptically identifies it, the King's English.[4]

Introductory summaries of the vicissitudes of Wessex in the ninth century abound, but I ask the reader's patience for a review of the extraordinarily steep trajectory from momentary West Saxon ascendancy to fragmentation and then back again to more lasting consolidation over the course of Alfred's life.[5] Alfred's grandfather Egbert had won for his kingdom ascendancy over the previously dominant kingdom of Mercia in the years 825–829. Egbert's dominance quickly evolved into what appears to have been an equal alliance between Wessex and Mercia by the time Alfred's father Æthelwulf acceded to the West Saxon throne in 839. During the same period, however, the depredations of seasonal Norse raiding parties already posed an escalating threat to the kingdoms south of the Humber. Beginning in 850 Viking tactics shifted to the overwintering of substantial military forces, as opposed to the more random smaller forays of the previous decades.

West Saxon political authority itself meanwhile was splintered by Æthelwulf's division of power, first between himself and his eldest son, and then, upon the latter's death and just before his own departure for Rome in 855, his subsequent division of authority with his next two eldest sons, Æthelbald and Æthelberht. Confusion ensued with the refusal of Æthelbald to surrender the territory entrusted to him upon his father's return, the death of Æthelwulf in 858, Æthelbald's death in turn in 860, the assumption of sole authority in territories under West Saxon control by Æthelberht, Æthelberht's death in 865, and the accession of Alfred's only surviving brother Æthelred. Meanwhile, the year of Æthelred's accession saw also the arrival of the massive Viking forces that within six years had exacted tribute in East Anglia, established a puppet regime at York, secured the capitulation of Mercia, returned once again to conquer East Anglia definitively, and begun an assault on Wessex itself.

At this low ebb of West Saxon fortunes, Alfred himself in 871 acceded to the throne upon the death of Æthelred. The following years saw him reduced to a struggle for survival and guerilla resistance against the invaders. A rout of the Viking forces in 878, under circumstances understood only imperfectly, resulted in peace and an exchange of hostages with Guthrum, the Viking king, and the settlement of the Norse in East Anglia, soon to become the Danelaw. The year 879 saw the departure of a third Viking force for the Continent, leaving Alfred's Wessex to some thirteen years of relative tranquility, which ended with the return of the Vikings and renewed assaults in 892. The 880s saw Alfred's consolidation of authority through the construction or renovation of a series of strategically placed fortified towns. By the early 880s Alfred had secured the overlordship of Mercia and the submission of all the English not under Danish rule. He recaptured London from the Vikings in 886. By the late 880s Alfred's charters styled him not simply as King of Wessex but by the new title *rex Angulsaxonum*—king of a now singly conceived people here denoted, by a hybrid nomenclature recently minted on the Continent and never before used in England itself, as the Anglo-Saxons.[6]

The same years also saw Alfred's recruitment of the team of scholars associated with his project for the first Great Books in Translation program of European history. Alfred himself would undertake, with levels of assistance that we cannot definitively establish, the translation of Gregory's *Pastoral Care*, Augustine's *Soliloquies*, Boethius's *Consolation of Philosophy*, and Psalms 1–50. The Alfredian program also included a translation of Gregory's *Dialogues* by Bishop Wærferth of Worcester, the anonymous West Saxon translation of Orosius's *History Against the Pagans*, and arguably the anonymous translation of Bede's *Ecclesiastical History,* whose dialectical features suggest the Mercian origins of its translator. The 880s also saw the initial compilation of the Anglo-Saxon Chronicle, though the latter was not distributed in the hyparchetypes of the surviving manuscripts until some time after the return of the Vikings from the Continent in 892.

While much of Alfred's scholarly team seems to have come to him from Mercia, Alfred recruited Asser from the church of St. David's (as he himself tells us in Chapter 79), where he was certainly a monk and may in fact have been bishop, and where his confreres encouraged the association in the hopes that Alfred might offer protection from the incursions of the king of the southern Welsh kingdom of Dyfed. The southern Welsh kings themselves had at a somewhat earlier date accepted Alfred's overlordship, choosing subordination to West Saxon authority as defense against the depredations of Rhodri Mawr, king of the ascendant northern Welsh kingdom of Gwynedd. (An alliance between Rhodri's son Anarawd and the Viking king of York would subsequently collapse around 893, leading to the submission of Anarawd as well to Alfred's overlordship.) Asser concluded his first extended stay as a member of Alfred's retinue at the end of 886. His *Life of Alfred* dates from 893.

Asser himself first documents and gives enduringly cogent shape to this triumphal march of Alfredian authority from the brink of extinction in 871 to West Saxon ascendancy over all the English as over most of the Welsh. Our sense of the distinctive and inextricable Alfredian linkage of royal authority, spirituality, and learning is itself dependent on Asser. While Alfred's own words, most famously in his preface to the translation of the *Pastoral Care*, attest many of the king's preoccupations, and while the Anglo-Saxon Chronicle accounts for the military and political aspects of Alfred's reign, it's virtually impossible for us to abstract our sense of Alfred from a synthesized nexus of documents organized around Asser's biography. The reception history of the texts substantiates the enduring power of such a nexus, beginning with the first printing of the preface to the English *Pastoral Care* as an appendix to the 1574 *editio princeps* of Asser by Matthew Parker[7] and continuing through the anthology of supporting documents arranged around Asser's text by Lapidge and Keynes in their 1982 Penguin Classics volume.

But lest we see the accretion of additional texts around Asser's as extraneous to his own work's textual strategies, it's worth recalling that sanctioned anthologization is already instantiated by Asser's text—a formally and substantively anomalous, disunified hybrid of chapters translated from an early version of the Anglo-Saxon Chronicle, on the one hand, with sections participating, on the other, in a more synthetic mode of biography ultimately Suetonian in lineage but more directly inspired by, albeit not substantially modeled on, Einhard's *Life of Charlemagne*.[8] Departing from previous considerations of the text's peculiarities as accidental to the vicissitudes of its composition and transmission, Seth Lerer argues that the principle of authorized anthologization is quintessential to Asser's articulation of discursive power.[9] Such an articulation affords us ample warrant to think intertextually about Asser's rhetorical strategies. On his own terms these are inextricably bound up with the rhetorical pragmatics of other texts supportive of Alfred's newfound status as governor of all the Christians of Britain and king of the Angles and Saxons, as Asser addresses him in his initial dedication.[10] In other words, we can and should think through Asser's staging of unity's triumph over diversity in relation both to the historical Alfredian subsumption of diverse polities and to the Alfredian submersion of linguistic difference through programmatic translation.

Secondary literature of recent years has variously addressed the supersessionist consequences of the Alfredian translation project. Sarah Foot traces the development of Alfredian notions of the *gens Anglorum* from its roots in Bede. She points out that the cultural force of Alfred's literary program imparted to the strategy of ethnic unification a conceptual depth that activity in the political field alone could not have achieved—an observation further and richly elaborated by Kathleen Davis.[11] Nicole Guenther Discenza's study of the Boethius translation derives a conceptual framework from Pierre Bordieu to address Alfred's accumulation of cultural capital. In other articles Discenza similarly addresses as well the construction of Anglo-Saxon authority in the Englisc[12] Bede and in the translation program as a whole. Robert Stanton also examines the Alfredian symbiosis of literary and political authority.[13]

Malcolm Godden surveys more specifically the translation pragmatics of the anonymous Orosius and of Alfred's translations of Boethius and Augustine, with particular attention to how they highlight the Latin source texts' authorial personae even as they depart dramatically from the substance of the originals. The continuously applied tag *cwæð Orosius* [so said Orosius] at once foregrounds the translated status of the Englisc version of the *History against the Pagans* while simultaneously obscuring many of the anonymous translator's very substantial interventions of content. The translator, Godden concludes, appeals to Orosius as wholly present in the translation as its author, even as s/he modifies Orosius's account of history for the Alfredian audience.[14] Godden also observes that Alfred "has gone out of his way to strengthen the impression, for a reader, that Boethius is present as narrator of the text—all three references to his relationship with Theoderic, for instance, are additions by the translator. Yet beneath this pretence of a Boethian voice and an early sixth-century situation, Alfred is rewriting very substantially." He later concludes that "in fictionalising Boethius, ironising Wisdom, radically changing Wisdom's arguments, and...taking issue, in the voice of Boethius, with the main thrust of Wisdom's views, while all the time maintaining and strengthening the fiction that this is a work of the sixth century, Alfred shows a remarkably confident, one might even say cavalier, belief in his right as author to remake the original text and to objectify it and its original author as products of their time and circumstance."[15]

Alfredian translation, then, ostensibly calls attention to the gap between Latin source and Englisc simulacrum. Yet ironically, it in practice collapses difference into the self-sufficiency of Alfredian culture as a presence into which alterities of time and language have been successfully and unproblematically assumed. This is nowhere more true than in the transformations of Bede's *Ecclesiastical History*, the only text in the Alfredian program itself of Englisc origin. Nicole Guenther Discenza's analysis of the Englisc Bede's translational pragmatics adduces parallels to the dynamics observed by Godden in the case of other texts, namely the presentation of Bede's persona as though he spoke here in his own voice, in Englisc, and the consistent omission of Latin documents in support of the narrative. The effect of such omissions, Discenza observes, "is to leave Bede as the sole authority for each of the events and sentiments marked by the letters."[16] The anglicization of the Church in Great Britain, carefully qualified in the original Latin text, is here rendered unequivocal. As Discenza goes on to conclude: "to all appearances, Bede speaks to the reader directly in Old English, with no translator mediating between the monk and his audience. Bede becomes the authority, the guarantor of truth for statements which had in his Latin *Historia* been guaranteed by the documents which he incorporated. The translator has no need of continental authorities or Latin documentation when England has its own history now available in its own legitimate language."[17] This supplantation is perhaps most dramatically embodied in one of the best-known episodes of Bede's work, which Discenza does not discuss, namely the miraculous origin of Christian Englisc poetry through the inspiration of Cædmon, the illiterate Whitby cowherd of Book 4, Chapter 24.

Katherine O'Brien O'Keeffe has splendidly elucidated the transmission history of Caedmon's nine-line Hymn.[18] As she reminds the reader, the Hymn comes down to us in two forms, as also reflected in the edition presented in the Anglo-Saxon Poetic Records: a Northumbrian version that travels as a marginal gloss to Bede's Latin paraphrase in manuscripts of the original text of the *Historia Ecclesiastica*; and a West Saxon version incorporated directly into the text of the Englisc translation.[19] Bede himself is scrupulous to point out that his translation of the Hymn into Latin is an approximation of the sense but cannot capture the fullness of the original text: "This is the sense but not the order of the words which he sang as he slept. For it is not possible to translate verse, however well composed, literally from one language to another without some loss of beauty and dignity."[20] Translation renders unnecessary this acknowledgment of linguistic difference, and all that remains of Bede's elaborate distancing of paraphrase from original is the introductory comment, "þære endebyrdnis þis is"—"of which this is the sequence."[21] But lest we read this movement of an originary text from periphery to centre, from gloss to primary document, as an unproblematic wresting of literary agency away from a metropolitan centre in favour of local positionality, it's salutary to remember that the Northumbrian specificity of a venerable text already two centuries old is in this very moment of ostensible privileging erased, buried in the relative linguistic uniformity of the Alfredian program and collapsed into an authoritative ninth-century West Saxon present that brooks temporal alterity no more than it tolerates linguistic difference.

Bede's glossing practices articulate a space for the sustained integrity of local language and local culture, amidst negotiations of identity bound up with the appropriation of a metropolitan language and with the internalization of a metropolitan vantage point as a means to consolidate "national" identity in eighth-century Northumbria. Adopting the Nigerian writer Gabriel Okara's taxonomy of postcolonial appropriations of English as neo-metropolitan or else experimental, Uppinder Mehan and I have elsewhere used his category of the neo-metropolitan to think through aspects of Bede's practice, namely his scrupulously correct Latin usage and his celebration of the authoritative metropolitan gaze of Gregory the Great as it hails the Angles into nationhood.[22] Bede carefully preserves linguistic and cultural difference, distinguishes between the universal and the particular, the metropolitan and the local, and articulates a space in which the particular and the local endure. In the Englisc *Ecclesiastical History*, by contrast, signs of difference collapse into the authoritative self-presentation of a formerly subaltern and now ascendant language that claims to speak for a newly consolidated national identity.

The contrast of Bede's early eighth-century Latin practice with the Alfredian program's articulation of authority bears consideration in light of Lawrence Venuti's meditations on the ethics of difference and assimilation in translation practice. Venuti's central concern to preserve the sign of the source text's heterogeneity, as a metonymy for the source culture that engenders it, leads him to advocate a "minoritizing" practice of translation. Such a practice calls attention to the translatedness of the translation, thus discouraging the reader from imagining that the translation's target language and culture have fully domesticated the alterity of the original. "This translation ethics does not so much prevent the assimilation of a foreign text as aim to signify the autonomous existence of that text behind (yet by means of) the assimilative process of the translation," he writes.[23] I don't intend to claim that Venuti's categories map precisely over the circumstances of Bede's Northumbrian original and its Alfredian rendering, or over the supersessionism of other texts in the Alfredian translation program. Still, there is little in the Englisc text—and this corroborates Discenza's observations cited above—to suggest a minoritizing practice of the sort Venuti's intercultural ethic leads him to promote, or that would hark back for that matter to the ostensible humility of Alfred's self-declared approach to translation in the preface to his *Pastoral Care*.

We might, then, invert the lens to focus not on the motivations behind Englisc versions of authoritative Latin texts, but rather on why, in 893, in the midst of the breakneck consolidation of vernacular authority in the service of West Saxon hegemony, Asser would in his biography of Alfred cleave to Latin. He could, after all, have excerpted annals from a newly composed and promulgated Anglo-Saxon Chronicle in their original form and added further anecdotal material in Englisc. The existing secondary literature has not engaged in any sustained way the question of why Asser didn't choose to initiate a practice of vernacular biography. One obvious answer is the continued prestige of the learned language of high culture: to borrow Discenza's appeal to Bordieu, the text's Latinity generates cultural and symbolic capital. Or perhaps Asser's own command of Englisc remained imperfect—although he in fact assisted Alfred in his translation of Boethius. But in the face of the abundantly charged meanings of burgeoning vernacularity, I'd argue that we should engage the meaning of Asser's Latinity as a central and polyvalent consideration. Nor, at a moment when a dominant vernacular has suddenly accrued cultural capital with spectacular success, is that meaning exhaustively explained by appeal to Asser's consciously articulated motivation. Rather, I'd suggest that the meaning of his Latinity, while including the text's celebratory construction of Alfredian authority, is likely to encompass as well, albeit as a less fully realized counterpoint, the residual misgivings of a Welsh churchman over the erasure of difference in that same West Saxon project to which he contributed so centrally. In other words, we should entertain the possibility that Asser's text includes elements subversive of West Saxon linguistic supersessionism and the proliferation of West Saxon cultural and symbolic capital.

Returning to Gabriel Okara's taxonomy, we might at least provisionally label Asser, like Bede before him, as a neo-metropolitan—that is, as a writer whose confidence in the essential solidity of local experience is joined to a faith that the metropolitan language can be made to express it fully. But let me be quick to repeat Uppinder Mehan's important point in connection with Bede, that the neo-metropolitan is not *tout court* the *comprador* who casts his lot with metropolitan power and metropolitan language. Such a stance, rather, can represent a bold appropriation, staking a claim, at the heart of the language of the privileged centre, for the integrity and autonomy of local subjectivity.[24] At the same time, the relation of metropolitan language to local subjectivity necessarily has for Asser shifted radically from Bede's Northumbrian circumstances of the 730s, with the sudden and politically charged rise of a privileged vernacular. In contemplating the changed circumstances of Asser's Latinity, we might thus consider analogies to the fortunes of modern English as the principal metropolitan language of the last century, at the other end of a trajectory initiated by Alfred's creation of the first King's Englisc—to wit, the provisional espousal of English in postcolonial contexts where a newly ascendant vernacular has threatened to swamp local difference. Such, for example, was the social and political role of English in Tamil Nadu in the years after Indian independence, as a defense against the imposition of Hindi.[25] English continues to function as a tool of cultural resistance in southern Sudan today, in opposition to Arabic as the lingua franca of the north.[26]

In analyzing the pragmatics of Asser's stance toward the expression of local diversity in the metropolitan tongue, we might begin by considering his bilingual or multilingual presentation of place names. The text offers sixteen such instances. Of these, three gloss an Englisc place name with its

Latin translation.[27] Four more gloss a Latin toponym with Englisc.[28] Two simply call attention to the place name as Englisc without providing a term in another language.[29] Seven adduce Welsh place names with Latin or Englisc or both as alternatives.[30] Finally, in two instances Asser gives Welsh names alone without comment or alternative.[31] It is a commonplace of scholarship that Asser's incorporation of Welsh place names establishes his intended historical audience as Welsh,[32] as may indeed have been the case. Here, however, I'd prefer to emphasize the intratextual rhetorical construction of ideal readership, the active fiction of Welsh readership that is textually prior to any historical Welsh readership—a readership the text in any case appears to have found with only very limited success, if any success at all. Much as is the case with Bede's glossing, Asser's supplementation of Englisc toponyms with Latin translations (and, *mutatis mutandis*, the reverse) establishes the fictive ideal reader of his text as requiring assistance with Englisc names and so obviously not himself Englisc by presumption. But while the authorization of Gregory's metropolitan gaze as constitutive of Englisc identity is essential to Bede's glossing practice,[33] here Asser's Latinity establishes that Englisc positionality is not unequivocally privileged, without Bede's recourse to a unitive and definitive Elsewhere of culture around which the field of local experience organizes itself. Asser like Bede invites the Englisc to see themselves being seen, but in contrast to Bede not so much from a unitive centre as from a multiplicity of provisionally validated locations.

After three bilingual Latin-Englisc glosses, Asser in Chapter 9 first introduces as a third term a Welsh toponym. He will continue to intersperse such trilingual glosses throughout the text, but they will achieve relative prominence as the text progresses, with the occasional elimination altogether of Englisc toponyms in favour of Welsh. Welsh toponymics, to be sure, carve out a place for local positionality in the heart of metropolitan Latinity, much as Bede's glosses had done; but more to my present point, they further relativize Englisc perceptions of place, establishing an implicit ethnography of multiple nations occupying a single island—and indeed, with Welsh place names occasionally applied deep within Englisc territory, like portals into the parallel Otherworld of Welsh narrative literature. Whether or not Asser intended these toponymics to render the text more intelligible to Welsh readers, they remind all readers—Welsh, English, and potentially Continental alike—that West Saxon subjectivity does not exhaust lived experience in the island of Britain.

The Continental triangulation of Asser's Latinity is indeed also relevant here. Alfredian aspirations to Carolingian prestige are yet another commonplace of scholarship. Asser's references to his sovereign as "rex Angulsaxonum," while borrowing the Frankish neologism more directly from Alfred's own recent charters, and so echoing Alfred's own extratextual pretensions to Carolingian affiliations, signal from the beginning of his text its ideal reader's Continental positionality. Asser's further affinities with ninth-century Continental biography include his debt to Einhard, his extensive inclusions of chronicle material, and the Frankish coloring of his lexicon.[34] These same Continental affiliations also serve to relativize Asser's use of the newly composed Anglo-Saxon Chronicle, translated back into the metropolitan language, against the literary expectations of an Elsewhere itself now destabilized—no longer the Rome of Gregory, as in Bede, but rather the already disjointed Francia of Charlemagne's late ninth-century successors—but whose gaze is turned upon all events in Britain, Englisc and Welsh alike.

Side by side with the Frankish coloring of Asser's language and the Frankish influences upon his text's formal arrangement, I invite reconsideration of two clear interlinguistic echoes of Welsh and English idioms. Asser repeatedly refers (in Chapters 32, 59, 79, and 80) to locations in the north or south as on the left or right hand, respectively, thus gesturing unmistakably to Welsh usage. In the instance of this in Chapter 79, the interlinguistic confusion of identity is even richer, and the momentary alignment of Welsh positionality with the metropolitan authority of Latin all the stronger, for the fact that the Latin designates the South Saxons as "the Saxons on the right" and then adds by way of gloss, "that is, in the Saxon tongue, the South Saxons." On the other hand, Asser in Chapter 18 translates literally from the Chronicle that the Christians in combat against the Vikings "held the place of slaughter" [et Christiani loco funeris dominati sunt]—an Englisc idiom that Keynes and Lapidge translate with the domesticated and less colourful "were masters of the battlefield." Secondary scholarship has paid ample attention to the former of these interlinguistic echoes as demonstrating Asser's ethnicity, and to the latter as evidence of a conscientious literal-mindedness in translation, as most students of the text would have it, while those still inclined to argue against Asser's authorship might claim the reverse. I'd propose to sidestep this debate for the moment and emphasize instead that the juxtaposition of Frankish lexical borrowings with both Welsh and Englisc idioms serve a neo-metropolitan practice that doesn't so much transcend the various specific cultural positionalities evoked by the text as set them all on equal footing. Asser's Latinity allows linguistic difference—all but fully suppressed in the Alfredian translation program—to lie barely dormant and imperfectly disguised.

Asser never more dramatically relativizes Englisc positionality than in the extraordinary and much discussed "misreading" of royal West Saxon genealogy in his opening chapter. Asser here adapts the Anglo-Saxon Chronicle's entry for 855, though departing in some details from the vernacular source. Having adduced Geat as a member of the West Saxon lineage, he immediately quotes the *Carmen Paschale* of Caelius Sedulius at the length of some ten lines, on the strength of Sedulius's reference to the "absurd Geta" of Roman comedy, dismissed by the Latin poet as he sets out instead to narrate the saving acts of God throughout biblical history and leading up to mankind's deliverance by Christ in his Resurrection. Seth Lerer says of this passage, "In offering Sedulius's comment on the 'absurd Geta,' Asser countermands the supposed authority of any genealogy of which it is a part. His interruption of a popular tradition with a learned text offers an inkling of his own intellectual method: one that places learned writings over oral lore and seeks to replace familiar credences with authoritative explanations."[35] I take no substantive issue with Lerer's assessment of this peculiar passage as a contestation of Englisc cultural capital—though it's worth pointing out that the West Saxon genealogy that Asser incorporates has already been reduced to writing, so that the opposition of oral to written source probably requires further qualification. But I do want to suggest that if we look at Asser's hijacking of West Saxon genealogy with the issue of cultural and linguistic difference in mind, rather than as a negotiation of issues of authority within a monocultural binary of orality and literacy, then a subversive and destabilizing aspect of Asser's practice comes to the fore. For it is not simply that he trumps oral legend with literate learning in a competition for cultural capital, but that he willfully misidentifies Alfred's legendary ancestor with a figure from Roman comedy and at the same time undermines the celebration of "national" secular authority with an appeal to metropolitan religious values. West Saxon cultural location is here rendered eccentric and subject to misinterpretation, in a way that might well leave us wondering how Alfred, reading his Welsh bishop's ostensible panegyric, might not experience at least a momentary frisson of affront.

Asser's Welsh difference, thus staged so extensively throughout his text, comes to the fore in Chapters 79–80, by which point he has abandoned paraphrase of the Anglo-Saxon Chronicle for a connected narrative in which he himself now figures as a player. Asser's account of contemporary Welsh internecine struggle, and within his home kingdom Dyfed of secular oppression of the Church of St. David, drives home a point central to my rereading of Asser's ideological stance—that Welsh fealty to Alfred remains partial, provisional, and contingent on circumstances within Wales. The submission of Welsh princes to Alfred has to do with alliances made for the sake of security in the face of threats from within Wales. Without aggression from the north, Dyfed and Brycheiniog would not have embraced Alfred's lordship in order to secure his protection; without the depredations of Æthelred, Ealdorman of Mercia, Glywysing and Gwent would not have done the same. Without the pressures exerted against St. David's by Hyfaidd, King of Dyfed, neither would Asser's confreres have encouraged him to seek out Alfred. Without the collapse of an alliance between Gwynedd and the Viking king of York, neither would the Northern Welsh have shifted their alliances to Wessex. Alfred's status as "governor of all the Christians of the island of Britain," announced in the dedication of Asser's text, by this point proves to be dependent on a multiplicity of political and cultural positionalities in an island that Asser emphasizes repeatedly is not coterminous with *Saxonia*, nor with the *Angelcynn* that will, in the following century, become more incontrovertibly England.[36]

This chapter has argued that we ought to read Asser's eccentric and yet pivotal biography of Alfred the Great not only as a foundational instrument in the consolidation of West Saxon hegemony, which of course it is, but also, imposing less hindsight upon it, for the surprising degree to which it entrenches the cultural diversity of an island it resolutely calls Britain. But in attending to the rhetorical pragmatics of Asser's Latinity in particular, I've also suggested at a more general level that we need to move beyond the unproblematic alignment of Latinity with monocultural authority as we think through negotiations of medieval cultural difference. We need a more flexible understanding of Latinity in Anglo-Saxon England, not as an unproblematic constant in the service of centralization and of dominant regimens of knowledge and power, but rather as a complex habitus, one that in this instance allowed a principal architect of West Saxon ascendancy simultaneously to articulate ongoing diversity and the plural location of culture and subjectivity.

In Asser's beginning is his end: in the dedication to Alfred, ostensibly an unproblematic honorific address, that prefaces his life—and that strangely enough mixes the conventions of epistolography with those of biography—he addresses the king of a foreign people as follows:

> To my venerable and most devout master, governor of all the Christians of the island of Britain, Alfred, king of Angles, of Saxons, Asser, last of all God's servants, wishes a thousandfold prosperity according to the vows of all his desires in either life.

> [Domino meo venerabili piissimoque omnium Brittanniae insulae Christianorum rectori, Ælfred, Anglorum Saxonum regi, Asser, omnium servorum Dei ultimus, millemodum ad vota desideriorum utriusque vitae prosperitatem.]

Asser celebrates his master as king of the Angles and Saxons (these two peoples brought together by a parataxis notably awkward in the Latin) only after he has first proclaimed him lord of all the Christians of Britain, a title that his work will go on to intimate is provisional indeed. He emphasizes here that the unity of the Anglo-Saxons, which he will reenforce in his later references to Alfred as *Angulsaxonum rex*, is also provisional. (Resisting what Michael Richter called the "Gregorian nomenclature" derived from Bede, and emphasizing his Celtic speaking position, Asser will resolutely throughout his work call the tongue of these Germanic parvenus "Saxon," not the Englisc of the *Angelcynn* that will rapidly become in the tenth century the preferred designation of "England.")[37] He makes reference to *utriusque vitae* [each life of the two]—surely meaning prosperity in this life and the next, but introducing at some level, however subconscious, the issue of other possible bifurcations of life: his own and Alfred's, the life of Welsh and of Saxons, the life of metropolitan Christendom and of local culture and language. He casts his lot with Empire, but we owe it to him to recognize that he does so provisionally; and that he might perhaps, some twelve centuries later, have found some coincidentally common ground with speakers of Dravidian languages in south India, or with the peoples of southern Sudan.

Notes

1. I am grateful to Ryan Harper of the University of Rochester for conversation without which this chapter might not have been written, and to Carin Ruff of Cornell University, whose careful erudition is matched by her generosity.

2. Allen J. Frantzen, *Desire for Origins: New Language, Old English, and Teaching the Tradition* (New Brunswick: Rutgers University Press, 1990).

3. William Henry Stevenson, ed., *Asser's Life of King Alfred, together with the Annals of Saint Neot's Erroneously Ascribed to Asser*, new impression (Oxford: Oxford University Press, 1959); V.H. Galbraith, "Who Wrote Asser's Life of Alfred?" in *An Introduction to the Study of History* (London: C.A.Watts, 1964), 88–128; Alfred P. Smyth, King Alfred the Great (Oxford: Oxford University Press, 1995) and *The Medieval Life of King Alfred the Great* (New York: Palgrave, 2002); Dorothy Whitelock, "The Genuine Asser," Stenton Lecture 1967 (Reading: University of Reading, 1968); Simon Keynes, "On the Authenticity of Asser's Life of King Alfred," *Journal of Ecclesiastical History* 47.3 (1996): 529–51; Seth Lerer, *Literacy and Power in Anglo-Saxon Literature*, Chapter 2, "The Beautiful Letters" (Lincoln: University of Nebraska Press, 1991), 61–96.

4. Nicole Guenther Discenza, *The King's English: Strategies of Translation in the Old English Boethius* (Albany: SUNY Press, 2005).

5. I have relied for what follows on Simon Keynes and Michael Lapidge, trans., *Alfred the Great: Asser's Life of King Alfred and Other Contemporary Sources* (London: Penguin, 1983), 11–44. See also Allen J. Frantzen, *King Alfred*, Twayne Authors Series 425 (Boston: Twayne, 1986).

6. On the neologism "Anglo-Saxon" as a significant departure in ethnic nomenclature, see Susan Reynolds, "What Do We Mean by 'Anglo-Saxon' and

'Anglo-Saxons'?" *Journal of British Studies* 24 (1985): 395–414. Reynolds discusses earlier self-designations of English groups and kingdoms as either "Saxones" or "Angli" and the emergence, first among Carolingian writers on the Continent, of the newer and never wholeheartedly adopted hybrid designation. Michael Richter, "Bede's *Angli*: Angles or English?" *Peritia* 3 (1984): 99–114 traces the path toward (and detours from) general adoption of the "Gregorian nomenclature" by which "Angli" becomes the comprehensive term; he points out that Celtic and Continental sources long continued to prefer "Saxones." On continued English dissent from Alfredian claims of English unity, see Patrick Wormald, "The Making of England," *History Today* 45.2 (1995): 26–32.

7. For Parker's edition, see pp. xiv–xxi of Stevenson's introduction.

8. For important caveats against unqualified linkages of Asser's text to the Suetonian tradition or to Einhard, see James Campbell, "Asser's Life of Alfred," in *The Inheritance of Historiography 350–900*, ed. Christopher Holdsworth and T.P. Wiseman, Exeter Studies in History No. 12. (Exeter: University of Exeter Press, 1986), 115–35.

9. Lerer, *Literacy and Power*, 70–74.

10. Stevenson, *Asser's Life*, 1: "omnium Brittanniae insulae Christianorum rectori, Ælfred, Anglorum Saxonum regi."

11. Sarah Foot, "The Making of *Angelcynn*: English Identity before the Norman Conquest," *Transactions of the Royal Historical Society*, 6th series, 6 (1996): 25–49; Kathleen Davis, "National Writing in the Ninth Century: A Reminder for Postcolonial Thinking about the Nation," *Journal of Medieval and Early Modern Studies* 28.3 (1998): 611–37; Kathleen Davis, "The Performance of Translation Theory in King Alfred's National Literary Program," in *Manuscript, Narrative, Lexicon: Essays on Literary and Cultural Transmission in Honor of Whitney F. Bolton* (Lewisburg: Bucknell University Press, 2000), 152.

12. I use hereafter the spelling "Englisc" to refer to languages and cultures of what we imagine as Anglo-Saxon England, with the intention of disrupting myths of continuity between the tenth century and modern constructions of English linguistic and ethnic identity.

13. Discenza, *The King's English*; "Wealth and Wisdom: Symbolic Capital and the Ruler in the Translational Program of Alfred the Great," *Exemplaria* 13.2 (2001): 433–67; "The Old English *Bede* and the Construction of Anglo-Saxon Authority," *Anglo-Saxon England* 31 (2002): 69–80; Robert Stanton, *The Culture of Translation in Anglo-Saxon England*, Chapter 2 (Woodbridge: D.S. Brewer, 2002), 55–100.

14. Malcolm Godden, "The Translations of Alfred and his Circle, and the Misappropriation of the Past," H.M. Chadwick Memorial Lectures 14 (Cambridge: Department of Anglo-Saxon, Norse, and Celtic, 2004), 6–11.

15. Godden, "The Translations of Alfred," 11–12 and 15–16.

16. Discenza, "The Old English *Bede*," 77.

17. Discenza, "The Old English *Bede*," 80.

18. Katherine O'Brien O'Keeffe, "Orality and the Developing Text of Cædmon's Hymn," in *Visible Song: Transitional Literacy in Old English Verse*, Cambridge Studies in Anglo-Saxon England 4, Chapter 1, (Cambridge: Cambridge University Press, 1990), 23–46.

19. Elliott Van Kirk Dobbie, ed., *The Anglo-Saxon Minor Poems*, Anglo-Saxon Poetic Records 6 (New York: Columbia University Press, 1942), 104–105.

20. Bertram Colgrave and R.A.B. Mynors, ed. and trans., *Bede's Ecclesiastical History of the English People* (Oxford: Clarendon Press, 1969), 416–17: "Hic est sensus, non autem ordo ipse uerborum, quae dormiens ille canebat; neque enim possunt carmina, quamuis optime conposita, ex alia in aliam linguam ad uerbum sine detrimento sui decoris ac dignitatis transferre."

21. Thomas Miller, ed., *The Old English Version of Bede's Ecclesiastical History*, Part I.2, Early English Text Society, Original Series 96 (Oxford: Oxford University Press, 1891), 344.

22. Uppinder Mehan and David Townsend, "'Nation' and the Gaze of the Other in Eighth-Century Northumbria," *Comparative Literature* 53.1 (2001): 15–16; Gabriel Okara, "Towards the Evolution of an African Language for African Literature," in *Chinua Achebe: A Celebration*, ed. Kirsten Holst Petersen and Anna Rutherford (Oxford: Heinemann, 1990), 11–18.

23. Lawrence Venuti, *The Scandals of Translation: Towards an Ethics of Difference* (London: Routledge, 1998), 11.

24. Mehan and Townsend, "'Nation' and the Gaze of the Other," 7–11.

25. Franz Ubleis, "Sprachprobleme in Tamil Nadu: Eine sprachliche und sprachsoziologische Untersuchung," *Lingvaj Problemoj kaj Lingvo-Planado/ Language Problems and Language Planning* 1.3 (1978): 153–165.

26. Muhammad Sid-Ahmad, "English as a Marker of Southern Sudanese Nationalism: History, Politics and Language in the Sudan," <http://www.chass.utoronto.ca/~cpercy/courses/eng6365-sid-ahmad.htm> accessed April 8, 2008; Liza Sandell, *English Language in Sudan: A History of its Teaching and Politics* (London: Ithaca, 1982).

27. 3.6–7: hiemaverunt pagani in insula, quae vocatur Sceapieg, quod interpretatur "insula ovium"; 5.6–7: in loco, qui dicitur Aclea, id est "in campulo quercus," diutissime pugnaverunt; 37.3–5: in loco, qui dicitur Æcesdun, quod Latine "mons fraxini" interpretatur, totis viribus et plena voluntate ad proelium prodeunt.

28. 4.3–4: Doruberniam, id est Cantwariorum civitatem; 21.6–8: et in regno Orientalium Saxonum, quod Saxonice "East-Engle" dicitur, hiemavit; 69.2–3: in regionem Antiquorum Saxonum, quae Saxonice dicitur Eald Seaxum; 79.4–5: usque ad regionem Dexteralium Saxonum, quae Saxonice Suth-Seaxum appellatur.

29. 66.5–7: civitatemque quae Hrofesceastre Saxonice dicitur...obsedit; 81.21–2: in duobus monasteriis, quae Saxonice cognominantur Cungresbyri et Banuville.

30. 9.3–5: in insula, quae dicitur in Saxonica lingua Tenet, Britannico autem sermone Ruim, animose et acriter belligeraverunt; 30.2–5: et Snotengaham adiit (quod Britannice "Tigguocobauc" interpretatur, Latine autem "speluncarum domus"); 49.6–8: in paga, quae dicitur Britannice Durngueir, Saxonice autem Thornsæta; 49. 21–24: ad alium locum, qui dicitur Saxonice Exanceastre, Britannice autem Cairuuisc, Latine quoque civitas Exae, quae in orientali ripa fluminis Uuisc sita est; 52.5–6: in orientali ripa fluminis, quod Britannice dicitur Abon; 55.6–8: quae est in orientali parte saltus, qui dicitur Seluudu, Latine autem "silva magna," Britannice "Coit Maur"; 57.4–5: Cirrenceastre adiit, quae Britannice Cairceri nominatur.

31. 42.17–19: in monte, qui dicitur Wiltun, qui est in meridiana ripa fluminis Guilou; 54.6: ante arcem Cynuit.

32. Keynes and Lapidge, *Alfred the Great*, 56–57; contrast Smyth, *The Medieval Life*, 117–31.

33. Mehan and Townsend, "'Nation' and the Gaze of the Other," 7–11.

34. For affinities with Einhard, see Stevenson, *Asser's Life*, lxxx–lxxxii; Keynes and Lapidge, *Alfred the Great*, 54–55; Janet Nelson, "Waiting for Alfred," *Early Medieval Europe* 7 (1998): 122 and n. 25; Smyth, *King Alfred the Great*, 222–29. For the Frankish convention (of Einhard as well as of other Frankish biographers) of incorporating annals into biography, see Stevenson, *Asser's Life*, lxxx–lxxxii and xcviii–xcix. For the Frankish elements in Asser's lexicon, see Stevenson, *Asser's Life*, xciii–xciv; Keynes and Lapidge, *Alfred the Great*, 54–55; Smyth, *The Medieval Life*, 137–40.

35. Lerer, *Literacy and Power*, 89.

36. Foot, "The Making of *Angelcynn*."

37. Foot, "The Making of Angelcynn"; Michael Richter, "Bede's *Angli*: Angles or English?" *Peritia* 3 (1984): 99–114.

CHAPTER 4

GREEN CHILDREN FROM ANOTHER WORLD,
OR THE ARCHIPELAGO IN ENGLAND

Jeffrey Jerome Cohen

*T**his chapter argues that a mysterious episode of green children emerging from the earth in twelfth-century England carries to the text's surface a historian's anxiety about the cultural diversity beneath the story of his nation.*

At some time during the reign of King Stephen, not far from the East Anglian village of Woolpit, two children emerged from the ground and stepped blinking into unaccustomed sunlight. Dressed in clothing of odd hue, uttering an unintelligible tongue, the siblings possessed skin entirely green. Once taught to deliver their history in words comprehensible to their auditors, they spoke of a world impossibly remote from yet inexplicably contiguous to the England in which they found themselves resident.

In the twelfth-century historian William of Newburgh's narration of this remarkable tale, the Green Children of Woolpit bring to the surface with them a living reminder of England's difference-riddled history. They offer a narrative divergent from the kings, triumphs, and unmourned vanishings that dominated contemporary English historiography. Just as the nation seems to have settled into a comfortable sense of its own perdurability, they emerge into the *History of English Affairs*—arriving just in time to remind their entranced narrator that his beloved homeland had even recently experienced political discontinuity and vexing heterogeneity. The Green Children spectacularly embody the cultural diversity from which the kingdom had been formed, the hybridity it had long disowned, the capaciousness of the insular expanses of which England remained but a single part.

Island Identities

"Race is a dangerous word." Thus Rees Davies initiated his Cecil-Williams lecture of 1973, and his declaration holds even more true decades later. Despite its perils Davies did not back down from employing the term, arguing that race is the only descriptive noun able to capture the profundity of the medieval distinction between the Welsh and the English, a separateness held to be elemental.[1] Like Davies I believe that the word is appropriate to a medieval context, especially in eleventh- and twelfth-century Britain, and not only because differences among the island's peoples were imagined as primal and enduring. Race is the only modern term expressing the paradoxical obduracy (at any particular moment) and instability (over a long stretch of history) of communal identities, underscoring that differentiation is deeply linked to embodiment, typically through acts of violence.[2]

Race, scientifically speaking, belongs to the realm of fantasy, where it demonstrates a powerful ability to give enduring substance to what would otherwise be abstract, volatile. Yet despite its seemingly chimerical nature, race is as bluntly corporeal as it is psychically wounding (or satisfying, depending on one's perspective). Race is constructed not only through inert signs like dermal pigmentation, but also through the embodied performance of identity: food consumed, language spoken, customs observed, sexuality practiced.[3] Because it buttresses uneven distributions of power while emplacing the distinction between dominating and subaltern groups in the body, race is (as Davies states) dangerous—and therefore also the best term for capturing the *force* of differences thought to separate medieval peoples.

Although at any given moment a seemingly impermeable boundary, as solid as it is constraining, race over time tends to be elastic, altering its contours as it is adopted and adapted. This historical malleability, generally disavowed, can enable a previously divided or heterogeneous group to cohere, enabling the proud embrace of a communal identity or the foisting of such a union upon peoples who do not necessarily desire such circumscription. In the latter case race tends to harden around the newly defined group, locking them in alien terms. Embrace of a collectivizing designator by a dominating group, on the other hand, tends to rely upon the unspoken plasticity of race, enabling a series of strategic inclusions and exclusions. In the twelfth century the Welsh, Irish, and Scots found themselves trapped in a suffocating English circumscription of their identity: inferior, feral, barbarian. The Normans, meanwhile, took advantage of a flexibility within Englishness to disappear into that powerfully ascendant term.[4]

England

Because it possessed from at least the ninth century onward a strong sense of itself as a corporate entity, James Campbell has labeled England Europe's most precocious nation-state.[5] Its unity owed much to belief in both a shared past and a deep continuity between rulers and ruled, a mythology of integration given eloquent voice by the monk Bede in his *Ecclesiastical History of the English People*. The Normans changed everything in 1066, shaking the kingdom out of its solitariness and terminating its imagined homogeneity. In the wake of rapid conquest, political and ecclesiastical power suddenly belonged to an alien-born, francophone minority. The lauded English race was brutally reduced to subaltern status. A bifurcated, postcolonial society took abiding root. Norman England began almost immediately to expand into Wales, Scotland, and Ireland, forcibly annexing land without exactly incorporating it. Decades after William the Conqueror had conjoined its ancient throne to a transnational empire, England still struggled with a forced and uneasy multiculturalism.

Twelfth-century writers like William of Malmesbury and Henry of Huntingdon did not compose their texts because they could, from some dispassionate vantage, arrange the events of former years into serene chronicle. Unsettled times elicit the calming powers of historiography. Both William and Henry were men of compound heritage: English on their maternal side, Norman in paternity. Trilingual and bicultural, both seem to have been haunted by England's unforeseen hybridity, a discomfort experienced all the more acutely since they were the biological products of this fusion. As Hugh M. Thomas has emphasized, however handy designations like "Anglo-Norman" might be for us, the medieval lexicon of race did not allow for hyphenated terms.[6] A people might vanish, as the Picts were supposed to have done. They might persevere under a changed name, as when diasporic Trojans became Romans or Britons. Races did not amalgamate and mutually transform; they did not engender middle categories. That is, however, exactly what the Normans had done through their policy of intermarriage, changing both themselves and their subjects in the process. Absorbed into the land they conquered, the Normans profoundly altered England and Englishness.

In his *History of the English Kings* William of Malmesbury ordinarily described Britain's races in terms inherited from Bede: the English burgeon at the utter expense of other insular peoples. The fifth-century advent of the Angles and the Saxons marks the definitive end of the hegemony of the Britons, Picts, and Irish [Scoti]. Under the dominion of Edward, son of Alfred the Great, the English lose whatever small variations with which they were endowed and become a unity. Thus East

Angles, West Angles, Northumbrians, and Danes "grow into one people" [iam in unam gentem coaluerat]. The Scots "who dwell in the northern part of the island" and the "Britons (whom we call the Welsh)" are not integrated into this emergent people but subdued and permanently excluded.[7] Small variations can be harmonized, but larger diversity in language, culture, and history form an insurmountable barrier, keeping some races perpetually distinct. Old enemies are therefore either "wiped out" [perempti]—the apparent fate of the Scots and Britons too close to home—or "spared and called English" [sub nomine Anglorum reservati]. The latter formulation seems meant for the Danes who had long lived among the English. Such a vanishing minority is something of a departure for William. For the most part enlargement of community is not possible, the designation "English" marking an absolute rather than a traversable limit. English, moreover, retains its limited flexibility only in the distant past. Later Danes, for example, are Vikings whose eradication is essential to the survival of the nation. They might influence English character through bad example and loose morals, but they do not become English themselves.

William of Malmesbury's admission that a racial line might be redrawn, as when enemies are spared but survive sub nomine Anglorum, is all the more remarkable for its rarity. True, the Normans had an originary myth placed in literary form by Dudo of St. Quentin that proclaimed an origin in intermixture.[8] Yet the moment they became Normans they remained a discrete group thenceforth, a people possessed of enduring "racial distinctiveness," Normanni ex Normannis.[9] Though reality was a great deal more complicated, insular histories spoke of Britain's races as abidingly separate, typically from time out of memory. Thus when William of Newburgh narrates the ancient past of Britain, he draws upon Bede and Gildas, each the historian of his own race. The gens Britonum, William observes, were the first inhabitants of "our island" [nostrae insulae primi incolae].[10] To protect themselves from the Picts and Scots, the Britons invited as mercenaries the "Saxons or Angles" (Saxones vel Angli, a conjunction that stresses primal equivalence). These hapless Britons were in time "crushed" by their guests, the "wretched remnant" finding themselves "penned...in trackless mountains and forests." Diminished and marginal, "they are now called the Welsh" [nunc Walenses vocantur] (1.Prologue).[11] The story of the Britons reaches its definitive terminus. Having confined the Welsh to a rugged pastoral life, having relegated them to an eternal premodernity, William turns his attention to the powerful kings who ensured that these dispossessed aborigines would never again occupy more than a small, wild corner of the island. The future—and paninsular dominion—belong to the Angli.[12]

With such brutal reductiveness did race work in British history, at least when British history was imagined from the English point of view. A new people arrive and wholly eradicate the old, banishing survivors to an uncivil geography, a spatial analogue to their inveterate brutishness. In William's account the diminished Welsh [*miseras reliquias*] seem so distant as to inhabit another world entirely, a roadless [*inviis*] expanse offering no path of return from the wild space to which their difference has been exiled—at least, no return that could find England by traveling the paved and predictable surface of the land.

Britain

William of Malmesbury and Henry of Huntingdon, the most highly regarded historians of the twelfth century, composed their works in a tumultuous era: struggles over succession to the crown, prolonged civil war, bloody resistance to England's movements west and north through the island and across the Irish Sea. Their histories were aimed in part at reconciling the Normans and English, disseminating a shared past that could bring about a more harmonious time to come. Both supported the English claim of dominance over the whole of the island, emphasizing the barbarity of non-English Britain.[13] As the century came to a close, however, Wales and Scotland no longer posed so fierce a challenge to English supremacy. The conquest of Ireland was swiftly proceeding. No prospect of renewed internal strife was evident at home. England now considered itself not only the island's cultural center, but *Britannia* itself. Henry of Huntingdon could therefore write nonchalantly that "this most celebrated of islands" might once have been called Albion, might later have been labeled Britain, but was now simply named England—a *pars pro toto* culmination that robbed Britain of the possibility of owning a present tense.[14] King Arthur begins the century as Geoffrey of Monmouth's mythic and exigent Briton, probably disseminated in an attempt to inspire Welsh pride, but by century's close has been converted into a serenely English monarch.[15]

Yet the "victory of Englishness" over the diversity of the island to which it belonged came at a price.[16] Glossing *Britain* as *England* ensured that the more recent term would always be haunted by its predecessor, a descriptor naming a geography too vast to be contained by a single kingdom, no matter how dominant. Britain was, after all, still inhabited by peoples who did not share with the English an identity, history, or political mythology. England could never fully harmonize itself, let alone the island it shared with Wales and Scotland, or the history it shared with Romans, Britons, Picts, Danes, the Irish, the Normans. Arthur could be translated into an English regent, Albion could be rendered *Anglia*, a history of cultural intermixture and alliance could be replaced by a myth of arrival and eradication, but there would always be an archipelago dwelling within England.

Because he was narrating a period in which his native land had survived conquest, subjugation, and civil unrest, William of Newburgh knew that his *History of English Affairs* was a story of blood. This sanguineous flow coursing through the insular past was not exactly news. Geoffrey of Monmouth, William's predecessor in historiography and the author responsible for bestowing a powerfully heroic vision of Arthur to history, had come to the same conclusion six decades earlier. An unforgettable scene from Geoffrey's *History of the Kings of Britain* has the boy sorcerer Merlin nearly sacrificed to subterranean dragons locked in eternal battle.[17] These two monsters represent the ever-antagonistic Britons and the Saxons. Some magicians declare, wrongly, that Merlin's blood must be sprinkled into the mortar of a tower to make it rise above the shaky ground the dragons underdwell, enabling a stable edifice to be built upon unremittingly contested soil. Missing the point of the political allegory, William of Newburgh declared such stories utter nonsense ("gushing and untrammelled lying," to be exact; 1.Prologue). Whereas Geoffrey imagined a Britain where different versions of the insular past might jostle in competition, where a king of the Britons could surpass English champions like Alfred and Athelstan, William was certain that the island's antiquity was large enough to contain precisely one history, an English one. To William of Newburgh, Geoffrey of Monmouth was a somnolent cartographer of unknown universes, his head ridiculously populated by *infinita regna*, realms without number, kingdoms without boundaries (1.Prologue).

William turned to the past to find stories that culminated, grandly and ineluctably, in the England of his day. Geoffrey of Monmouth, on the other hand, had unleashed upon twelfth-century Britain a version of insular history that proliferated alternatives. Millennia about which English historians had been silent were suddenly populated by charismatic figures like the Trojan refugee Brutus, sailing to Britain's shores to found a new nation; the quarrelsome brothers Belinus and Brennius, annexing a humbled Rome to their burgeoning empire; the magnificent Arthur, uniting the British archipelago under his command and blazing in military glory across the known world. For William of Newburgh, the fact that England had emerged as the supreme power on the island was reason enough to assume his nation's inevitability. Geoffrey of Monmouth, however, was a lover of ambiguity and sly multiplier of possibility. By providing an unanticipated history of the island, one in which England was dwarfed by a realm even more resplendent, Geoffrey restored to British history its contingency, its potential to have unfolded otherwise.

William realized that in introducing a rival kingdom, a Britain with a captivating history, Geoffrey of Monmouth had interjected into twelfth-century historiography the possibility that the past might indeed contain *infinita regna*. This endlessness of histories in clamorous competition could erode the supposed bedrock upon which the English present had been founded, could undermine England's solitary preeminence. Through the *History of the Kings of Britain* Geoffrey had challenged not only England's smug superiority, but the very historical support upon which contemporary Englishness was built. In the process of undercutting the renown that inhered in tracing lineage from the Angles and Saxons, moreover, Geoffrey wove a mantle that the Welsh could assume with pride, a mantle that had the potential to transform them from a denigrated people to a race enrobed in a glorious history all their own. Geoffrey had offered the Welsh that road denied them by William of Newburgh's dismissal of the Britons to pathless [*inviis*] mountains and remote pastures.

The English quickly realized that the only way to neutralize the challenge Geoffrey's history posed was to absorb and anglicize its content. They did so with gusto. If Geoffrey's ambition was to offer a viable alternative to England's self-approving narration of the island's history, a narration as venerable as Bede himself, he did not succeed. At the time his text appeared (c. 1138) Britain's racial categories were rapidly hardening, becoming carceral. Like the Irish, Scots, and Jews, the Welsh were being systematically dehumanized by the English. No revisionist history, as it turned out, was powerful enough to reset the cultural cement of this category once it solidified. Only a century ago England had been a country riven by foreign conquest, its population divided into francophone elites and *Englisc* subalterns. As the country began to imagine itself a harmonious collective again, as Norman difference faded and English identity was reinvigorated, a host of others, both external to England (Welsh, Irish, and Scots barbarians) and living within (Jews), found themselves excluded by their supposedly patent and intractable differences, their monstrosity, their blood.

This kingdom in the island's southeast corner had, at the end of the twelfth century, two historical vanishings to account for, one more desired than real: the conquering Normans who had transformed the land and then faded; and the aboriginal Britons, to whom Britain had once belonged and who reminded England of its own belatedness. For the most part England responded to these challenges in the way that domineering powers typically respond in the face of ethical complexities, by ignoring them. Yet histories anxiously relegated to silence frequently

prove themselves to be like the undead who haunt the halls and bar-
rows of Icelandic sagas: eerily returning in strange forms, relentlessly
demanding that the unfinished business they incarnate be acknowledged. Just as in the sagas, moreover, such revenants enter the present
moment with disturbing stories about trauma, memory, and the violence
of community.

Green Children

An Augustinian canon who may never have traveled far from his native
Yorkshire, William of Newburgh endeavored in the *History of English
Affairs* to provide a detailed record of his nation from the days of the
Norman kings to the present. Today his narrative is cited most frequently
for two seemingly unconnected episodes: the account of viridescent children discovered in East Anglia with which I began this chapter, and his
vituperative condemnation of Geoffrey of Monmouth. Neither of these
episodes seems well connected to the kings, conquest, and civic tumult
occupying the first book of his *History*. There is something out of place
about both the Green Children of Woolpit and William's lengthy rant
against Arthurian history, something that remains unsaid and, within the
textual world William creates, almost unsayable.

Of the *History of the Kings of Britain* William sneered, "clearly all that
Geoffrey has published in his writing about Arthur and Merlin has been
invented by liars to feed the curiosity of the ignorant" (1.Prologue). His
contempt for Geoffrey's vision of the British past and his scorn for a
mode of historiography that implicitly buttressed Norman imperialism
is intimately connected to his inability *not* to tell the story of the Green
Children, a wonder that, he says, compels him to "believe and marvel
at what I cannot grasp or investigate by any powers of the mind" (1.27).
Dwelling at an epistemic edge, the Green Children figure two differences-
within-similarities that haunt William's unfolding story: the unspoken
conversion of the conquering Normans into ordinary English; and the
lingering presence of aboriginal peoples in a Britain over which England
has asserted complete dominion. On the one hand, the island had by the
end of the twelfth century been so long under a process of forced anglicization that English writers no longer bothered to distinguish between
Britain and England; on the other, the untimely intrusion of pre-English
indigenous presence suggests that, even if the Normans became English,
not every difference is so tractable. At once fragments of a fading past and
a spectacular embodiment of a living people consigned to mere antiquity,
the Green Children undermine William's usually confident narration of
English perdurability and ascendancy.

William of Newburgh introduces the Green Children late in the first book of his *History*, describing them hyperbolically as a "prodigy unprecedented since the world began." He locates their appearance during the turbulence of King Stephen's reign, and situates them thematically within a series of contemporary wonders and marvels. Here is the story of the Green Children [*De viridibus pueris*] in William of Newburgh's wide-eyed account:

In East Anglia there is a village which is said to lie four or five miles from the famous monastery of the blessed king and martyr Edmund. Close to the village some very ancient ditches are visible. In English they are called *Wlfpittes* or wolf-ditches, and they lend their name to the village close by [modern Woolpit, Suffolk]. At harvest-time, when the harvesters were busy in the fields gathering the crops, two children, a boy and a girl, emerged from these ditches. Their entire bodies were green, and they were wearing clothes of unusual colour and unknown material. As they wandered bemused over the countryside, they were seized by the reapers and led to the village. Many people flocked to observe this most unusual sight, and for several days they were kept without food. So they were now almost fainting with hunger, yet they paid no attention to any food offered to them. It then chanced that beans were brought in from the fields; they at once grabbed these, and looked for the beans in the stalks, but when they found nothing in the hollow of the stalks they wept bitterly. Then one of the bystanders pulled the beans from the pods and offered them to the children, who at once gleefully took and ate them.

For several months they were nourished by this food until they learned to eat bread. In the end they gradually lost their own colour when the qualities of our foodstuffs had their effect. They became like us, and also learned the use of our speech. Persons of prudence decided that they should receive the sacrament of holy baptism, and this was also administered. But the boy, who seemed to be younger, lived only a short time after baptism and then died prematurely, whereas the girl continued unaffected, differing not even in the slightest way from the women of our kind. She certainly took a husband later at Lynn, according to the story, and was said to be living a few years ago.

Once they had the use of our language, they were asked who they were and where they came from. They are said to have replied: 'We are people from Saint Martin's land; he is accorded special reverence in the country of our birth.' When they were next asked where that land was, and how they had come from there to Woolpit, they said: "We do not know either of these things. All we remember is that one day we were pasturing our father's flocks in the fields, when we heard a mighty din such as we often hear at St. Edmund's when they say the bells are ringing out. When we turned our attention to the sound which caused us surprise, it was as though we were out of our minds, for we suddenly found ourselves among you in the fields where you were harvesting." When they were asked whether people believed in Christ there, or whether the sun rose, they said that it was a Christian country and had churches. "But the sun does not rise among the natives of our land," they said "and it obtains very little light from the sun's rays, but is satisfied with the measure of its brightness which in your country precedes its rising or follows its setting. Moreover a shining land is visible not far from our own, but a very broad river divides the two." They are said to have made these and many other replies too long to narrate to interested enquirers. (1.27)

The story merits, as William says, to be "considered" or "reasoned over" [*ratiocinetur*] as best as an interpreter is able. I will do so not, as have some scholars, by seeing the episode as an intrusion of folklore into what is an otherwise sober chronicle of kings, nobles, bishops, and politics. Nor will I take the (admittedly fruitful) approach recently utilized by Laurie A. Finke and Martin B. Shichtman, an interpretive method that stresses the ordinariness of marvels in twelfth-century historiography.[18] As alien intrusions into both the English landscape and William's narrative, these Green Children are weirdly out of place. Yet the more they are examined, the more *extimate* they become: at once extraneous to and intimate with William's text as a whole. One converted into an ordinary English wife, the other perishing in order to retain his queerness, the boy and girl of verdant hue arrive to tell a complicated story about gender, race, conversion, and the historical fragility of English identity.

William of Newburgh's relationship to the Green Children is tortured. He does not want to include them in his *History*, but knows he must; he does not wish to believe in them, but feels compelled; he does not understand them, and yet is convinced of their abundant meaningfulness: "I myself had protracted doubts over this...I was compelled to believe and marvel at what I cannot grasp or investigate by any powers of the mind" (1.27). Rocks that when smashed apart reveal at their secret interiors small dogs or toads with golden chains, a subterranean feast witnessed by a late-night wanderer: these marvels William can confidently declare the magic tricks of fallen angels, wrought to ensnare humans.[19] "But an explanation of the green children who are said to have come forth from the earth," he writes in exasperation, "is more puzzling; the frailty of our intelligence is quite incapable of unearthing this" (1.28). The Green Children haunt William in the inscrutability of their abounding significance. The power they exert, I would argue, derives from the fact that the narrative William grants them resonates, quietly but profoundly, with anxieties about conversion, assimilation, and continuity that trouble his *History* throughout its unfolding.

Normans

Take, for example, the seemingly trivial (but all the same wholly opaque) assertion by the Green Children: "We are people from Saint Martin's land; he is accorded special reverence in the country of our birth." A fifth-century bishop whose worship was especially associated with France, Saint Martin is mentioned only one other time by William. Early in Book I of the *History*, Martin is the dedicatee of a great monastery built by William the Conqueror. Erected on the battlefield of Hastings, the edifice is supposed to commemorate eternally his victory. The problem for William of Newburgh, however, is that the construction of this monument seems more an act of forced forgetting. As he contemplated the events of 1066, William of Newburgh knew that his beloved kingdom had been defeated, its church colonized, its crown annexed to a transmarinal empire differing in language, custom, culture. Other twelfth-century historians typically narrated the Battle of Hastings as a struggle between patently different peoples. The ascendant Normans not only spoke an alien tongue, they at times seemed set apart in their very bodies, their short hair and clean-shaven faces contrasting sharply with the flowing tresses and moustaches of the native English—leading to an entire poetics of hairstyle, racial difference, and gender in the contemporary literature.[20] Having been born of mixed ancestry, William of Newburgh's most influential predecessors, William of Malmesbury and Henry of Huntingdon, felt themselves pulled in dual directions. Ambivalence and hesitation characterize their description of the Conquest and its aftermath. William of Newburgh, on the other hand, would have none of this equivocation. He identified simply and straightforwardly with the English, a people who were in his words *gentis nostrae, id est Anglorum*, "our race, that is, the English" (1.Prologue.1). Yet, by the time he was at work on his *History* (begun c.1196), the conquering Normans had long ago vanished, having become as proudly English as those whom they had once subjugated. How, then, to narrate the advent of a people who had conquered a race that did not need conquering, who had altered it profoundly, and who were no longer to be found in England but who had never left?

At first it seems that William turns to a patriotic nativism. Stigand, the last "Anglo-Saxon" archbishop of Canterbury, refuses to consecrate William of Normandy king of England, judging the duke *ille viro cruento*, "that bloody man" (1.1.1). The blood that tinges William the Bastard (*Guillelmus cognomento Nothus*, as William of Newburgh prefers to call him) likewise sullies his victory at Hastings, depriving the engagement of lasting glory. In a richly complicated description, William of Newburgh writes that the conquest came at the price of blood that continues to call out from the ground, as if the lifeforce of slaughtered Abel:

> William, though a Christian, assailed innocent Christians as an enemy, and gained his kingdom at the price of much Christian blood, and for this reason doubtless incurred in God's eyes as much guilt as he acquired glory before men. I have heard this proof from trustworthy witnesses; for in the place where the conquered English lay was built a splendid monastery named St Martin of Battle. Doubtless in men's eyes it would be a lasting proclamation of the Norman victory, and in God's eyes an atonement for shedding so much Christian blood. Finally, in that same monastery, the spot at which occurred the greatest slaughter of the English fighting for the fatherland sweats real and seemingly fresh blood whenever there is a slight shower of rain, as if it were openly proclaimed on the very evidence of this event that the voice of all that Christian blood is still crying out to God from the earth. (1.1.8)

For William of Newburgh, the violence at Hastings vividly endures one hundred and thirty years after its initial eruption. Having soaked the battleground, this effusion of English blood neither coagulates nor recedes. The Normans quickly erect a monument upon the field of war, the majestic monastery of St. Martin of Battle. William sees in the raising of this structure an act of obliteration more than remembrance, for its towering architecture signals triumph, not the loss upon which the victory depended. The Normans intend the monastery to be eternal, but William stresses that the subterranean gore upon which it rose likewise remains immune to time, remains real [*verum*] and fresh [*quasi recentem*], requiring only the smallest amount of precipitation to make it flow from the earth and stain the monastic grounds.

That the soil of Hastings should, so many years hence, continue to exude *recens sanguis* [fresh blood] implies that even if the Normans were no longer to be found among the English, even if these two people had conjoined to form a single kingdom, the blood through which this unity was forced cannot be forgotten, no matter how distracting an edifice is built upon its foundation. At first glance the sanguineous architecture at St. Martin of Battle might seem a symbol of England itself, a structure likewise formed through violent and permanent commingling of the Norman and English, foreign edifice stained with native blood, a composite wonder. At St. Martin's in Hastings those differences remain forever separate, a moment of conflict frozen in eternal repetition. In William's day, however, the partition of indigene and subjugator was no longer possible. The English and Normans had clearly amalgamated. Unlike the bleeding monastery, they did not become locked in unceasing struggle.

William therefore erodes the grounds for lasting English/Norman distinction with his vision of Hastings as a fratricidal battle in the mode of Cain and Abel. This biblical figuration implies that the Normans should long ago have recognized the very community that they achieved a century later, should have acknowledged immediately their Christian fraternity with the slaughtered English. The crimson flow at Hastings offers through its cry a story about warring collective identities, Norman and English, and the shared blood that ultimately binds them. It is a narrative about how "Norman" and "English" difference was predicated upon a fundamental misrecognition. If the Normans and the English had always been brothers, then the hybrid England engendered by the conquest can be represented as a family reunion. Because Norman difference cannot be easily accommodated within the continuist vision of history that William of Newburgh espouses, William insists that Hastings consisted of illicit violence, like against like. The vision of Norman and English difference familiar from William's source materials is implicitly dismissed as both distracting and specious: for William of Newburgh there are no salient racial markers like hair, custom, law, civility, manliness. What resurfaces in the Green Children is, then, what cannot be forgotten, despite William's disavowal: the Normans actually *did* interject difference into English community, transforming the English nation while fading into the identity of their subjects.[21]

Because they lose their otherness through assimilation, the Green Children who appear from the ground carry with them to the surface vague memories of how the Normans vanished—a process William must know took place, but never mentions. The phrase William employs to describe the conversion of the children into Englishness is *similes nobis effecti*, "rendered like us." The process includes learning to eat indigenous foods (native beans, local bread), nourishment that alters their skin color; recognizing that their style of clothing is foreign to their new home; starting to speak English words; and accepting baptism (though, as it turns out, they were already Christian). Significantly, they are called into their new land by a bell clanging at Bury St. Edmunds. This grandiose abbey was an early example of the conquering Normans' zeal for raising vast, Romanesque architectures upon newly acquired land. The building commemorated a revered English king, but it also served to colonize that national memory. Bury St. Edmunds was at the time of its completion among the largest structures in Christendom, a monumentally alien addition to a countryside otherwise dotted with modest wood and masonry structures. Like the abbey of St. Martin at Hastings, Bury St. Edmunds was a reminder congealed in towering stone of the Norman Conquest, of the influx of difference that came with the swift alteration in governmental power. Significantly, the church at Woolpit was intimately connected to Bury St. Edmunds. Jocelin de Brakelond records that about the time of the appearance of the Green Children, Sampson, a future abbot of the place, was journeying to Rome to have the pope validate ownership of the Woolpit church by the abbey (c. 1159–1162).[22]

The transformation that the villagers enact upon the children to draw them out of their green incomprehensibility is in fact a complete change of race. Medieval race consisted of, among other things, language, food choice, custom, clothing, religion, geographic location, bodily difference. Language was typically the most privileged of these markers. So closely allied were words and identities that Isidore of Seville had argued, "peoples arose from languages, not languages from peoples."[23] In the years after Hastings, speaking French was the primary marker of Norman difference, so much so that the Normans in England were typically denoted as *Franci*. The girl, proving a rapid learner of native customs and speech, eventually differs "not even in the slightest way from the women of our own race" [nec in modico a nostri generis feminis discrepante] (1.27). She even takes a local spouse, vanishing into an indigenous family. Although she carries with her the memory of a life once enjoyed in a dim and distant land, after her transformation into quiet domesticity she never voices sorrow at her loss. As a married adult she settles in the decidedly nonmagical city of Lynn [apud Lennam]. Just as intermarriage with the local population and subsequent anglicization ensured that there were no Normans living among the English when William was writing, so the green girl from St. Martin's land vanishes into mundane life in a Norman settlement. Significantly, the seaside port of Bishop's Lynn was a post-Conquest "new town," a Norman addition to the rapidly changing landscape of East Anglia.

Yet before it became the Norman economic engine christened "Bishop's Lynn," before its transformation into the thriving English port called "King's Lynn," *Lynn* was simply a Briton word for "pool." This geography alongside the Wash was inhabited by a past far more ancient than English and Norman histories on the island.

Britain

William of Newburgh knew that history is written in *verum sanguinem et quasi recentem*, real blood that long retains its freshness, its sting. What William did not and perhaps could not acknowledge, however, is that not all of this blood coursing through the kingdom's history was English or Norman. If Hastings was an illegitimate conquest, predicated upon a refusal to see a similarity that should have been obvious (even if it wasn't), then Hastings was nothing at all like the movement of post-Norman England into Wales, Scotland, Ireland. William of Newburgh never says this, but he certainly implies it—despite the fact that Scotland, Ireland, and Wales were occupied by people just as Christian as the Normans and English (indeed, people whose Christianity was far more ancient). The Angles and Saxons had not arrived on an empty island. Transformed into the *Wealh* or Welsh, many of the indigenous British found themselves deprived of their humanity, in part so that the very collectives deny-ing them membership could circumscribe their boundaries and establish community. To use William of Newburgh's biblical verb, their blood once shed never ceases to cry out. Just as Cain and Abel had ultimately to admit their kinship, intercultural violence tends to intermingle every-thing it was supposed to differentiate. Kingdoms like England are built upon myths of collective difference, but the spilled blood beneath such myths soaks the ground upon which they are erected and calls out with a different story altogether, a narrative of intricate hybridities.

Like most English writers of his day, William was no lover of the Scots, Irish, or Welsh. They are at best barbarians, at worst a monstrous people who amount to a national threat.[24] The Scots he describes as "thirsting for blood against the English people, through savage barbarity" (1.24; cf. 2.32, 2.34). The natives of Ireland are "uncivilized, and barbarous in their manners, almost totally ignorant of laws and order" (2.26). The Welsh are "a restless and barbarous people" (2.5). This last race, William explains, are

> the remnant of the Britons, the first inhabitants of this island, now called England, but originally Britain…when the Britons were being extermi-nated by the invading nations of the Angles, such as were able to escape fled into Wales…and there this nation continues to the present day. (2.5)

This passage makes it clear why Geoffrey of Monmouth's *History of the Kings of Britain* irritated William of Newburgh so much. William knows that the Welsh are the aborigines of the island; he knows that they once held the whole of Britain, and that they would argue strenuously against his declaration that "Britain" had been superseded by "England." William's rhetorical question ("Is he dreaming another world containing kingdoms without number?" 1.Prologue) is supposed to expose the pat-ent ridiculousness of Geoffrey's narration. Yet it also reveals an anxiety that William implicitly voices through his prolonged condemnation of that author: what if Geoffrey is right? What if British history has not been subsumed into and superseded by English history? What if Arthur resists assimilation into an English king? Despite the insistence of William and his contemporaries that it has been renamed and thoroughly anglicized (*similes nobis effecti*, "rendered like us"), could it be that the island of Britain remains so capacious that its territories are rife with other worlds, with kingdoms lacking number?

One such realm is revealed as contiguous to an ordinary East Anglian village. The land of Saint Martin might be so distant that the sun never manages to rise or set there, and yet its residents can hear the bells of the local abbey, and they sometimes find themselves transported up through the ground and surrounded by people who want to change their pastoral mode of life, their non-cereal based diet, their non-anglophone language—want, in the end, to acculturate them just as the contemporary Welsh (and Irish and Scots) were being forcibly anglicized. The children's declaration that they had always been Christian, their narration of a life that might not be agricultural but appears far from barbaric, constitute a rebuke that could as easily have come from a contemporary Welsh or Irish or Scottish mouth.[25] The Green Children resurface another story that William has been unable to tell, one in which English paninsular dominion becomes a troubled assumption rather than a foregone conclusion.

Even when absorbed into an ordinary household, the nameless young woman who had once been a green child does not exactly vanish. She becomes a living reminder of an otherness once held in her flesh: assimilated, yet marked still by difference, even if simply past difference, her story lingering long beyond her assimilation at Lynn.[26] Her young brother perishes shortly after his baptism. His green skin fading due to the influence of English food, his tongue just learning to wrap itself around English words, he nonetheless carries an otherness within him that seems incapable of transformation. A foreigner who retains his queerness, the little boy dies "prematurely," yielding his life in order to remain unchanged, in order to prevent his own fading into ordinariness. Yet even more than his sister, the deceased boy persists: as a memory, as a story that is still being told, as a narrative enclosed by but not integrated into the English history that William is composing. Suspended between the alien and the familiar, partially anglicized but not yet of England, this Green Boy dies too soon to be rendered *similis nobis*, "just like us." The boy's corpse may be buried in East Anglia, the economic heart of England, yet the uneasy alterity that he dies to retain is not so easily put to rest. Through his refusal to become something else—his refusal, really, to embrace adulthood, full Englishness, and the proper masculinity that is cultural shorthand for both—the little boy of verdant hue suggests that there are some differences that are inalienable, that will perish rather than submit to conversion.

The Archipelago in England

The boy and the girl describe their homeland as a place that "obtains very little light from the sun's rays." Dimly illumined by a distant star, this region would seem the furthest place on earth. Yet across a wide river, they declare, "a shining land is visible not far from our own." This shining land could easily be Britain, even England: there are no gradations of light between the home of the Green Children and that realm directly across the waters, just a barrier that seems insurmountable but is in fact fluid and traversable. Like the ever-fresh blood that William earlier described surfacing at Hastings, the marvel of the Green Children yields a compelling meditation on the protean vectors and vagrant trajectories of human identity. William's historiographic omissions find their most expressive voice in the Green Boy, an adamantly alien interloper who refuses assimilation, adulthood, history, Englishness, modernity. With his promise of an adjacent world that cannot be annexed, of an otherness that will perish to endure, the Green Boy also offers the possibility of viewing English history through a monster's eyes. The panorama that he opens trades all-encompassing and seemingly homogeneous identities for hybrid expanses where Englishness combines with differences at once distant and intimate, middle spaces as yet unmapped that begin suddenly to expand.

Notes

1. "Race Relations in Post-Conquest Wales: Confrontation and Compromise," *Transactions of the Honourable Society of Cymmrodorion* (1974–75): 32.
2. For an extended argument with more bibliography than space allows here, see my entry "Race" in the *Dictionary of the Middle Ages*, Vol. 14, First Supplement, ed. William Chester Jordan (New York: Charles Scribner's Sons, 2004), 515–18; *Medieval Identity Machines* (Minneapolis: University of Minnesota Press, 2003), 188–221; *Hybridity, Identity and Monstrosity in Medieval Britain: Of Difficult Middles* (New York: Palgrave Macmillan, 2006), 11–42; and the materials gathered at <jjcohen. blogspot.com>.
3. Customs, language, law, and descent were the typical start to the list, with origin (especially in its relation to climatic imprint), religion, humoral balance, and history not far behind. See especially Robert Bartlett, *The Making of Europe: Conquest, Colonization, and Cultural Change, 950–1350* (Princeton: Princeton University Press, 1993) and R.R. Davies, "The Peoples of Britain and Ireland, 1100–1400: I. Identities," in *Transactions of the Royal Historical Society*, 6th Series, 4 (1994): 1–20. David A. Hinton surveys the materials from an archeological viewpoint in *Gold and Gilt, Pots and Pins: Possessions and People in Medieval Britain* (Oxford: Oxford University Press, 2005), esp. 4–6.

4. I make this argument at greater length and supply relevant bibliography in *Hybridity, Identity and Monstrosity in Medieval Britain.*

5. "The United Kingdom of England: The Anglo-Saxon Achievement," in *Uniting the Kingdom? The Making of British History*, ed. Alexander Grant and Keith J. Stringer (Routledge: London, 1995), 31.

6. *The English and the Normans: Ethnic Hostility, Assimilation, and Identity, 1066–c.1220* (Oxford: Oxford University Press, 2003), 71. Thomas details convincingly the conquest's lasting wake of violence and the long span required for Norman and English hostilities to ameliorate.

7. *Britones omnes, quos nos Walenses dicimus*: the first person plural of that verb reveals much about William's audience and identification. *Gesta Regum Anglorum: The History of the English Kings*, 2 vols. ed. and trans. R.A.B. Mynors, completed by R.M. Thomson and M. Winterbottom (Oxford: Clarendon Press, 1998), 2:175.

8. On the rarity of such a genesis story, see Cassandra Potts, "*'Atque unum ex diversis gentibus populum effecit'*: Historical Tradition and the Norman Identity," *Anglo-Norman Studies* 18 (1996): 139–52.

9. G.A. Loud, "The 'Gens Normannorum'—Myth or Reality?" *Anglo-Norman Studies* 4 (1981): 114 and Eleanor Searle, *Predatory Kinship and the Creation of Norman Power, 840–1066* (Berkeley: University of California Press, 1988), 242–44.

10. William of Newburgh, *The History of English Affairs*, Book 1, ed. and trans. P. G. Walsh and M.J. Kennedy (Wilthsire: Aris and Phillips, 1988), 1.Prologue. For the complete Latin see *Chronicles of the Reigns of Stephen, Henry II and Richard I*, ed. Richard Howlett, Rolls Series 82, London (1884–1889), vol. 1–2; for a complete English translation, *The History of William of Newburgh*, trans. Joseph Stevenson (Felinfach: Llanerch Publishers, 1996).

11. William writes that the Britons are relegated to *inviis montibus et saltibus*, the last word suggesting rugged pastoral land. On relegating the Welsh to a nonagricultural, "primitive" identity (as opposed to England's field-clearing, cereal-based modernity), see R.R. Davies, *The First English Empire: Power and Identity in the British Isles, 1093–1343* (Oxford: Oxford University Press, 2000), 113–41.

12. For a sophisticated reading along these lines see Patricia Ingham, "Pastoral Histories: Utopia, Conquest, and the Wife of Bath's Tale," *Texas Studies in Literature and Language* 44 (2002): 34–46.

13. See especially the work of John Gillingham gathered in *The English in the Twelfth-Century: Imperialism, National Identity and Political Values* (Woodbridge: Boydell Press, 2000) and R.R. Davies, *The First English Empire.*

14. Henry of Huntingdon, *Historia Anglorum*, ed. and trans. Diana Greenway (Oxford: Clarendon Press, 1996), 12–13. Gervase of Canterbury, Wace, Chrétien de Troyes, and William of Newburgh made similar pronouncements.

15. R.R. Davies traces the conversion process in *The First English Empire*, 1–2, 41–43, 48–49. The best discussion of the ambiguities Geoffrey of Monmouth built into his history, allowing Arthur to appeal to both conquerors and the subjugated, is Patricia Clare Ingham's *Sovereign Fantasies: Arthurian Romance and the Making of Britain* (Philadelphia: University of Pennsylvania Press, 2001), 21–50. Christopher Baswell likewise makes clear the complexity of translating Geoffrey into English in his excellent essay "Troy, Arthur, and the Languages of 'Brutis Albyoun,'" *Reading Medieval Culture: Essays in Honor of Robert W. Hanning*, ed. Robert M. Stein and Sandra Pierson Prior (Notre Dame, IN: University of Notre Dame Press, 2005), 170–97.

16. R.R. Davies's term for the twelfth-century Anglicization of Britain: *The First English Empire*, 51.

17. Geoffrey of Monmouth, *Historia Regum Britanniae*, trans. Lewis Thorpe (Harmondsworth: Penguin Books, 1966), 171–72; Neil Wright, ed., *The* Historia Regum Britannie *of Geoffrey of Monmouth*, vol. 1, *Bern, Burgerbibliothek, MS. 568* (Cambridge: D.S. Brewer, 1985), 74–75.

18. See Laurie A. Finke and Martin B. Shichtman. *King Arthur and the Myth of History* (Gainesville: University Press of Florida, 2004). Compare the generically contextualizing approach to marvels taken in Nancy F. Partner, *Serious Entertainments: The Writing of History in Twelfth-Century England* (Chicago: University of Chicago Press, 1977) and Monika Otter, *Inventiones: Fiction and Referentiality in Twelfth-Century English Historical Writing* (Chapel Hill: University of North Carolina Press, 1996). All three works are invaluable contributions to understanding twelfth-century historiography in all its literary complexity.

19. William's worry is that such strange and enticing phenomena are brought about to grip observers in a "useless fascination" (*in quibus homines stupore inutili teneabtur*, 1.28)—as opposed to, it seems, a more profitable fascination that a prodigy sent by God might elicit. For some context of William's marvels, see the excellent section "Beings Neither Angelic, Human nor Animal," in *England Under the Norman and Angevin Kings, 1075–1225*, ed. Robert Bartlett (Oxford: Clarendon Press, 2000), 686–92.

20. Ann Williams surveys the contemporary depictions of Norman and English difference, stressing the strategic and performative aspects of these descriptions: *The English and the Norman Conquest* (Woodbridge: Boydell Press, 1995), 188–90.

21. Blood that flows with uncanny life reappears later in the *History of English Affairs* as William narrates the death of Geoffrey de Mandeville. A personification of the chaos that William discerned in the reign of King Stephen (1135–1154), Geoffrey is described as a "reckless, strong and crafty man" (1.11). His most spectacular crime is the storming of Ramsey Abbey, where he evicts the monks and transforms the ecclesiastical buildings into a private fortress and "den of thieves." Suddenly the walls of captured church and cloister run with real blood (*verum sanguinem*

sudarunt), a divine rebuke to Geoffrey's crimes. William takes the episode from his favorite source, Henry of Huntingdon's *Historia Anglorum*. The bleeding walls at Ramsey seem to have been a wonder well known throughout England, and Henry claimed to have seen the flow of blood himself (*et ipse ego oculis meis inspexi*, 8.22). During Stephen's turbulent years on the throne many of the wounds inflicted by the Norman Conquest reopened. No surprise, then, that as William narrates Stephen's reign we witness for a second time an efflux of *verum sanguinem*. This blood likewise runs as if it had just been shed, linking the turmoil of Stephen's tenure back to Hastings, violence, and the historical formation of collective identities.

22. See the *Chronicle of the Abbey of Bury St. Edmunds*, ed. and trans. Diana Greenway and Jane Sayers (Oxford: Oxford University Press, 1989). For more on Norman architecture as a kind of imperialism, see Eric C. Fernie, "Architecture and the Effects of the Norman Conquest," *England and Normandy in the Middle Ages*, ed. David Bates and Anne Curry (London: Hambledon Press, 1994), 105–116 and *The Architecture of Norman England* (Oxford: Oxford University Press, 2000).

23. For this quotation and more on language as a fundamental racial marker, see *Hybridity, Identity and Monstrosity*, 24.

24. Although I do not have the space to explore the entanglement of England in contemporary Scotland and Ireland, concentrating instead upon Wales, it is worth keeping in mind that William knew very well how enmeshed the Scottish royal family was with the English, and how nebulous Scottish identity could be. For a meditation upon Irishness and partial assimilations that, though later than the materials I analyze, nonetheless resonates deeply with their themes, see Claire Sponsler, "The Captivity of Henry Chrystede: Froissart's *Chroniques*, Ireland, and Fourteenth-Century Nationalism," *Imagining a Medieval English Nation*, ed. Kathy Lavezzo (Minneapolis: University of Minnesota Press, 2004), 304–39.

25. Cf. R.R. Davies: "In a world where the advance of bread-grains was much the dominant feature, these societies appeared to be culpably backward and underdeveloped" (*First English Empire*, 124). He then quotes William of Newburgh on the Irish: "The soil of Ireland would be fertile if it did not lack the industry of the dedicated farmer; but the country has an uncivilized and barbarous people, almost lacking in laws and discipline, lazy in agriculture, and thereby living more on milk than on bread" (2.26).

26. In the only other version of the story of the Green Children—a version independent of that related by William of Newburgh—the young woman is not so compliant. She proves herself quite "lascivious and wanton": no happy domesticity here. See Ralph of Coggeshall, "De quodam puero et puella de terra emergentibus," *Chronicon Anglicanum*, ed. Joseph Stevenson, Rolls Series 68 (London 1875), 118–20.

CHAPTER 5

BEYOND BRITISH BOUNDARIES IN THE HISTORIA REGUM BRITANNIAE

Michael Wenthe

In Geoffrey of Monmouth's Historia Regum Britanniae, *King Arthur's preeminence as the greatest king of the Britons paradoxically depends on his challenge to the traditional understanding of British peoplehood as defined by precise boundaries of geography and ethnic identity. His efforts to extend Britishness are resisted by a desire for expression of identity that depends on exclusion.*

In the 1130s, civil war for the throne of Anglo-Norman England, left vacant by Henry I's death without legitimate male issue, pitted Henry's nephew Stephen of Blois against Henry's daughter (and designated heir) Matilda. During their struggle, the rival cousins both passed through Oxford, where the cleric Geoffrey of Monmouth wrote his *Historia Regum Britanniae* [*History of the Kings of Britain*] (c. 1136–1138). An account of the British rulers who had preceded the Anglo-Saxons, the *Historia* stretches from the Trojan-Italian origins of the eponymous nation-founder Brutus to the domination of Britain by Angles and Saxons in the seventh century. Geoffrey dedicated his work to figures on both sides of the civil war, perhaps because the history he chronicled provided numerous examples of the dangers of internecine conflict and the benefits of national unity. It also demonstrated the longstanding difficulty of maintaining a widespread empire centered on a Britain with an ethnically diverse population, a difficulty no less pertinent to the cross-Channel kingdom of Geoffrey's Anglo-Norman contemporaries than it was to the cross-Channel empire of Arthur, the greatest champion among Geoffrey's British kings.[1]

The intersection of geography and identity determines much of the conflict in the *Historia*, and Geoffrey presents British history as a series of binary struggles between the Britons and their ethnic opponents (chiefly Romans and Saxons), struggles that turn on the sovereignty of the island of Britain itself. He nevertheless reveals the weakness of such binary thinking, both as a structure that promotes conflict and as an oversimplification of the complex engagements with multiple groups that characterize real cultural contact. As Homi Bhabha notes, "[t]he 'locality' of national culture is neither unified nor unitary in relation to itself, nor must it be seen simply as 'other' in relation to what is outside or beyond it. The boundary is Janus-faced and the problem of outside/inside must always itself be a process of hybridity, incorporating new 'people' in relation to the body politic [and] generating other sites of meaning."[2] So it is that Geoffrey's Arthur, who distinguishes himself as a king not only of the Britons but also of many other subject peoples, both inside and outside Britain, fashions new "sites of meaning" beyond the received boundaries of British ethnic identity and Britain's natural borders.

Arthur can attempt to win over the victims of his conquests by promoting a new image of community to which others besides Britons can accede. In this, he revisits the nation-building efforts of his ancient predecessors Brutus and Corineus, who joined their separate communities of Trojan exiles, established them in a new land (Albion/Britain), and gave them a new name ("Britons," after Brutus). Britain is an "imagined community" in Benedict Anderson's sense in that its Britons are too numerous for each to know all the others, but Geoffrey's Britons are also "imagined" inasmuch as the bases of their community image are found in creative acts of differentiation that are not absolute, given, or natural, but the products alike of chance and will.[3]

Geoffrey's Arthur develops from a local, chauvinistic champion of national and ethnic interests to the leader of an international, multiethnic empire that challenges the hegemony and ideology of Rome. Arthur begins his reign as the latest in a long line of xenophobic defenders of the Britons in Britain, but as he directs his attention to foreign conquests he comes to revise his understanding of Britishness. Yet the glorious extension of Arthur's British empire beyond the natural physical boundaries of Britain's coastline exposes Britishness to the risky indeterminacy of the imaginary political boundaries dividing continental Europe into regions of permeable contiguity. The resultant threat to British identity as traditionally conceived is answered in the treachery of Arthur's nephew Mordred, whose otherwise shocking alliance with the historical enemies of the Britons within Britain is a way of reasserting the familiar group identities and inflexible boundaries that previously enabled the construction of Britishness. In Arthur's successes, Geoffrey shows the potential for British greatness to grow greater still through fruitful (if exploitative) contacts with outsiders beyond Britain; and in Arthur's final failure, Geoffrey shows the difficulty for Britons to abide such contacts if they should dilute British identity as traditionally understood and fiercely maintained, despite—or because of—its factitiousness.

The self-destructive tenacity of British identity is revealed shortly before Arthur's first appearance, when Geoffrey interrupts his history to insert a series of enigmatic prophecies uttered by the boy Merlin while in a trance before the treacherous, Saxon-loving usurper Vortigern. The first of these prophecies expounds the weird scene found below the foundations of a tower that Vortigern has tried to erect. Under a a subterranean pool that has swallowed up the foundations, a pair of dragons, one red, one white, sleep in two hollow stones. Once the pool is drained, the dragons emerge and begin to struggle for supremacy, each driving the other back by turns. A tearful Merlin explains that the dragons represent the two peoples then at war for dominance in Britain:

> Alas for the Red Dragon, for its end is near. Its cavernous dens shall be occupied by the White Dragon, which stands for the Saxons whom you have invited over. The Red Dragon represents the people of Britain, who will be overrun by the White One: for Britain's mountains and valleys shall be levelled, and the streams in its valleys shall run with blood.

For a while, the White Dragon of the Saxons will be overcome by "the Boar of Cornwall," a British champion whose rule will extend to other islands and Gaul and who will even threaten Rome before his mysterious end; but in time to come, "the Red Dragon will revert to its true habits and struggle to tear itself to pieces" [in proprios mores reuertetur rubeus draco et in seipsum seuire laborabit].[4]

Merlin's animal imagery is suggestive, not only for the ferocity of the conflict between Britons and Saxons but for the similarity of the foes. For much of the *Historia*, the Britons betray a chauvinistic confidence in their superiority that demands a corresponding denigration of all others, from continental Franks, Romans, and Saxons to insular giants, Scots, and Picts. Their privileging of an inside group against outsiders takes on literal force in the frequent efforts to purge the British Isles of all those peoples who arrive after them. But since the Trojan-derived Britons did not themselves originate in Britain, as Geoffrey makes clear early in his text, these interlopers in fact recapitulate part of the Britons' history, resembling their bitter foes as the White Dragon resembles the Red. Indeed, apart from color, nothing in Merlin's prophecy distinguishes the dragons from each other.

Notable, too, is the dependence of the Red Dragon on another figure, the Boar of Cornwall, for the temporary restoration of its fortunes. This boar represents Arthur, the first individual to be invoked in Merlin's prophecies, and it "shall be extolled in the mouths of its peoples" [in ore populorum].[5] The plural form of *peoples* suggests that Arthur's reach will extend beyond the Britons whom first he defends, and it contrasts with the singular forms used throughout the prophecies for the collective of Britons represented by the Red Dragon. Yet the Red Dragon's struggle with itself reveals that its true nature is also multiple. Merlin's prophecies conceal the sad fact that Arthur will himself be undone by dragonish treachery on the part of his nephew Mordred, not least because Arthur's expansionary efforts expose the fiction behind any simple image of Britishness.

By furthering his interests beyond the British Isles, Arthur must realize that British identity is not reducible to a single binary such as Britain versus Saxon. The very multiplicity of binaries—Briton versus Saxon, versus Gaul, versus Roman, and so on—demonstrates the insufficiency of mere binarism as the engine of identity (an insufficiency already apparent in the resemblance of the two dragons). This recognition of multiple others entails a corresponding multiplicity in self-knowledge. The fullest picture of Arthur's majesty, his plenary court at Caerleon, likewise offers the clearest picture of the British king's multiple constituencies as he listens to many voices from many lands, voices that he unifies in his singular pronouncements as king over them all.

When the fifteen-year-old Arthur first takes the crown, the Britons face a national, existential crisis. The Saxons within Britain have summoned their continental countrymen to join them in an effort to "exterminate" [*exterminare*] the Britons—a terminal enmity that establishes the Saxons as the most hostile and implacable of the Britons' Others. But Arthur turns the tables on the Saxons, besieging a large contingent of them in Caledon Wood. When the starving Saxons plea for mercy, he allows them to leave Britain unmolested, provided they leave behind hostages and treasure. Despite a history of violent and treacherous Saxon behavior, Arthur stops short of slaughtering them altogether, an opportunity that his predecessor Maximianus would not have let slip. Rather than exterminate those who sought to exterminate his people, Arthur would simply have them leave his country en masse.[6]

In this expulsion of an entire people, Arthur echoes his Trojan forebears, who first drove off the native giants that awaited them on their arrival in Albion. At this point, Arthur's defense of the Britons suggests a simple geographical understanding of Britishness and British interests: the Britons belong in Britain, sovereign and safe. But just as the giants returned to attack the first Britons, so do the expelled Saxons return, murdering the peasantry in flagrant violation of the truce whereby they had left Britain peacefully. No longer does Arthur show them mercy: he puts his hostages to death and prepares for a decisive campaign to destroy the Saxons.

During this successful effort, Arthur seizes the opportunity to dominate the other peoples of Britain, the Scots, Picts, and Irish. Having overcome the Britons' foes at home, Arthur attacks the outlying islands in a preemptive strike, quickly overcoming Ireland and Iceland. Thereafter, his reputation begins to win him bloodless conquests, for "[a] rumour spread[s] through the other islands that no country [nulla prouincia] could resist [him]." Consequently, the kings of Gotland and of the Orkneys come to Arthur "of their own free will to promise tribute and to do homage." Their lands escape the ravages inflicted by Arthur's armies, and Arthur returns to Britain. There he restores his kingdom to lasting peace [statumque regni sui in firmam pacem renovans] and enjoys a twelve-year hiatus before next launching battle.[7]

This extended *pax Arthuriana* represents Arthur's first great achievement, but it remains within a limited area, a group of islands on the margins of Europe. This isolation argues for Arthur's willingness, for these twelve years at least, to keep British affairs among the Britons. It also confines his dominion to islands, land masses with definitive (and defensible) natural borders as opposed to the indeterminate extension of lands eastward in continental Europe. There may be an element of imperialistic expansion in Arthur's first foreign conquests, but his motives seem as much defensive as aggressive or venal: by subduing the other islands, Arthur preserves the Britons from their nearest threats.

Meanwhile, Arthur enjoys an unusual degree of loyalty from his compatriots, ruling over his lands with the steadfast support of his advisers, allies, and relatives, notably Duke Cador of Cornwall and Duke Hoel of Brittany. This unified front contrasts sharply with the many previous episodes of factionalism and treacherous infighting, the usual pattern for Britons in the absence of campaigns directed against outsiders. While concentrating his rule to a Britain dominated by Britons, Arthur may not relish a worldwide fame, but he does enjoy twelve years of unprecedented peace and unity. Only when he turns to foreign knights for comradeship does Arthur begin to gain a reputation among the nations of Europe; only then does he embark on continental conquests; and only thereafter, as the provincial chieftain threatens to absorb the Roman Empire, does Arthur lose the unified support of the Britons with the rebellion of his nephew Mordred.

The resumption of combat after long peace in Britain reveals that there can be no final answer to the question of British identity; any apparent settling of the issue is exposed as temporary, contingent, incomplete. Arthur brings twelve years of peace to an end by launching a campaign of conquest against "the whole of Europe" [totam Europam], and fighting lasts nine years, with quick victories in Scandinavia followed by a prolonged effort to subdue Gaul.[8] At campaign's end, Arthur is master of a widespread domain with significant cross-Channel holdings. James Noble summarizes the view, advanced by scholars since J.S.P. Tatlock, that "the imperialism of the *Historia* is unprecedented in any of the earlier or contemporary histories Geoffrey might have read."[9] Tatlock himself claimed that "[n]o interest stands out in the *Historia* more prominently than imperialism," meaning "the extension of a king's rule beyond the realm he began with, perhaps to provide apanages for *his* younger sons as well as revenue and feudal prestige for himself."[10] The progression of Arthur from restorer of his people's fortunes within Britain to master of a host of nations beyond its borders represents the apogee of the imperialistic theme that runs through the *Historia*, and that is part of Arthur's great glory among the other kings; but his more federated approach to rule and his accommodation of foreigners among his counselors temper the force of British domination and ultimately color his sense of Britishness itself, sacrificing the simple clarity of an identity defined as a single *populus* in a precisely bounded *patria*.

Significantly, Arthur's major campaign of continental imperialism is apparently motivated from the outside. Rather than extend his rule in order "to provide…feudal prestige for himself," Arthur is led to attack other nations thanks to the feudal prestige he already enjoys. As his court gains renown, foreign kings begin to fear invasion by Arthur's armies. Geoffrey states that Arthur only conceives of such invasions after learning of the foreigners' fears,[11] so his subsequent activity serves to confirm the reputation that has already developed. In effect, the imperial Arthur is less the apotheosis of the Britons than a creation of his foes, a figure who adapts himself to comport with what others say about him.

Some foreigners meet Arthur halfway, as when Arthur conquers Gaul with the aid of Gaul's fighting men. The "better part of the army of the Gauls" supports Arthur in his final fight against Frollo, the tribune who rules Gaul in the name of the Roman Emperor Leo.[12] The success of Arthur's British army thus depends in part on the collusion and participation of Gallic forces, who are not the only foreigners to have joined him. At his Parisian court after Frollo's defeat, Arthur summons the clergy and the rest of the populace [clero et populo] and "settle[s] the government of the realm peacefully and legally" [statum regni pace et lege confirmauit].[13] This language recalls that used to describe Arthur's reimposition of peace in Britain after his conquest of the islands twenty-one years earlier [statumque regni sui in firmam pacem renovans] (cited above), and the echo both reinforces the association of Gaul with Britain and suggests the onset of a second era of *pax Arthuriana*.

Arthur's inclusion of local laypeople and religious in establishing the government in Gaul further testifies to Gaul's importance (perhaps a reflex of twelfth-century politics). Nowhere else does Geoffrey depict Arthur holding court outside of his chief cities in Britain, and the role afforded the locals suggests that Gaul's provinces will enjoy a measure of autonomy under their British governors. Indeed, only here does Geoffrey show how conquered states within Arthur's far-flung polity must be governed, as vassal states ruled by Arthur's subordinates with some participation by elements of the local population. We hear little about the nonelite mass of humanity in Arthur's world save when it suffers the depredations of savage armies (including Arthur's), but Geoffrey insists that the conquered towns and peoples of Gaul are "pacified."[14]

Subsequently, in one of the only Arthurian scenes not devoted to combat, Geoffrey portrays something of both the culture of Arthur's Britain and the governance of his empire. Arthur, having pacified Gaul and established its system of governance, returns to Britain and prepares to hold a plenary court at Pentecost. He mentions his plans to his entourage (*familiaribus suis*, "his familiars," among whom must be some foreigners), and they recommend that he hold court in Caerleon. Arthur agrees, deciding to place the crown of the realm [regnique diadema] on his head while he reestablishes the firmest peace [firmissimam pacem renouaret] with the kings and dukes subject to him.[15] Again Geoffrey echoes the language of Arthur's first extended period of peace [statumque regni sui in firmam pacem renouans], reaffirming the impression that the Gallic victories have affixed a seal to his imperialistic campaigns. Lewis Thorpe takes the reference to "the crown of the realm" to mean that Arthur wears it in state, since he had already been crowned at age fifteen with "the crown of the kingdom" [diademate regni].[16] But Arthur's kingdom is no longer what it was then, suggesting that this later ceremony constitutes a new coronation. Arthur is now the imperial master of a realm that extends well beyond his British inheritance, a reach demonstrated by the diverse geographical origins of his attendants.

In describing the plenary court at Caerleon, Geoffrey lists over forty kings, dukes, and leaders of cities who come to pay homage to Arthur; the sheer accumulation of names suggests that the wearing of his crown before this princely gathering represents the culmination of Arthur's ambitions. Arthur apparently believes that he has successfully conquered "the whole of Europe"—at least, the whole of Europe that matters to him. Arthur appears to have forgotten about Rome, but Geoffrey recalls it in describing Caerleon's gilded gables, with which it "imitates Rome" [ita ut...Romam imitaretur].[17] Arthur has fashioned an alternative to the Roman Empire in a northwestern European polity privileging Britain, Gaul, and Scandinavia over the lands of southern and eastern Europe, the Iberian peninsula, and the Mediterranean littoral. Geoffrey writes that "no prince of any distinction this side of Spain [citra Hispaniam]...did not come when he received his invitation": Arthur having triumphed over all the princes "this side of Spain," he must not have bothered to invite any others.[18]

In the varied gathering of the plenary court, Arthur shares his dignity with a grand assortment of peoples. As Michael J. Curley writes, "the Caerleon idyll projects an image of social unanimity, benevolent monarchical hegemony, conciliar consensus politics, a static social hierarchy, and solidarity between secular and ecclesiastical powers, all of this founded on the king's distribution of lands and titles to the deserving members of his court."[19] Having fought savage wars to dominate the nations that surround Britain, Arthur now aims to establish peace and order and to reinforce his military imperialism with a cultural imperialism that would make Britons of their erstwhile others.

By conquering Gaul, however, Arthur has caught the attention of the Roman Empire that is cousin to his British empire, the original Other-term against which Brutus first defined himself as newly independent. A delegation sent to Arthur's court by the Roman procurator Lucius demands the restoration of Gaul and the payment of ancient tribute. For Rome to take note of Arthur now is to recognize him and his empire as a threatening alter ego, one that dares replace Rome by forcibly acquiring Roman territory. By asserting Rome's former domination, Lucius attempts to reduce Britain to its historical subjection, unwilling to allow a full-fledged imperial competitor since, as he reminds Arthur in his letter of warning, "the entire world owes submission" [famulatum] to the Roman Senate.[20]

The tribute that Rome demands may recall that which Arthur expects from Gotland or the Orkneys, but Rome and Arthur differ in their manner of governing and imposition of authority. Where Lucius speaks of *famulatus* [servitude], Arthur turns to his *familiares* [entourage], those other kings and dukes whom he draws close. Lucius's letter reveals Rome's attitude toward its subjects to be arrogant condescension: the Senate simply makes decisions about the Empire's inhabitants, apparently without their involvement. Arthur acts violently to establish his sway over other countries, but having done so he involves local populations in creating a system of governance that answers to him. Likewise, Arthur acts with the consent of his counselors, and he polls his *consocii* [companions] before he resolves to attack Rome in defiance of its demands.

Arthur's advisers declare that the war against Rome will be a struggle to defend their liberty [*libertatem nostram*, "our freedom"] against Roman aggression.[21] Though the speakers directly quoted by Geoffrey are both of British descent (Hoel of Brittany and Auguselus, king of Albany), numerous other leaders echo their sentiments in another impressive catalogue of Arthur's followers listed chiefly by nation rather than name as the leaders volunteer their armies' services. This scene contrasts with the picture of decision-making in Rome that follows, where the Senate directs Lucius to issue a proclamation commanding the Kings of the Orient to assemble their forces.[22] The enthusiasm of Arthur's subjects to defend his cause shows that the cause is theirs too.

The territories of these "Kings of the Orient" lie along the southern and eastern coasts of the Mediterranean littoral, including lands that, geographically speaking, are not European.[23] Many of their peoples can be assumed to be non-Christian, given such rulers' names as Mustensar, king of the Africans, and Aliphatima, king of Spain.[24] Geoffrey does not portray Arthur's Roman war as anything other than a dispute over sovereignty and territory; still, the geographical division of the opponents suggests a northwestern European crusade against Mediterranean infidels, even if they are allied with Rome, seat of the papacy.[25] Earlier, Geoffrey had used the terms *pagan* and *Christian* as equivalents for *Saxon* and *Britain* to describe social mixing under Vortigern, which made it difficult to know "who was a pagan and who was a Christian" [quis paganus esset, quis christianus].[26] Given the Britons' pagan origins and continuing hostility after the Saxons' conversion to Christianity, the apparently religious dimension of the pagan–Christian opposition is less operative than the fact of opposition itself. Since Arthur's dispute with Rome is also essentially nonreligious, the usual binary opposition of Christian and pagan is further confused, since seeming Muslims fight alongside Rome against Christian Britain and its allies. Indeed, the social mixing suggested by linking the Romans with these more marked outsiders offers further evidence of the lack of uniformity among them, which, from the British perspective, only confirms their wickedness.[27]

With regard to this seeming diversity of faiths under Rome, consider the reminder of Scott L. Waugh and Peter D. Diehl that "Latin Christendom had always encompassed great variety within its nominal unity of religious faith. The vision of a uniform Christendom under the leadership of a single Church barely concealed the heterogeneity of the peoples it embraced or the diversity of beliefs they held."[28] Such a vision is lacking in Geoffrey's portrayal of Rome, but it finds its analogue in Arthur's vision of his British empire. Arthur promotes a uniform dominion under the leadership of a single king who conceals or otherwise tries to reduce the heterogeneity of his subject peoples—a policy that is contrary to all the previous moves of British history, which have insisted on British exceptionalism and distinctiveness from other peoples and their customs.

Indeed, the radical nature of Arthur's exploits can be seen in his emulation of the nation's founders Brutus and Corineus, who made a new land safe for their merged peoples by killing off the giants in Albion (by single combat, in Corineus's case). So, too, does Arthur combine various peoples and expand their lands; moreover, he even kills a giant himself at Mont Saint-Michel, his first victim in the war against Rome. To some extent, these actions crown Arthur as the epitome of British kings: his recapitulation of foundational acts confirms his exemplary Britishness. At the same time, Arthur's exploits challenge the prior understanding of Britishness within Britain. Much as his predecessor King Lud renamed Trinovantum (New Troy) as Kaerlud (Lud's city, whence London), stamping the British capital with his own image and thereby stamping out its Trojan heritage,[29] so Arthur's emulation of Brutus and Corineus is not simple repetition but rather a potential replacement, or—what is worse, from the standpoint of Britons in Britain—a literal displacement, a removal of British interests from the *patria* itself to a territory unbounded by the sea and open to penetration from unfamiliar areas.

One stranger who penetrates Arthur's continental lands is precisely the giant of Mont Saint-Michel, a monster that has kidnapped Duke Hoel's niece (who dies of fright) and devoured many of the men Hoel has sent to fight it. There is no question of Arthur's socializing this giant, but more important to its exclusion than its diet are its origins and the recurrence of gigantomachy in British history. Since the giant is said to have "emerged from certain regions in Spain" [ex partibus Hispaniarum], its otherness is polyvalent, inasmuch as a Spain ruled by Aliphatima would suggest (to a contemporary audience) a Muslim origin.[30] While it would be a mistake to claim that this monster is himself Muslim, Spain remains outside the Arthurian orbit (recall that his plenary court summoned all the major princes "on this side of Spain").[31] Tatlock describes Spain as both "clearly in Geoffrey's mind...a Moslem region" and "outside the pale, a natural origin for uncanny creatures."[32] Geoffrey does not dispatch Arthur on a *Reconquista* against the giants and Muslims of Spain; it suffices to make sure that they are kept out of the more northerly lands that properly constitute Arthur's realm. The giant is a foreign intruder in lands ruled by Arthur's trusted ally and relative Hoel. Arthur's single-handed defeat of the giant vindicates his rule over ineffective subordinates by defending the land and people that Hoel cannot protect.

The Trojans' destruction of Albion's giants had ensured their new identity as Britons in the homeland they renamed Britain; what, then, does Arthur's gigantomachy entail for British identity or reveal about his ambitions? Arthur repeats the essential task of eliminating giants who threaten to occupy the same space as the British (or their subjects, allies, and relatives), and the echoes of the earlier contest invest his victory with the sense that a space is again being secured for the proliferation and development of a ruling British society whose ideal is conformity with or resemblance to itself. But the earlier gigantomachy enabled the Britons to settle a newly empty land as theirs alone. Arthur's battle offers a less dramatic result, but the reappearance of a giant in British history after the elimination of those under Brutus warns that Arthur's territorial expansion beyond the fixed borders of Britain has newly exposed his subjects to long-forgotten threats. This latest fight between Briton and giant portends the return of a struggle to secure British identity, a struggle renewed by Arthur's readiness to look outside his native land and beyond his native people to establish his identity as the most illustrious king of the Britons. In other words, Arthur defends British interests in response to a crisis of identity that he himself has provoked, and by fighting for Britishness outside of Britain he threatens to overturn the originary conception of that identity as partly shaped in ridding Albion of its giants. Under Brutus, the first Britons established themselves by destroying their enemies at home; under Arthur, the latest Britons extend themselves by discovering new foes abroad. Though similar in some respects, the gigantomachies differ crucially in their distinction between native-born foes and a foreign interloper.

This distinction between native and foreign likewise informs the progress of Arthur's renown, which spreads among foreigners abroad partly thanks to the foreigners among his entourage in Britain. Of Arthur's twelve years of peace in Britain after conquering the islands of the ocean, Geoffrey has nothing to say other than that Arthur "moram .xii. annis ibidem fecit": he spent twelve years in the same place, in the same way.[33] But then Arthur begins "to increase his personal entourage [familiam suam] by inviting very distinguished men from far-distant kingdoms [ex longe positis regnis] to join it."[34] Geoffrey does not indicate why Arthur should want to enlarge his household in this way, but he is clear enough about the consequences: the importation of foreigners soon leads to the spread of Arthur's fame and the exportation of Arthurian customs, customs that have themselves been influenced by these newcomers.

Arthur begins to have such elegance [*facetiam*] in his household that he inspires imitation in peoples abroad [ita ut emulationem longe manentibus populis ingereret].[35] The only specific example Geoffrey gives of such imitation involves clothing and ways of bearing arms,[36] so we cannot claim that various distant peoples emulated other Arthurian cultural practices. But the adoption of such external and visible signs as clothing and arms recalls the confusion between Britons and Saxons under Vortigern that resulted from their social mixing, and once again such similarity between different groups stems in the first instance from their proximity. Arthur's influence on people in foreign lands follows his absorption of foreign knights within his *familia* [entourage, household, vassals]; only thereafter do foreigners abroad begin to take after the British elite, revealing the dynamic of mutual influence between outside and inside in shaping a new Arthurian cultural identity.

Both Arthur's welcome of foreigners and foreigners' imitation of Arthur lead to a homogenization of culture (at least warrior culture), but that does not in turn reduce bellicosity. On the contrary, the spread of Arthur's fame abroad only emboldens him against those unfortunate foreign rulers who must watch as their best men join his court. They must also watch as the best knights who remain to them adopt the dress and military techniques of Arthur and his knights. While the latter might be explained as a sort of sixth-century arms race, the former suggests a sympathy for Arthur that undermines the confidence of foreign kings in their own capacity to lead their knights and defend their rule.

When Arthur's fame has finally spread to the furthest poles of the earth [per extremos mundi cardines], these "kings of countries far across the sea" [transmarinorum regnorum] dread invasion and the loss of their lands, so they "re-buil[d] their towns and the towers in their towns, and then [go] so far as to construct castles on carefully-chosen sites" for refuge from Arthur. Ironically, their frantic defensive preparations urge Arthur to go on the attack, for he learns from this construction boom that he is feared.[37] Furthermore, these civic building projects show that Arthur exercises a sort of civilizing (if not necessarily humane) effect on the societies around him even before he conquers them. Already, his reputation prepares foreign lands for absorption into his empire, for both the physical makeup of towns and the cultural practices of the knightly classes are transformed, the better to resemble Arthur's warlike society.

Such cultural imperialism thus prepares for the political variety. Arthur's installation of Britons as lieutenant rulers of Gaul and Norway reveals that uniformity of culture marches hand-in-hand with uniformity of rule, both emanating from Britain. At the same time, his armies welcome fighters from all lands, some of whom fight in national brigades commanded by their countrymen, but all in the service of their British conqueror. Arthur's political dominance may not allow for equality between British masters and foreign subjects, but his armed forces do foster a comradeship among soldiers from different peoples, including those that Arthur has conquered.

Arthur fosters this sense of comradeship in the language he uses to inspire his men before battle against both the Roman armies and, ultimately, the allies of his nephew Mordred. The formerly chauvinist champion of British ethnicity appeals to all his soldiers by insisting on their liberty and on the defense of their singular *patria*, not discriminating between native Britons and others but rather deliberately shaping a concept of British identity that incorporates those he has attracted from abroad. Thus, in a speech just before his decisive victory over the Romans at Saussy,[38] Arthur addresses a diverse company of soldiers, from Denmark, Norway, and Gaul as well as Britain, as "domestici mei," which Thorpe plausibly renders as "my countrymen." The Latin may also be translated "members of my household" or even "my servants"; the latter would play off Arthur's subsequent statement that his *domestici* "have made Britain mistress [*domina*] of thirty kingdoms."[39] But Arthur goes further to associate his retainers with his own people and homeland, urging them to resist the Romans' threats to their liberty [*libertatem*] and to defy their efforts to make their homeland [*patriam*] a tributary of the Romans.

Despite the fact that Denmark, Norway, and Gaul had submitted to Arthur only after campaigns marked by their savagery [*seuicie*] and their protraction, Arthur reminds his *commilitones* [fellow fighters] of those very campaigns, insisting that their subjection to his rule [*potestati*] has meant the liberation of these lands from the shame of Roman mastery [ab eorum pudendo dominio].[40] Since among his addressees are the soldiers of Denmark, Norway, and Gaul, Arthur's mention of a single *patria* to defend argues for a wider sense of mission that joins them all, a unity that Geoffrey reflects in his narrative by conveniently referring to this mixed company simply as "Britons."[41]

An even greater demonstration of the unity of Arthur's diverse forces comes when he must abandon his triumphant entry into Rome in order to quell Mordred's rebellion back in Britain. Having learned that his nephew-regent has seized both crown and queen during his absence, Arthur must now invade Britain from the continent, with the support of the other kings of the islands ("cum insulanis...regibus," including the king of Denmark). Mordred on his side musters an army of all those who hate his uncle, including not just treacherous Britons of his own but also Saxons—to whom he offers restoration of the British lands they lost to Arthur's earliest campaigns—as well as the Scots, Picts, and Irish also dispossessed by Arthur. Mordred's forces are an alliance of both pagans and Christians, *tam paganorum quam christianorum* in the binary pairing familiar for its threatening implications for the integrity of British identity.[42]

Before the climactic battle against Mordred's armies, Arthur inspires his men by castigating their enemies as foreigners ["de externis regionibus," from external regions] come to "steal their lands"[43]—a strange way to inspire his soldiers from regions outside Britain, and more striking still when it is remembered that Mordred's allies all have their own histories of residence in Britain prior to Arthur's birth. Arthur continues by emphasizing the disunity and variety of their foes: "He told them, too, that this miscellaneous collection of barbarians, come from a variety of countries [diuersos diuersorum regnorum barbaros]—raw recruits who were totally inexperienced in war—would be quite incapable of resisting valiant men like themselves, who were the veterans of many battles."[44] Arthur makes explicit the martial contrast between the inexperience of Mordred's men and the expertise of his own, but he leaves another contrast implicit. Arthur stresses the difference of Mordred's men not only from his own but also from each other—they are "*divuersos diuersorum regnorum barbaros*," where the repeated adjective *diversus* can offer a semantic range that includes "remote" and "hostile" as well as "different," "unlike." But having mentioned this diversity in his foes (which may be either geographical or ethnic or both), he neglects to specify the origin(s) of his own men, implying in his silence that their difference has either been overcome or is no impediment to their success on the battlefield, which may be their real home.

Geoffrey continues to contrast the diversity of Mordred's men with the unity of Arthur's when he lists the fallen of the final battle. On Mordred's side, he discriminates the dead by ethnic origin, first listing four Saxon leaders, then four Irishmen, then collectives of Scots, Picts, and almost all those whom they commanded.[45] On Arthur's side, Geoffrey names only four soldiers altogether: the King of Norway, the King of Denmark, Cador Limenich, and Cassivelaunus. Even the two kings are identified not by their peoples (as with the leaders of the *Saxones* and *Hibernenses*) but by their realms. Together with these leaders died many of their soldiers, *both* Britons *and* men from the other peoples that they brought with them: "cum multis militibus suorum *tam* Britonum *quam* ceterarum gentium quas secum adduxerant."[46] Where the difference in Mordred's allies is underlined by the twice-repeated adjective "diverse," the variety of Arthur's followers is described with the neutral term *ceterae* [other]. Where Mordred's allies appear to command their own ethnically distinct battalions, each fighting for the ethnically specific lands promised by the usurper, Arthur's lieutenants lead mixed forces, numbering Britons and non-Britons alike among their soldiers. Both sides field mixed armies, but Mordred's side is constituted by its differences while Arthur's side is united beyond them.

The resistance by other Britons under Mordred's banner implies Arthur's failure to persuade his ethnic compatriots of the openness or catholicity of "British" identity. That Mordred should ally himself with such traditional enemies of the Britons as the Saxons and the Picts only argues for the greater existential threat of Arthur's reconception of Britishness—a threat not to individual Britons but to "the Britons" as formerly conceived. Since Britons before Arthur traditionally defined themselves in opposition to ethnic others within Britain, Mordred's overtures to the Saxons and Picts paradoxically support the maintenance by traditional means of British identity in its primitive form, *even if* (read: *precisely because*) he promises to cede land to the Britons' historical foes.[47]

Mordred achieves a Pyrrhic victory, for though he dies and his side suffers defeat, he manages to restore British identity to its status quo ante Arthur, complete with the return of Saxons to struggle with the Britons for dominance. Meanwhile, Arthur is mortally wounded and departs for the other world of Avalon, having failed to sustain a new vision of the Britons and their others. Over time, the Saxons grow ever more powerful, and at the close of the *Historia* the beleaguered Britons have abandoned their plague-infested island for Brittany. Having temporarily lost their land, they finally suffer the loss of their name, for, as reported in one of the final sentences, the *Britones*, "Britons," come to be known as the *Gualenses*, "Welsh." This word Geoffrey derives eponymously from such later Welsh rulers as Gualo or Galaes, but it actually stems (as Geoffrey might have known) from Old English *wealh,* plural *wealas*, meaning "foreigner," "stranger," "slave"—a bitterly ironic name for those who had been the native rulers of Britain.[48]

Some manuscripts of the *Historia* conclude with a paragraph describing how the Welsh returned to Wales but incessantly caused internal or external strife, fighting either with the Saxons or with themselves.[49] This final recurrence to Merlin's vision of the Red Dragon's true habits demonstrates the dangers of a bellicosity that demands an outlet or must otherwise turn inward.[50] The *Historia* also shows how the construction of identity via binarism is ultimately destructive (even if simultaneously determinative), in part because it can never be definitive. Individual lives are more often multiple than singular, as community bonds intersect in complicated Venn diagrams, and "the Other" more often consists of "others."[51]

Arthur's move toward hybridization—a kind of strength in numbers, where the number is greater than two—is rejected by an atavistic British desire for exclusion and ethnic purity. Mordred's self-destructive gambit of self-definition reveals the dangers of a parochialism that promotes the simplistic understanding of Britishness as staged through binary opposi- tions, oppositions at work throughout the *Historia* but always revealed to be inadequate to the task of either fixing British identity or preventing the arrival of other Others, let alone protecting the Britons from turning on each other. The insistent figuring of British identity through conflict leads to a supersessionistic historiography that chronicles the replacement of one group of Britain's rulers by another: giants are replaced by Britons who are replaced by Saxons, who will themselves be replaced by the Normans to whom Geoffrey dedicates his work.

A similar supersession of Arthur himself recurs almost immediately in such daughter texts of the *Historia* as Wace's Anglo-Norman *Roman de Brut* and Layamon's early Middle English *Brut*. The former decorates Arthur's court with Normanesque trappings; the latter makes Arthur a hero of the English who descend from the Britons' bitterest foes. In a sense, though, Arthur's literary posterity represents his final escape from the shackles of a bounded identity, as his story spreads among non- Britons, many outside of Britain. The fictional Arthur's loss of political prominence at home goes hand in hand with his real-world literary pre- eminence abroad, much as Geoffrey's Arthur suffers British treachery at the height of his Continental success.[52] Though Arthur may never escape the doom of Mordred's betrayal, later writers will elaborate on Geoffrey's hints of his international appeal by concentrating less on Arthur's wars than on his Round Table fellowship, uniting knights of diverse origins from within British boundaries and beyond.

Notes

I would like to thank Katherine Terrell and Jeffrey Jerome Cohen for their comments and suggestions on an earlier version of this chapter.

1. For background on ethnic conflicts and territorial matters in Anglo- Norman England, see Robert Bartlett, *England under the Norman and Angevin Kings, 1075–1225*, The New Oxford History of England (Oxford: Clarendon Press, 2000), chapter 2: "England and Beyond," and Hugh M. Thomas, *The English and the Normans: Ethnic Hostility, Assimilation, and Identity, 1066–c. 1220* (Oxford: Oxford University Press, 2003).
2. Bhabha, "Introduction: Narrating the Nation," in *Nation and Narration*, ed. Homi K. Bhabha (1990; reprint, New York: Routledge, 1995), 4 [1–7].
3. Benedict Anderson, *Imagined Communities: Reflections on the Origin and Spread of Nationalism*, rev. ed. (New York: Verso, 1991).
4. Geoffrey of Monmouth, *Historia Regum Britanniae*, trans. Lewis Thorpe (Harmondsworth: Penguin Books, 1966), 171–72, corresponding to Neil Wright, ed., *The* Historia Regum Britannie *of Geoffrey of Monmouth*, vol. 1,

Bern, Burgerbibliothek, MS. 568 (Cambridge: D.S. Brewer, 1985), 74–75, §112. I will normally cite in English from Thorpe's translation, noting when I differ from his rendering. Here, his translation is more colorful than the Latin, which does not literally mean "tear itself to pieces" so much as "vent its rage against itself." References to Thorpe's translation (cited as Thorpe) will therefore be cross-referenced to the appropriate page and section numbers in Wright's edition of Geoffrey's Latin (cited as Wright). References to editorial matter include a short title.

5. Thorpe, 172; Wright, 74, §112.
6. Thorpe, 215; Wright, 102–3, §145.
7. Thorpe, 222; Wright, 107, §153.
8. Thorpe, 222 and 225; Wright, 107, §154 and 109, §155.
9. Noble is one of various scholars who sees echoes of Norman campaigns in some of Arthur's battle sites. He argues that this "would seem to be indicative of a conscious attempt on Geoffrey's part not only to invite comparison with, but also to establish sound historical precedent for, the imperialistic practices and ambitions of William the Conqueror and his successors, William Rufus and Henry I" (James Noble, "Patronage, Politics, and the Figure of Arthur in Geoffrey of Monmouth, Wace, and Layamon," in *The Arthurian Yearbook II*, ed. Keith Busby [New York: Garland Publishing, 1992] 161–62 [159–78]).
10. J.S.P. Tatlock, *The Legendary History of Britain: Geoffrey of Monmouth's Historia Regum Britanniae and Its Early Vernacular Versions* (Berkeley and Los Angeles: University of California Press, 1950), 305. The childless Arthur need provide no lands for sons, though he establishes his brother-in-law Loth, Gawain's father, as king of Norway (Thorpe, 223; Wright, 107–8, §154).
11. Thorpe, 222; Wright, 107, §154.
12. Thorpe, 223.
13. Thorpe, 225; Wright, 109, §155.
14. Thorpe, 225; Wright, 109, §155.
15. Wright, 109, §156.
16. Thorpe, *History*, 226 n, referring to the passage at Thorpe, 212; Wright, 101, §143.
17. Thorpe, 226 (who renders it "a match for Rome"); Wright, 110, §156.
18. Thorpe, 228; Wright, 111, §156.
19. Michael Curley, *Geoffrey of Monmouth* (New York: Twayne Publishers, 1994), 86–87.
20. Thorpe, 231; Wright, 113, §158.
21. Wright, 115, §161.
22. Thorpe, 236; Wright, 116, §163.
23. Granted, the precise boundaries of Europe have shifted, since what we designate a continent is little more than the western end of the Asian land mass. Many medieval Europeans would hardly have known they were part of an entity known as "Europe" (Siân Jones and Paul Graves-Brown, "Introduction: Archaeology and Cultural Identity," in *Cultural*

Identity and Archaeology: The Construction of European Communities, ed. Paul Graves-Brown, Siân Jones, and Clive Gamble, Theoretical Archaeology Group [London: Routledge, 1996] 11 [1–24]). J.R.S. Phillips writes that "[f]or [the Romans'] descendants in the west the empire was no more, and Europe was merely a geographical expression with little political or emotional content" (Phillips, *The Medieval Expansion of Europe* [Oxford: Oxford University Press, 1989] 18). In the meantime, those Roman allies from North Africa and the Levant are more certainly "non-European" (at least geographically) than the Greek forces. As Edward W. Said observes, invoking Denys Hay's *Europe: The Emergence of an Idea* (1957; reprint, New York: Harper and Row, 1966), "[o]rientalism is never far from what Denys Hay has called the idea of Europe, a collective notion identifying 'us' Europeans as against all 'those' non-Europeans." Certainly Arthur's disparaging comments about the sluggishness of "oriental types" ("orientalium generum," Wright, 124, §169; Thorpe, 249, gives "Eastern peoples") corresponds to what Said claims is the "major component" that made European culture "hegemonic both in and outside Europe: the idea of European identity as a superior one in comparison with all the non-European peoples and cultures" (Said, *Orientalism* [1994; reprint, with new preface, New York: Vintage Books, 2003] 7).

24. Tatlock observed that these (pseudo-)Arabic names appear to derive from the eleventh-century Muslim ruler Abu Tamîn Ma'add al-Mustansir, "the Fatimite caliph of Egypt from 1036 to 1094," and from some vague knowledge of Shi'ite tradition (conflating the male and female names of 'Ali and Fatima). Even the classical names describe those who were "enemies of western Europeans, being in Geoffrey's time partly subject to the Orthodox Church and the Byzantine emperor, but mostly Moslem; and all except one are actually named in accounts of the first Crusade" (Tatlock, *Legendary History*, 122–23).

25. See Tatlock, *Legendary History*, 261–62.

26. Thorpe, 161; Wright, 68, §101. Jeffrey Jerome Cohen has examined this confusion in terms of not social but racial mixing, focused on the essentializing materiality of blood—though Geoffrey characteristically complicates the seemingly straightforward essences he invokes (*Hybridity, Identity, and Monstrosity in Medieval Britain: On Difficult Middles*, The New Middle Ages [New York: Palgrave Macmillan, 2006] 69–76; for British women mixing with Saxon men under Vortigern, see p. 72).

27. "The religious frontier had to be defended at the level of personal relations, where daily contact might lead to a blurring of differences" (Scott L. Waugh and Peter D. Diehl, *Christendom and its Discontents: Exclusion, Persecution, and Rebellion, 1000–1500* [Cambridge: Cambridge University Press, 1996] 9).

28. Waugh and Diehl, *Christendom and its Discontents*, 1.

29. Thorpe, 74 and 106; Wright, 15, §22 and 34, §53.

30. Thorpe, 237; Wright, 117, §165. It is unlikely that Geoffrey or his readers would have recognized the anachronism of sixth-century Muslims. On the disinclination even of Christians in the crusader kingdoms to learn

about their Muslim neighbors, see Phillips, *Medieval Expansion*, 52. Geraldine Heng has addressed the "curious" plural form of *Hispaniarum* in her *Empire of Magic: Medieval Romance and the Politics of Cultural Fantasy* (New York: Columbia University Press, 2003), 19, 35–37, arguing that the contemporary ambiguity of the term "Hispania" (referring to both Spain and "the interior regions of Syria") enabled Geoffrey to use Arthur's triumph against a monster in the past to recuperate the crusaders' struggles against Muslims in the present. Heng's wider discussion of cannibalism and Islamic echoes in Arthur's giant fights are provocative, though she does not address their relation to Corineus's gigantomachies under Brutus.

31. One manuscript of the fourteenth-century *De origine gigantum*, which details the pre-British history of Albion, identifies the human mothers of Albion's giants as the daughters of a Spanish king. Since *Hispanie* is written over the erased *Grecie* that is the reading in other manuscripts, the choice is surely deliberate. Ruth Evans cites the opinion of James P. Carley and Julia C. Crick, editors of the Latin, that the change is "most probably in line with the text's ideological use by Scottish nobles...since it picks up a detail from the Scota story, 'where the founding race travels from Egypt to Spain'" (Evans, "Gigantic Origins: An Annotated Translation of *De origine gigantum*," in *Arthurian Literature* 16, ed. James P. Carley and Felicity Riddy (Cambridge: D.S. Brewer, 1998), 202 [197–211]).

32. Further: "Save as the origin of the Irish and as subdued by Rome..., Spain appears only thus" (Tatlock, *Legendary History*, 113–14).

33. Wright, 107, §153; "moram" may also convey a sense of delay.

34. Thorpe, 222; Wright, 107, §154.

35. Wright, 107, §154. Thorpe's translation (222) states that "in this way [Arthur] developed such a code of courtliness [tantamque facetiam] in his household that he inspired peoples living far away to imitate him." Fiona Tolhurst cautions that Thorpe's translation may offer a misleading anticipation of later developments in Arthurian romance ("Geoffrey of Monmouth's *Historia Regum Britanniae* and the Critics," *Arthuriana* 8 [1998]: 4 [3–11]). For the historical development of courtliness, see C. Stephen Jaeger, *The Origins of Courtliness: Civilizing Trends and the Formation of Courtly Ideals, 939–1210*, The Middle Ages (Philadelphia: University of Philadelphia Press, 1985).

36. "[E]ven the man of noblest birth...thought nothing at all of himself unless he wore his arms and dressed in the same way as Arthur's knights" (Thorpe, 222; Wright, 107, §154).

37. Thorpe, 222; Wright, 107, §154.

38. Thus Thorpe interprets "Siesia" in his source manuscript; Wright's manuscript gives "Sessia" (123, §168). See Thorpe, *History*, 247 n, for comment on his interpretation; contra Thorpe, see Hans E. Keller, "Two Toponymical Problems in Geoffrey of Monmouth and Wace: Estrusia and Siesia," *Speculum: A Journal of Medieval Studies* 49 (1974): 693–98 [687–98].

39. Thorpe, 248; Wright, 123, §169.

40. On the savagery in Denmark and Norway, see Wright, 108, §154; on the prolonged campaign in Gaul, see Wright, 109, §155. For the "liberation" of these countries in being made subject to Arthur, see Wright, 124, §169. Thorlac Turville-Petre asks: "[D]id the Trojans, in becoming patrons of European provinces, win domination by conflict or free peoples from their enslavement? In fact they did both in Geoffrey of Monmouth's account" ("Afterword: The Brutus Prologue to *Sir Gawain and the Green Knight*," in *Imagining a Medieval English Nation*, ed. Kathy Lavezzo, Medieval Cultures, vol. 37 [Minneapolis: University of Minnesota Press, 2004] 344–45 [340–46]). Compare Ernst Renan, foundational scholar of nationalism: "Indeed, historical enquiry brings to light deeds of violence which took place at the origin of all political formations, even of those whose consequences have been altogether beneficial. Unity is always effected by means of brutality" (Renan, "What Is a Nation?" trans. Martin Thom, in Bhabha, ed., *Nation and Narration*, 11 [8–22]).

41. As, for example, Thorpe, 251; Wright, 125, §171. Geoffrey likewise refers to the combined forces of Rome and its allies simply as *Romani*, "Romans," but their leader Lucius invokes only the Republic's overlordship, never a homeland's liberty.

42. Wright, 130, §177.

43. Thorpe, 260, translating "suos eis honores demere affectabant" (Wright, 131, §178); here *honores* likely bears its feudal sense of "lands held of a lord," parallel to the *possessiones* that Mordred promises his soldiers in the previous sentence.

44. Thorpe, 235; Wright, 131, §178.

45. Wright, 131–32, §178.

46. Wright, 132, §178; emphasis added. Thorpe gives: "many thousands of the King's troops, some of them Britons, others from the various peoples *he* had brought with *him*" (Thorpe, 236, emphasis added); the plural verb in Wright's edition makes better sense and is better coordinated with the plural verb in the preceding sentence.

47. This should not imply that Mordred is correct or even consistent in implicitly insisting on ethnic unity: his paramour (and Arthur's wife) Guinevere is, like many wives of noble Britons before her, of mixed ethnic stock, being of Roman descent. Rather, Mordred's villainy should imply the inadequacy of his (traditional) conception of Britishness.

48. On Geoffrey's use of English and other languages in the *Historia*, see T.D. Crawford, "On the Linguistic Competence of Geoffrey of Monmouth," *Medium Aevum* 51 (1982): 152–62.

49. Wright, 147, §207.

50. At the same time, there remains an overall unity of Britishness inasmuch as the dragon attacks itself. Benedict Anderson addresses the ideological bases for figuring such divisive group-based conflicts as those between Catholics and Protestants in early modern France as "reassuringly fratricidal wars between—who else?—*fellow Frenchmen*" (*Imagined Communities*,

200–202, with similar observations about the American Civil War; emphasis in original).

51. Cf. Homi Bhabha's remarks about the "locality of culture" being more complex and contingent than the monolithic certainties propounded by a more ideological nationalism: it is also "more *hybrid* in the articulation of cultural differences and identifications…than can be represented in any hierarchical or *binary* structuring of social antagonism" ("DissemiNation: Time, Narrative, and the Margins of the Modern Nation," in *Nation and Narration*, ed. Bhabha, 292 [291–322]; emphasis added).

52. Thus, too, Arthur is imagined by the continental Bretons and by the English to be the messianic champion of the Britons—but not by the Welsh, who look rather to the return of Cynan and Cadwaladr for their redemption; see Kristen Lee Over, *Kingship, Conquest, and* Patria: *Literary and Cultural Identities in Medieval French and Welsh Arthurian Romance*, Studies in Medieval History and Culture (New York: Routledge, 2005), 9, 18, and 24–25.

CHAPTER 6

ARTHUR'S TWO BODIES AND THE
BARE LIFE OF THE ARCHIVES

Kathleen Biddick

*T*his chapter studies how the History of the Kings of Britain *by Geoffrey of Monmouth constitutes a formative moment in the medieval fabrication of the king's two bodies and shows how contemporary archival practices were intrinsic to such political-theological invention. It also considers archives of trauma as conceptualized in mid-twelfth century Jewish notions of archival disciplines.*

> Truly the Jew is able to have nothing which belongs to himself, because whatever he acquires is not for himself but for the king, because they do not live for themselves but for others and so they acquire from others and not for themselves.[1]
>
> [*Iudaeus vero nihil proprium habere potest, quia quicquid acquirit non sibi acquirit sed regi, quia non vivunt sibi ipsis sed aliis et sic aliis acquirunt et non sibi ipsis.*]

Thus a famous English legal tract of thirteenth century defines the status of Jews. This chapter seeks to write in between the singular body, "the Jew" [*Iudaeus*], and plural bodies embodied in the verb, "they live" [*vivunt*]. It wagers that this medieval legal text (and others like it) need to be folded into genealogies of contemporary sovereignty and biopolitics argued by the philosopher Giorgio Agamben.[2] Crucial to Agamben's understanding of biopolitics is the Roman juridical concept of *homo sacer*—that is, the one who cannot be sacrificed but may be murdered without penalty. Such a legal exception reduces the human body to what Agamben calls "bare life" [*bios*], a biopolitical condition that, he argues, has now become the rule of contemporary sovereignty. Also intrinsic to sovereignty, according to Agamben, is the archive (the said and the unsaid) and by implication history itself. This chapter asks: What might the one *who may have nothing*, the Jew, a kind of *homo sacer* imagined by thirteenth-century English law, have to do with the constitution of Western sovereignty and its archives?

Medieval historians have already expended much painstaking scholarship on the juridical status of Jews under English law.[3] Rather than take sides in the debate over the question of their freedom or unfreedom, this chapter, instead, offers a biopolitical perspective on the question of Jews in the constitution of archive and constructions of temporality in Anglo-Norman England. My starting point is Geoffrey of Monmouth's *History of the Kings of Britain* (*Historia Regum Britannie*, hereafter *HRB*) (c. 1138).[4] This study refrains too from lively contemporary debates over the purported ethnic (Welsh, Breton, Anglo-Norman, or English) identifications and border writing at stake in Geoffrey's history. Hugh M. Thomas has offered a good overview of this scholarship in *The English and the Normans: Ethnic Hostility, Assimilation, and Identity 1066–c. 1220*, and rich examples of such border tracings may be found in the works of Jeffrey Jerome Cohen, Laurie A. Finke and Martin B. Shichtman, Patricia Clare Ingham, and Michelle Warren.[5] Instead, I am asking about the biopolitics of Geoffrey's invention of King Arthur as a "twin person," that is, one who is both mortally wounded [letaliter vulneratus est][6] and yet lives—he is taken to be healed on the isle of Avalon [qui illinc ad sananda vulnera sua in insulam Avallonis evectus].[7] Geoffrey's concept of a royal twin person offers, I argue, not only a formative biopolitical moment in the medieval fabrication of the king's two bodies (a juridical concept that would become central to medieval sovereignty), but also a stunning example of how mundane contemporary bureaucratic practices lodged themselves in such biopolitical inventions. By tracing out the sovereign archival palimpsest of Geoffrey's text, it is possible to write a secret history of its spectral debt.

The Infinite Labors of the Archive

These duties [Master of the Exchequer Writing Office] need but few words to explain, but demand almost endless labors.[8]

[que quidem officia, licet paucis exprimantur verbis, infinitis tamen vix expleri possunt laboribus.]

When in 1129 Geoffrey of Monmouth witnessed the first charter at Oxford to bear his signature, royal archivists were radically transforming their temporal capacities to monitor income and debt on a continuous annual basis.[9] Henry I (1100–1135) introduced new linking technologies designed to join the discrete bureaucratic activities of reviewing customary receipts (often in the form of notched wooden tallies) rendered by sheriffs with an efficient fiscal computation based on the principle of the abacus. Scribes recorded the royal sources of income and debt (county by county), as well as the names of creditors and debtors, on carefully prepared parchment rolls and then preserved these documents for ongoing consultation. By inaugurating the archival series known as the Pipe Rolls, the royal bureaucracy precociously embodied the temporal concept of "continuity" (from 1158 onward, the Pipe Rolls, are available in a virtually continuous series).[10] In his famous study, *The King's Two Bodies: A Study in Medieval Political Theology*, Ernst Kantorowicz argued that the fabrication of just such a notion of continuity was crucial to the medieval imagining of the corporate, undying body of the sovereign, the king's second body.[11]

The Pipe Rolls secured this temporal continuity through its "scriptural" archival procedures (not even erasures were allowed) described in the late 1170s by Richard Fitz Nigel but already materially in evidence in the organization of the 1130 Pipe Roll.[12] The scribe first pricked and ruled each parchment sheet to be bound in Roll and then further broke down the space of the page by labelling compartments in which relevant information was to be entered (see figure 1). The Rolls were thus conceived as graphic modules that cast a fiscal grid (with all the normalizing pretensions of such coordinates) over the English counties (and, in 1130, the Welsh territories of Pembroke and Carmarthen). Although seeming to encode a diversity of local arrangements, the bureaucratic practices embodied in the Rolls, in fact, actually worked to deterritorialize local difference.[13]

The earliest preserved Pipe Roll (but not the *inaugural* roll of this accounting system) from 31 Henry I (1130) can be studied as a map tracing out the archival coordinates of the archdiaconal milieu of Geoffrey of Monmouth.[14] Walter the Archdeacon (Geoffrey's mentor, provost of his Oxford college of St. George, and purported owner of the ancient book upon which Geoffrey based his "translation") appears in the 1130 Pipe Roll (hereafter *PR*) charged with a large sum of 180 marks (equivalent to the cost of the farm of the town Stamford that year) for a plea [pro placitum] between himself and Restold, the former sheriff of the county.[15] Walter paid roughly half of his charge (sixty-eight shillings), and his balance owing was recorded for future audit. This brief entry does two things: it locates Walter enmeshed in the royal justice system, and it inscribes him in the continuous archival discipline of the Pipe Rolls, since the payment of his outstanding balance can be checked annually. Although it is

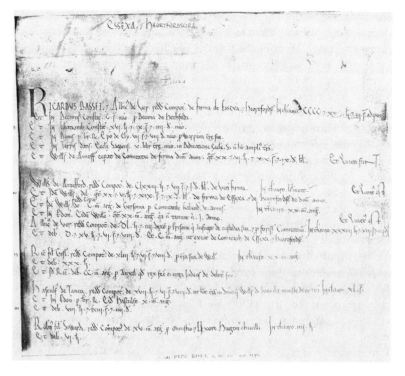

Figure 1 Public Record Office, Pipe Roll, 31 Henry 1 (1130), membrane 6.

Source: From the facsimile printed in Charles Johnson and Hilary Jenkinson, *English Court Hand 1066–1500* (Oxford: Clarendon, 1915), Plate IV A.

impossible to know the exact nature of Walter's business with the former sheriff, the greedy competition of the archdiaconate for court fees was already established by this date.[16]

An older intellectual contemporary of Geoffrey, Adelard of Bath, also appears in the 1130 Pipe Roll. Scribes record his pardon, by courtesy of royal writ, of a murder fine (4 shillings 6 pence) levied against the hundreds of the county of Wiltshire.[17] Renowned Arabist and author of treatises on the abacus and astrolabe, Adelard has been associated with the new computational technologies used in generating the Pipe Rolls, and some historians place him as a clerk in the Exchequer and thus intimately involved with its archival disciplines.[18] Historians have also speculated that the very form of the Pipe Rolls, a *rotulus* [roll], and not the folded quire of parchment typical of the construction of the book [*libellus*], bears the traces of the contacts that Adelard and those like him had with Spanish Jews educated in Arabic sciences and for whom the roll would be a familiar format for writing.[19] Geoffrey of Monmouth undoubtedly had Adelard in mind when he praised the astronomical computations and prognosticating studies undertaken at the Caerlon college of the two hundred philosophers: "The city also contained a college of two hundred learned men, who were skilled in astronomy and the other arts, and who watched with great attention the courses of the stars and so by their careful computations prophesied for King Arthur any prodigies due in his time" [preterea ginnasium ducentorum phylosoforum habebat qui astronomia atque ceteris artibus eruditi cursus stellarum diligenter obseruabant et prodigia eorum temporum ventura regi Arturo veris argumentis predicebant].[20]

The Pipe Rolls of 1130 also map the coordinates of King Henry's royal control over Jews. The reader of the Pipe Rolls can track Henry as he used his arrogated sovereign right over Jews in England to broker indebtedness. For instance, Richard, son of Giselbertus, owed the king 200 marks of silver for the help that the king gave him against his debt to the Jews.[21] Rubi Gotsche (the Pipe Roll rendering of the name of Rabbi Yosi of Rouen) and other Jews, to whom Ranulf, Lord of Chester, was indebted, are recorded as owing ten marks for the help of the king regarding the count's debts.[22] The largest fine (£2,000, or 13.25 percent of the total fees demanded by the royal treasury for the year) in the 1130 Pipe Roll is levied against the Jews of London for killing [interficerent] a sick man.[23] Rabbi Yosi of Rouen is among those Jews listed defraying this fine and he is the earliest rab or master to be linked to Rouen, the capital of Normandy and a center of Jewish learning distinguished enough to have been visited by Abraham Ibn Ezra around 1149.[24] The entries discussed so far show how the Pipe Rolls inscribed clerics like Geoffrey of Monmouth with archival practices that fabricated continuity and also bore the material traces of forms of knowledge and writing practices gained by contact of the Anglo-Norman court with Muslims and Jews.

During the 1130s, as Geoffrey was composing the *HRB*, his arch-diaconal circle was also busy confecting its own archival innovations. Their work took the form of inventing new legal archives.[25] The *Leges Edwardi Confessoris* (hereafter, *LEC*), composed most likely at Lincoln around 1136 (remember that Walter of Oxford, Geoffrey's mentor, was an archdeacon of Lincoln), claimed to record the *laga Edwardi* [law at the time of Edward the Confessor]. The opening of the tract constructs a deterritorializing fiction of continuity.[26] It tells how in 1070 William the Conqueror summoned English nobles [*Anglos nobiles*], twelve from each county, and asked them to declare [*edicarent*] the rules of their laws and customs [incidentes legem suaram et consuetudinum].[27] Upon hearing them, William with the advice of his barons authorized them [et sic auctorizate sunt legis Regis Aedwardi].[28] The modern editor of the *LEC*, Bruce R. O'Brien, shows, this text to be an imposture: "the *Leges Edwardi* is not a translation of Old English laws, nor is any part of it derived from a preconquest English legal text, as is the case with all the other codes. When the author does use another source, it is, like those used in *Leges Henrici Primi*, a Frankish work."[29]

The *LEC* describes the king boldly as the vicar of the highest King (Christ) [rex autem, qui vicarius summi Regis est].[30] Such a legal vision of royal embodiment resonates with the contemporary theology of kingship articulated by the author of the *Norman Anonymous*, a collection of treatises attributed to William Bona Anima, Archbishop of Rouen (1079–1110) or his archdiaconal circles.[31] Among his associates, the Archbishop of Rouen could count leading English churchmen: Lanfranc, William Giffard (Bishop of Winchester), and Gerard (Archbishop of York). William had been a monk at Bec, an abbot at Caen, and also a sometime supporter of the abbey of Fécamp (archival material from which abbey ended up bound with Geoffrey's *History* in the Bern manuscript).[32] As archbishop of Rouen, William was also acquainted with Norman dukes and kings including Henry I, who spent more than half his reign in Normandy. Under the archbishop's watch, Crusader bands from Normandy entered Rouen in the autumn of 1096 and massacred the Jews of the city who refused baptism.[33] In his treatises, William Bona Anima intertwined his theology of the kingship (the king as vicar of Christ) with his speculations on the king's two bodies. William conceived of the king as a *gemma persona*: a twin person. When Geoffrey imagined Arthur as a *gemma persona* with a personal body that could be mortally wounded and a theological body that could not die, he echoed the legal and theological concepts circulating among Anglo-Norman canons in the earlier part of the twelfth century.

As a legal treatise, *LEC* is also noteworthy for setting a European precedent for defining the legal status of the Jew as property of the king:

> It should be known that all Jews, in whichever kingdom they may be, ought to be under the guardianship and protection of the liege king; nor can any one of them subject himself to any wealthy person without the license of the king, because the Jews themselves and all their possessions are the king's. But if someone detains them or their money, the king shall demand [them] as his own property if he wishes and is able.[34]

> [Sciendum est quod omnes Iudei, in quocumque regno sint, sub tutela et defensione Regis ligii debent esse; neque aliquis eorum potest se subdere alicui diviti sint licencia Regis, quia ipsi Iudei et omnia sua Regis sunt. Quod si aliquis detinuerit eos vel pecuniam eorum, requirat rex tanquam suum proprium, si vult et potest.]

LEC was a potent archival invention. It deterritorialized the Anglo-Saxon legal archive in order to territorialize the kings as a twin body and to produce Jews as a juridical category. *LEC* elides Jews and their possessions with the king's double body. We have already seen the capacity of the king to "possess" the possessions of the Jews in the 1130 Pipe Rolls where the king exercised his rights to administer the debt of the Jews through various appeals by both Christians and Jews. Such legal appeals over debt cost money, and thus the king "doubled" his juridical control over debt. A half century later, in the next generation of English law books, pleas of debts would be very precisely defined as belonging to the king's two bodies, that is his crown [*corona*] and his dignity [*dignitas*]—so claimed Rannulf Glanvill, Chief Justiciar, in *The Treatise on Laws and Customs of the Realm of England*: "pleas concerning the debts of laymen also belong to the crown and dignity of the lord king" [placitum quoque de debitis laicorum spectat ad coronam et ad dignitatem domini Regis].[35]

Several decades ago, in his important discussion of *LEC*, Gavin Langmuir observed how this clause on possession of Jews, in its departure from Carolingian discourses, marked a break in the "rightlessness" of the Jews in medieval Europe. This break coincides, I argue, with cleaving the king's body into two persons in contemporary legal (*LEC*) and literary (*HRB*) texts. So far, I have been tracing the dispersed strands of archival technologies threaded through this cleavage: 1) the deterritorialization of geographic regions and local time through the Pipe Rolls that gridded space and marked time as a continuity for fiscal surveillance and dispersed over that grid the juridical right of the king over the debts of the Jews; and 2) the deterritorialization of the laws of the different Anglo-Saxon kingdoms through the fiction of the *LEC*.[36] Through this strategy, the law tract produced the juridical category of the Jew, over which category the king exercised sovereign right. This is not coincidence. The "it should be known" [sciendum quod] of the clause on Jews is intertwined with the "was established for this" [hoc constitutus est] of the king's body as the vicar of the highest king [vicarius summi Regis est].

The Tears of the Archive

...the King ordered Ambrosius Merlin to explain just what the battle of the Dragons meant. Merlin immediately burst into tears. He went into a prophetic trance and then spoke as follows.[37]

[precepit rex Ambrosio Merlino dicere quid prelium draconum portendebat. Mox ille in fletum prorumpens spiritum hausit prophetie et ait.][38]

In his important essay on the contexts and purposes of the *HRB*, John Gillingham emphasized the role of history as the sign of civilization in the twelfth century: "to be without history was the mark of the beast. Yet the Britains had virtually no history."[39] So far this chapter has suggested that the accomplishment of *HRB* was not simply to provide such a history, as Gillingham has observed, but rather to render it as a *continuous* archival event—a consecutive and orderly narrative [actus omnium continue et ex ordine perpulcris orationibus].[40] In so doing the *HRB* enmeshes itself in the kinds of contemporary archival practices so far considered. At the same time Geoffrey's history also recounts what the neatly ruled membranes of the Pipe Rolls foreclosed and what the fictions of legal continuity the *LEC* suppress— the violence of founding this sovereignty in and through archival continuity, and thus, the violence of founding the king's second body, the body that cannot die. Put in other words, *HRB* enacts the violence of traversing what Agamben has called the sovereign zone of indistinction: "sovereign exception is the fundamental localization (Ortung), which does not limit itself to distinguishing what is inside from what is outside, but instead traces a threshold (the state of exception) between the two, on the basis of which outside and inside, the normal situation and chaos, enter into those complex topological relations that make the validity of the juridical order possible."[41]

I now want to consider how Geoffrey casts this "taking of the outside" as massacre. He brackets his history with tales of massacres, and he uses the Latin cognates of *caedes* [carnage, slaughter] to form the brackets. The *HRB* opens with two massacres in which the parricide Brutus and his Trojans slaughter *unarmed* [inermis] Greeks: "the Trojans were fully equipped; their enemies were virtually unarmed. Because of this the Trojans pressed on all the more boldly and the slaughter that they inflicted was very heavy. They continued to attack in this way until almost all the Greeks were killed and they had captured Antigonus [brother of Pandrasus, king of the Greeks] and his comrade Anacletus [Nam Troes armis muniti erant, certeri uero inermes. Unde audatiores insistentes cedem miserandam inferebant nec eos hoc modo infestare quieuerunt donec cunctis fere interfectis Antigonum et Anacletum eiusdem sotium retinuerunt].[42] The Trojans then treacherously launch their second attack. By ruse, they enter the Greek camp during the night and slay the sleeping (once again, unarmed) soldiers in their tents. Brutus "beside himself with joy" [fluctuans gaudio] surveyed the carnage [*caedis*] in the morning light.[43]

Geoffrey uses cognates for *caedes* for the last time in *HRB* to describe the fatal battle between Mordred and Arthur:

> In the end, when they had passed much of the day in this way, Arthur, with a single division in which he had posted six thousand, six hundred

and sixty-six men, charged at the squadron where he knew Mordred was. They hacked a way through with their swords and Arthur continued to advance, inflicting terrible slaughter as he went. It was at this point that the accursed traitor was killed and many thousands of men with him.[44]

[Postquam autem multum diei in hunc modum duxerunt, irruit tandem Arturus cum agmine uno, quo sex milia et sexcentos sexaginta sex posuerat, in turmam illam ubi Modredum sciebat esse et uiam gladiis aperiendo eam penetravit atque tristissimam cedem ingessit. Concidit namque proditor ille nephandus et multa milia secum.][45]

Geoffrey not only brackets his history with massacre, he closely binds slaughter and prophecy. The Saxon massacre of the unarmed British nobility at the council meeting at the Cloister of Ambrius[46] precipitates the events that lead up to the prophecies of Merlin. The story is familiar. Merlin, a "fatherless" child from the union of a woman and an incubus, is on the verge of becoming a kind of inverted Passover sign, because King Vortigern wishes to sprinkle his blood on the collapsing foundations of a massive defensive tower. Merlin halts the proceedings and orders an archaeological excavation—"iube fodere terram";[47] archaeology and the archive are also closely bound.[48] When King Vortigern asks Mordred to explain the fighting dragons uncovered by this excavation, Merlin first bursts into tears, and then his spirit is prophetically seized.

Geoffrey is careful to fashion an archival pedigree for Merlin's prophecies. He informs his reader that he has translated them from British to Latin, and he sends his edition by letter to Alexander, Bishop of Lincoln. Geoffrey thus aligns Merlin's prophecies (as he has aligned his history, *HRB*) with the "sayable" of the archive and thus with the imagined continuity of archival utterance. His painful and awkward suturing of massacre and prophecy seems to work feverishly: I, Geoffrey, recognize the violent foundational moment of the archive, but nevertheless I love the archive. What is the "unsayable" of the archive that beats in the pulse of Geoffrey's fever? Like a Derrida before Derrida, Geoffrey prompts us to think about the relations of archivization and anarchivization: "the anarchive, in short the possibility of putting to death the very thing, whatever its name, which *carries the law in its tradition*: the archon of the archive, the table, *what* carries the table and who carries the table, the subjectile, the substrate, and the subject of the law."[49]

Songs of the Unsayable

If the reader listens closely, the unsayable of Geoffrey's archive floats in the Whitsun air above King Arthur's crown-wearing feast at Caerlon, a momentous event assembled at a center of scholarship and music. Geoffrey unabashedly lures his readers with descriptions of the musical glory of this occasion at which the assembled clergy processed "chanting in exquisite harmony" [miris modulationibus precinebat],[50] and organ music filled the naves of the churches where Arthur and his queen celebrated their coronal sovereignty. In twelfth-century England, Pentecost (an understudied liturgical feast of tongues and one aptly focused on by Geoffrey, the wizard of translation) was a powerful communal event during which local clergy paraded with their parishioners to the cathedral church where they were obliged to make oblations. In large dioceses that covered several counties, such as Lincoln, to which Oxford belonged, the bishop allowed Pentecostal processions to congregate at Eynsham, where the men of Oxfordshire received an indulgence equivalent of the trek to Lincoln.[51] Important to this feast, and of special meaning for crown-wearing ceremonies with their special quasi-liturgical royal garments, was the singing of the hymn, Te Deum. This early medieval hymn is redolent with the images of processing martyrs robed in white garments washed by the precious blood of Christ.

The imagery and performance of Christian feast of Pentecost doubled and interacted with a concurrent Jewish celebration, the Feast of Weeks (Shavuot), a harvest festival of first fruits that commemorated the giving of the Torah. At Shavuot, Jewish families presented young schoolboys for induction into the yeshiva.[52] Israel Jacob Yuval has traced the traumatic festal intersections of Pentecost and Shavuot in his readings of the Mainz memorials in the Hebrew Chronicles of the Crusades, which commemorate the Jewish martyrdoms there when Crusader bands, intent on forced baptism, attacked the Jews of Mainz during the feast of Pentecost/Shavuot.[53] When Ashkenaz paytanim [liturgical poets] subsequently mourned this slaughter in liturgical hymns, they did so by imagining an archival device capable of recording and remembering traumatic events. They drew upon the Midrashic image of the porphyrion [royal purple cloak] and attributed to it the capability of precise transcribing: "every drop of blood of Jews killed by Gentiles is recorded in a divine 'ledger' in the form of a scarlet garment."[54] This splattered woven textile, an archive of trauma, reverberates with the words of Isaiah 63:2: "why is thy apparel red, and thy garments like his that treads in the wine press?"

Muffled echoes of this proof text resound in the Te Deum, the liturgical hymn that would have been intoned at Arthur's Pentecostal crown-wearing. The proof text also baffles one of Merlin's prophecies: "a man shall wrestle with a drunken Lion, and the gleam of gold will blind the eyes of the onlookers. Silver will shine white in the open space around, causing trouble to a number of winepresses. Men will become drunk with the wine which is offered to them; they will turn their backs on Heaven and fix their eyes on the earth" [Amplexabitur homo leonem in vino et <fulgor> auri oculos intuentium excecabit. Candebit argentum in circuiti et diversa torcularia vexabit. Imposito vino inebriabuntur mortales postpositoque caleo in terram respicient].[55] This verse from Isaiah can also be found incised on an artifact contemporary with Geoffrey's composition of Merlin's prophecies—the remarkable ivory processional cross, known as the Cloisters Cross, or the Bury St. Edmunds' Cross.[56] The central front medallion of this exquisitely carved cross depicts Moses raising the Brazen Serpent surrounded by figures bearing tituli intended to develop the typology of the scene. The prophet Isaiah bears a scroll carved with the familiar verse: "Why then is thy apparel red and thy garments like theirs that tread in <the winepress>" (Isaiah 63:2).[57]

Taken together as an ensemble, the numerous titular inscriptions of the Cloisters Cross foreground the problem of translation. The Cross is exceptional for featuring the earliest representation of the dramatic scene recounted in the Gospel of John in which Caiaphas, the Jewish High Priest, and Pontius Pilate, the colonial governor, debate the wording of the titulus to be affixed to the head of Christ's Cross. The studied depiction of this scene renders the specific inscription of the titulus on the Cloisters Cross even more weighty. The artist has changed the gospel text from "Jesus of Nazareth, King of the Jews," to read "Jesus of Nazareth, King of the Confessors." This change invokes, I argue, the overtones of the *Te Deum* hymn, a hymn of confessors, sung during the liturgical processions of Easter and at Pentecost: "Te deum laudamus te dominum confitemur" [We praise you, God, we confess you to be Lord].

The dating of the Cloisters cross is disputed. Some scholars attribute it to the abbacy of Anselm of Bury (1121–1148); others consider its anti-Semitic typology more relevant to the abbacy of the illustrious Abbot Samson (1188–1211), whose office is associated with the massacre of the Jews in Bury St. Edmunds. The earlier date gains support when the convergence of the archival projects of the Cloisters Cross and Geoffrey of Monmouth is considered along with early-twelfth-century schism of the "Jewish" pope.[58] That schism ended in 1138 (around the time that Geoffrey was composing his *History*) with the death of Anacletus II (Peter Pierleone of Rome) who was the great-grandson of a converted Jew.[59] During this schism, Peter the Venerable and Bernard of Clairveaux championed the antipope, Innocent II. Geoffrey of Monmouth invoked this schism when he cast "Anacletus" as the comrade of Antigonus, son of Pandrasus, King of the Greeks. It is Anacletus whom Brutus forces into betraying the Greek camp. Anselm of Bury, as papal legate, was in Normandy in 1119 when the Pierleone family served Pope Calixtus at the

Council of Rheims and caused a scandal among northern prelates. Oderic Vitalis recounted the racializing comments made by prelates attending the council at Rheims. They were offended by the Pierleone physique and their irredeemable family history of usury.[60] When Innocent II, the antipope, traveled from Rome to France to secure support, he celebrated Easter at St. Denis in 1131 at which time he received a delegation of Parisian Jews bearing a Torah scroll. The Jews of Rouen also offered Innocent II gifts upon his triumphant arrival in that city.

Geoffrey's *HRB* and the Cloisters Cross converge distinctively on problems of translation, continuity, and archive. Both projects grapple with translation as a form of conversion. As it purports to translate an ancient British book, the *HRB* converts its British source into an archive a continuous Latin history. The Cloisters Cross probes the limits of the archive and of conversion. Rather than translate the titulus of Pilate according to the gospel text "Jesus of Nazareth, King of the Jews," it edits those words to read in the Latin and Greek inscriptions: "Jesus of Nazareth, King of the Confessors" [Rex confessorum; Basileos examolisson]. The Hebrew version of this phrase inscribed on the titulus marks the "untranslatable" since this line on the titutlus is a cipher of misoriented upside down letters.[61] The Cross accomplishes what Dominique Iogna-Prat has analyzed as a new impulse of this period, not simply to denounce the execution of the "King of the Jews" (a common trope of anti-Judaic polemic dating from early Christianity), but to demonstrate the ongoing, "continuous" nature of Jewish deicide.[62]

A contemporary Jewish archival project, the *porphyrion*, hovers at the edges of the Cloisters Cross, It is just such a processional cross that would have accompanied the dramatic liturgies of Easter and Pentecost at Bury and that embodied the problems of translation, continuity, and archive with which Geoffrey of Monmouth grappled as he imagined Arthur's Whitsun crown-wearing. The twin-person of a sovereign Arthur fabricated by Geoffrey—his personal body that could be mortally wounded and his theological body that could not die—was confected, I have argued, out of an archival project enmeshed in the fantasies of translation based on the stability of the signified, on archive as continuity, and on radical possession of that which was untranslatable, "the Jew." The "infinite" bureaucratic labors of recording and preserving the fiscal data in the sayable archive of the Pipe Rolls, the juridical allocation of sovereign rites over Jews, the Pentecostal processions that traversed diocesan space to "confess" at the metropolitan cathedral, the infinite realms imagined by Geoffrey formed the flesh of Arthur's second body. The painstakingly fabricated and complexly rendered corporate flesh of the sovereign's second body remains indebted to the bare life of the unsayable shadow category constituted by this archival project of the twelfth century: the singular archival Jew [*Iudaeus*] who, nevertheless, lived in the plural [*vivunt*].

Notes

1. Henry de Bracton, *On the Laws and Customs of England* [*De Legibus et Consuetudinibus Anglie*], ed. George E. Woodbine and trans. Samuel E. Thorne, 4 vols. (Cambridge, MA: Harvard University Press, 1968–1977), 4:208. Note that this oft-cited passage is an *addicio* to a section on warranty and Thorne publishes it in fn. 3 on p.208. Thorne lists the manuscripts that contain this *addicio* in volume 1, p. 417. The core of this treatise was written in the 1220s and 1230s and then was subsequently much revised according to Paul Brand, "The Age of Bracton," in *Proceedings of the British Academy* 89 (1996): 65–89. The dating of this particular passage is in need of more scholarly work.

2. Giorgio Agamben, *Homo Sacer: Sovereign Power and Bare Life*, trans. Daniel Heller-Roazen (Palo Alto: Stanford University Press, 1998); and his *Remnants of Auschwitz: The Witness and the Archive*, trans. Daniel Heller-Roazen (New York: Zone Books, 1999).

3. See footnote 34.

4. Latin citations are from *The Historia Regum Britanniae of Geoffrey of Monmouth, I. Bern, Burgerbibliothek, MS 568*, ed. Neil Wright (Cambridge: D.S. Brewer, 1984) (hereafter Wright), and to enable comparisons for readers, I cite from the English translation, *History of the Kings of Britain*, trans. Lewis Thorpe (New York: Penguin, 1966) (hereafter Thorpe).

5. Hugh M. Thomas, *The English and the Normans: Ethnic Hostility, Assimilation, and Identity 1066–c. 1220* (Oxford: Oxford University Press, 2003); Jeffrey Jerome Cohen, *Hybridity, Identity and Monstrosity in Medieval Britain* (New York: Palgrave Macmillan, 2006); Laurie A. Finke and Martin B. Shichtman, *King Arthur and the Myth of History* (Gainesville: University of Florida Press, 2004); Patricia Clare Ingham, *Sovereign Fantasies: Arthurian Romance the Making of Britain* (Philadelphia: University of Pennsylvania Press, 2001); and Michelle R. Warren, *History on the Edge: Excalibur and the Borders of Britain, 1100–1300* (Minneapolis: University of Minnesota Press, 2000).

6. Wright, 132.

7. Wright, 132.

8. Richard Fitz Nigel, Treasurer of the Exchequer (c. 1158) and former archdeacon of Ely (c. 1160) wrote about the procedures of the Exchequer in the late 1170s—cited from Richard Fitz Nigel, *Dialogus de Scaccario* (*The Course of the Exchequer*), ed. and trans. Charles Johnson with corrections by F.E.L. Carter and D.E. Greenway (Oxford: Clarendon Press, 1983), 26.

9. For the charters witnessed by Geoffrey see, H.E. Salter "Geoffrey of Monmouth and Oxford," *English Historical Review* 34 (July 1919): 382–85.

10. Kathleen Biddick, "People and Things: Power in Early English Development," *Comparative Studies in Society and History* 32 (1990): 3–23. The literature on the Pipe Rolls is enormous; basic references may be found in my 1990 article—also see, M.T. Clanchy, *From Memory to Written Record: England, 1066–1307* (Cambridge: Harvard University Press, 1979). Note that Clanchy underscores the use of the Domesday Book (bound as a book): "seems to have been principally symbolic, like the regalia, since it cannot be shown that it was frequently consulted at the time Fitz Neal was writing in c. 1179 [that is time of the composition of the *Dialogue of the Exchequer*]" (122). The Pipe Rolls inaugurate the kind of continuous bureaucracy that is relevant to this discussion of Geoffrey of Monmouth.

11. Ernst H. Kantorowicz, *The King's Two Bodies: A Study in Medieval Political Theology* (Princeton: Princeton University Press, 1957); see Chapter 4 on continuity and corporations, but note that when Kantorowicz discussed the importance of annual taxation (284–91) that he neglects to mention the Pipe Rolls. Patricia Clare Ingham drew attention to the resonance between Geoffrey's Arthur and Kantorowicz in her *Sovereign Fantasies*, 4–5.

12. The ruling and compartmentalizing of the parchment for the Pipe Rolls is described in Richard Fitz Nigel, *Dialogus de Scaccario*, 29–30.

13. For discussion of how such deterritorialization and reterritorialization worked in both archive and in the landscape of settlement see, Biddick, "People and Things."

14. *The Pipe Roll of 31 Henry I* (Michaelmas 1130) transcriber Rev. Joseph Hunter for the Record Commission in an edition of 1833 and reprinted (London: H.M. Stationery Office, 1929), hereafter *PR*. Figure 1 is a reproduction of membrane 6 from the Pipe Roll of 31 Henry 1. This facsimile is printed in Charles Johnson and Hilary Jenkinson, *English Court Hand 1066–1500* (Oxford: Clarendon, 1915), Plate IV.A.

15. *PR*, 3. Restold was sheriff of Oxfordshire between 1122 and 1127: Judith A. Green, *English Sheriffs to 1154*. Public Record Office Handbooks, 24 (1990). London: H.M. Stationery Office, 70.

16. Jean Scammell, "The Rural Chapter in England from the Eleventh to the Fourteenth Century," *English Historical Review* 86 (1971): 1–21.

17. *PR*, 22.

18. For basic work on Adelard of Bath see Charles Burnett, *Adelard of Bath: An English Scientist and Arabist of the Early Twelfth Century* (London: Warburg Institute Surveys and Texts, 1987), 14; Charles Homer Haskins, *Studies in the History of Mediaeval Science* (Cambridge: Harvard University Press, 1924), 20–42; Reginald L. Poole, *The Exchequer in the Twelfth Century* (Oxford: Clarendon, 1912), 44, 50–53, 56–57.

19. There are elusive discussions of Jewish and Arabic influences on the actual roll format of the Pipe Rolls in Clanchy, *Written Record*, 108–110; Poole, *Exchequer*, 52–57. For an overview, see Brigitte Bedos-Rezak, "The Confrontation of Orality and Textuality: Jewish and Christian Literacy in the Eleventh and Twelfth Century in Northern France,"

Rashi 1049–1990, ed. Gabrielle Sed-Rajna (Paris: Les Éditions du Cerf, 1993), 541–58 and Jeremy Johns, *Arabic Administration in Norman Sicily* (Cambridge: Cambridge University Press, 2002), 1–10.

20. Thorpe, 227; Wright, 110.
21. *PR*, 53.
22. *PR*, 149.
23. *PR*, 149. The total for different forms of income and the overall totals for the 1130 Pipe Roll are tabulated by Judith A. Green, *The Government of England under Henry I* (Cambridge: Cambridge University Press, 1986).
24. Norman Golb, *The Jews in Medieval Normandy* (Cambridge: Cambridge University Press. 1998), 225. For a discussion of the Jewish population in England in the mid-twelfth century, see Kevin T. Streit, "The Expansion of the English Jewish Community in the Reign of King Stephen," *Albion* 15 (1993): 177–92. Important also is the collection of essays in Patricia Skinner, ed., *The Jews of Medieval Britain: Historical, Literary and Archaeological Perspectives* (Rochester: Boydell & Brewer, 2003).
25. Indeed, later versions of the *Leges Edwardi Confessori* (hereafter *LEC*) written at the end of the twelfth century interpolated extracts from Geoffrey's *HRB*: Walter Ullmann, "On the Influence of Geoffrey of Monmouth on Legal History," *Speculum Historiale: Geschichte im Spiegal von Geschichtsschreibung und Geschichtsdeutung*. ed. C. Bauer, L. Böhn, and M. Müller (Freiburg: Verlag Karl Alber, 1965), 258–76.
26. This section is indebted to the following study: Bruce R. O'Brien, *God's Peace and King's Peace: The Laws of Edward the Confessor* (Philadelphia: University of Pennsylvania Press, 1999). O'Brien dates the composition of the *LEC* to around 1136 (49) and thinks Lincoln the most likely place for its composition (53). His argument for it being the product of archdiaconal circles is persuasive. This treatise enjoyed great popularity during the twelfth century (at least six manuscripts in three versions survive, p. 3). For a perceptive overview of law texts drawn up in the twelfth century, see Patrick Wormald, *The Making of English Law: King Alfred to the Twelfth Century*, 2 vols. (Oxford: Blackwell, 1999), 1:465–76.
27. *LEC*, 192–93.
28. *LEC*, 192–93.
29. *LEC*, 29.
30. *LEC*, 174–75.
31. The articulation of notions of the king's body in the *Norman Anonymous* (Cambridge: Corpus Christ College MS Lat. 415) were of great interest to Kantorowicz, *King's Two Bodies*, 42–92. The authorship has been worked out by George H. Williams and has been widely accepted: *The Norman Anonymous of 1100 A.D.: Towards the Identification and Evaluation of the so-called Anonymous of York*, Harvard Theological Studies, 18 (Cambridge: Harvard University Press, 1951). Sections of the key tract (J24A) on the theology of kingship have been translated by Oliver O'Donovan and Joan Lockwood O'Donovan, *From Irenaeus to Grotius: A Sourcebook in Christian Political Thought* (Cambridge, UK: William B. Eerdmans, 1999), 250–59.

32. Williams, "*Norman Anonymous*," offers biographical details of William
    Bona Anima, 102–27. It should be noted that Norman Cantor disagreed
    with this attribution in *Church, Kingship and Lay Investiture in England*
    (Princeton: Princeton University Press, 1958), 181–85. The fact that the
    tract came from a tightly enmeshed Anglo-Norman archdiaconal circle
    is not disputed. For the entanglement of this circle, see M. Brett, *The
    English Church under Henry I* (Oxford: Oxford University Press, 1975), 9.
    Wright describes the Fécamp materials bound in Bern, Burgerbibliothek,
    MS. 568, xxviii–xxxi.

33. Golb, *Jews in Medieval Normandy*, 117.

34. *LEC*, 185. O' Brien, *God's Peace*, 184. Gavin Langmuir succinctly sum-
    marized the implications of this clause in his essay "The Jews and the
    Archives of Angevin England: Reflections on Medieval Anti-Semitism,"
    Traditio 19 (1963): 183–244. He observed: "we thus seem to be confronted
    with a clearly degraded legal status of Jews in England by about 1135,
    well before similar continental developments, and it should doubtless be
    seen as a result of the early strength of the English government" (200).
    Much subsequent debate about this clause has floundered on the status of
    property in twelfth-century England, for instance, Paul R. Hyams, "The
    Jews in Medieval England," *England and Germany in the High Middle Ages*,
    ed. Alfred Haverkamp and Hanna Vollrath (German Historical Institute
    London: Oxford University Press, 1996), 181–85; for important conti-
    nental perspective see William Chester Jordan, "Jews, Regalian Rights,
    and the Constitution in Medieval France, *AJS Review* 23 (1998): 1–16.
    No historians have asked how this clause might have been *constitutive*
    of shaping notions of property. For an important discussion of the his-
    toriographical debate over the concept of property in twelfth-century
    England see, John Hudson, "Anglo-Norman Land Law and the Origins
    of Property," *Law and Government in Medieval England and Normandy*
    (Cambridge: Cambridge University Press, 1994), 198–223.

35. G.D.G. Hall, ed. and trans., *The Treatise on Laws and Customs of the Realm
    of England commonly called Glanvill*, 2nd edn. (Oxford: Oxford University
    Press, 1993), 116 (with a note on further reading by M.T. Clanchy).

36. Jeffrey Jerome Cohen points to precisely this kind of deterritorialization
    process in his discussion of Geoffrey of Monmouth in his *Hybridity, Identity
    and Monstrosity*, 68: "Geoffrey's revisionist historiography employed a
    dual strategy: explosive recovery of Britain's full history, and silent pass-
    ing over of the richness of the English past." Here I would simply deepen
    this observation to say that Geoffrey deterritorializes an Anglo-Saxon
    past to fabricate a *continuous* history.

37. Thorpe, 171.

38. Wright, 74.

39. John Gillingham, "The Context and Purposes of Geoffrey of Monmouth's
    History of the Kings of Britain," *Anglo-Norman Studies* 13 (1990–91): 105
    [99–118], citation. Laurie A. Finke and Martin B. Shichtman emphasize
    Geoffrey's exercise in rendering the scattered into a "coherent narrative"

in their *King Arthur and the Myth of History*, 38. I am urging that we deepen this observation to apprehend the implications of a *continuous* narrative.

40. Thorpe, 51; Wright, 1.
41. Agamben, *Homo Sacer*, 19.
42. Thorpe, 58; Wright, 4.
43. Thorpe, 61; Wright, 7.
44. Thorpe, 261.
45. Wright, 131.
46. Thorpe, 164–65.
47. Wright, 73.
48. Jacques Derrida, *Archive Fever: A Freudian Interpretation* (Chicago: University of Chicago Press, 1995), 92: "As we have noted all along, there is an incessant tension here between archive and archaeology."
49. Derrida, *Archive Fever*, 79.
50. Thorpe, 228; Wright, 111.
51. M. Brett, *The English Church under Henry I* (Oxford: Oxford University Press, 1975), 162–64. For comments (all too brief) on Pentecostal liturgical dramas at Barking Abbey, England and at Rouen in Normandy (they include the use of doves that figure in Geoffrey's procession) see Diane Dolan, "Le drame liturgique de Pâques en Normandie et en Angleterre au moyen age," *Publications de L'Université de Poitiers Lettres et Sciences Humaines* 16 (1975): 130.
52. Naomi Seidman has drawn attention to the narrative of Pentecost (Acts 2) as a site of doubling and difference that inflects the translation of Jewish-Christian difference: *Faithful Renderings: Jewish-Christian Difference and the Politics of Translation* (Chicago: University of Chicago Press, 2006), 21–24. For a description of the excavations of the "school of the Jews" at Rouen see Golb, *Jews in Medieval Normandy*, 154–69, 563–76.
53. Israel Jacob Yuval, *Two Nations in Your Womb: Perceptions of Jews and Christians in Late Antiquity and the Middle Ages* (Berkeley: University of California Press, 2006), 135–204. Note that Caroline Walker Bynum's recent publication on the theology of blood addresses a later period–the long fifteenth century (1370s to 1520s)—in areas mostly east of the Rhine: *Wonderful Blood: Theology and Practice in Late Medieval Northern Germany and Beyond* (Philadelphia: University of Pennsylvania Press, 2007).
54. In *Two Nations*, Yuval traces the complicated Ashkenazic reworkings of this motif in the post-1096 liturgical hymns, 92–109.
55. Thorpe, 184; Wright, 83.
56. See Elizabeth C. Parker and Charles T. Little, *The Cloisters Cross: Its Art and Meaning* (New York: Harry N. Abrams, 1994) who publish the inscriptions of the cross and offer detailed bibliography; Thomas Hoving, *King of the Confessors* (New York: Simon and Shuster); revised in 2001 as an e-book available for download at http://www.ebooks.com/ebooks/book_display.asp?IID=118433 (accessed March 16, 2007). I am persuaded by arguments for earlier dating of this cross to the abbacy of Anselm of Bury (1121–1148), who had been an abbot at the Greek-Latin monastery

of St. Saba in Rome and a cardinal papal-legate to England. See Norman Scarfe, "The Walrus-Ivory Cross in the Metropolitan Museum of Art: the Masterpiece of Master Hugo of Bury?" *Suffolk in the Middle Ages* (Dover, NH: Boydell Press, 1986), 81–98. Under Anselm (1123), Bury obtained the privilege that should the monastery become the seat of a bishopric it would be served only by monk-bishops. With its immunities from the diocesan at Norwich, the monastery at Bury functioned as a bishopric manqué (Brett, *English Church*, 61).

57. Parker and Little, *Cloisters Cross*, 244–45.

58. Anselm of Bury waged an unpopular campaign to establish the Immaculate Conception as an official feast. This feast was approved in a Legatine Council held in London in 1129. Frederick K. Maurice Powicke, ed., *Councils & Synods with Other Documents Relating to the English Church. Part II. 1066–1204*, (Oxford: Clarendon University Press, 1981), text no. 134:750–54; Brett, *English Church*, 82, 190.

59. Innocent II secured the support of Peter the Venerable of Cluny, Bernard of Clairveaux, and Abbot Suger. The death of Anacletus II in January 1138 brought an official end to the schism. Mary Stroll, *The Jewish Pope: Ideology and Politics in the Papal Schism 1130* (Leiden: Brill, 1987); Golb, *Jews in Medieval Normandy*, 198–202.

60. Dominique Iogna-Prat, *Order and Exclusion: Cluny and Christendom face Heresy, Judaism, and Islam (1000–1150)*, trans. Graham Robert Edwards (Ithaca: Cornell University Press, 2002), 320–22.

61. Parker and Little, *Cloisters Cross*, 69–75 discuss the inscriptions on the titulus at length. Judith Olszowy-Schlanger treats the knowledge and practice of Hebrew in preexpulsion England in her essay "The Knowledge and Practice of Hebrew Grammar among Christian Scholars in Pre-Expulsion England: The Evidence of 'Bi-lingual' Hebrew-Latin Manuscripts," *Hebrew Scholarship and the Medieval World*, ed. Nicholas De Lange (Cambridge: Cambridge University Press, 2001), 107–30. For the question of the untranslatable Jew and Christian concepts of translation and conversion, see Seidman's excellent chapter on conversion and translation from Jerome to Luther in her *Faithful Renderings*, 115–52.

62. Iogna-Prat, *Order and Exclusion*, 279.

CHAPTER 7

THE INSTRUCTIVE OTHER WITHIN: SECULARIZED JEWS IN *THE SIEGE OF JERUSALEM*

Randy P. Schiff

Far from being anti-Semitic, the alliterative Siege of Jerusalem *presents secularized Jews whose martial courage and civilian suffering undermine the theological pretensions of a mercenary Roman war machine. Both conqueror and besieged speak to anxieties about the late medieval expansionist energies of English empire.*

In *passus* IX of the B-text of *Piers Plowman*, Wit turns to the ethical example of Jewish behavior in order to chastise Will's contemporaries for allowing fellow Christians to starve. Wit's reference to exemplary Jewish behavior clearly depends upon a view of Jews as both ignoble and uncharitable: it should be shocking, says Wit, that any Christian could be unkind to another, since Jews, whom "we jugge Judas felawes" [deem the companions of Judas], would not "for alle the mebles on this moolde" [wealth of the world] allow another Jew to beg if they might "amende" the situation.[1] Wit goes so far as to debase his Christian audience by asserting that Jews herein maintain a position of superiority to Christians, as their instructors—for they "ben oure loresmen" [are our teachers] which is "shame to us alle!" (IX.88).

Jews play a similarly instructive yet simultaneously debased role in a poem roughly contemporary with Langland's work—the fourteenth-century alliterative poem *The Siege of Jerusalem*.[2] The Jews facing the might of the suddenly and ferociously Christianized Roman war machine are presented in remarkably secularized terms, in a poem that both invokes and forecloses a direct link between divine will and earthly violence. In many ways haunting the consciousness of the Christian West by being the one group that might conceivably lay claim to a more antique right to divine favor in the realm of force, medieval Jews are, insofar as they are represented in the discourse of the Christian West, characterized by ambivalence as it is deployed in the work of Homi K. Bhabha.[3] The *Siege*-poet's Jews evoke admiration every bit as much as they do repulsion portrayed in a fundamentally ambivalent relation of military aggressors to others who, without appeal to the brutal ideology of total, theologically authorized warfare, might become something more like neighbors or even trading partners. Bhabha's linkage of ambivalence with excess can help us read the proliferating images of violence in *The Siege of Jerusalem* as something more than mere expression of hatred, but rather as a tactic aimed at turning the gaze of audiences hungering for such violence to the injurious effects of militancy closer to home. For the violence of the *Siege of Jerusalem*, far from appearing to be the measured punishment of Jerusalem's Jews for the killing of Christ, as it is initially contextualized, emerges more like the purely arbitrary violence of divinity that Walter Benjamin argues transcends by its nature law and reason.[4]

The Siege of Jerusalem's version of the well-worn story of the first-century sacking of Jerusalem by Roman armies under Titus and Vespasian can then be seen as a mirror in which a militarized Christendom is made to look back and question its own confidence in a monopoly on divine favor in the arena of violence. Considering the poem's overwhelming focus on the military skills and on the civilian sufferings of the Jews coupled with the almost complete evasion of the question of conversion central to other versions of the narrative, we can trace the ways in which the anonymous composer of *The Siege of Jerusalem* depends upon such cultural anxieties about the rejecting Jewish other, even as he empties the tale of nearly all theological content, instead channeling its narrative to a regional reflection on the ingloriousness of mercenary expansionism. Indeed, the Jews of the *Siege* seem ready to stand in quite as readily for Scottish as for English citizens caught up in Anglo-Scottish conflict played out in the war-torn north in which numerous manuscripts of the *Siege* circulated.[5] Through parallels with yet another defiant ethnic other whom they had dispossessed—the Celts and their legendary hero King Arthur, the Jews of the *Siege* may even bear uncanny resemblance to the hyper-militaristic English who mythologized themselves through the fraught appropriation of Arthur as symbol of the Crown, the ambivalence of which narratives has been incisively analyzed by literary scholars such as Patricia Clare Ingham and historians like R.R. Davies.[6] *The Siege of Jerusalem* would thus reveal common interests with a number of alliterative texts taking on the vexed narrative of Arthurian conquest, in which the costs of militarism haunt otherwise seemingly nationalistic narratives of British Empire born through the bloody displacement of Celtic populations.[7]

Ambivalent Aggression: Divinely Personal Violence in *The Siege of Jerusalem*

The *Siege of Jerusalem* was clearly a popular poem in its day, with eight relatively full- and one-fragmented texts surviving—thus in terms of attestation standing second only to *Piers Plowman* among alliterative texts.[8] The *Siege* has generated as much critical fascination as discomfort, with the work's volatile mixture of violence and seeming religious partisanship leading to Ralph Hanna's understandably oft-cited description of the poem as the "chocolate-covered tarantula of the alliterative movement"[9]—a description that cannily combines the simultaneous attraction and repulsion of the ambivalent at the heart of the *Siege*. The poem's putative anti-Semitism is often seen as a—if not the—key question, and its often inventive and high-fueled descriptions of violence upon militants and civilians alike has been foregrounded in most recent commentaries. Many critics have read raw anti-Semitism as at the heart of the *Siege of Jerusalem*. Thorlac Turville-Petre might be heard as speaking for many commentators in calling it a "spiteful poem" that "rejoices" in the sufferings of the Jews, with the vividness of imagery of violence committed upon Jewish bodies leading David Lawton to call the *Siege* a poem that "even its editors cannot love."[10] Ralph Hanna goes so far as to suggest that the poem's portrayals of violence against Jews (who he believes can be seen as standing in as figures for Lollards as targets of communal aggression) is literally beyond the pale, suggesting that the *Siege* be consigned to the "suppressed margins of critical attention, unaccompanied by commentary."[11]

It is not difficult to see why so many critics come to such conclusions, insofar as gory details punctuate the narrative of a blood-soaked siege. A small sampling of scenes can give an idea of the unrelenting violence that permeates the poem: we see seven hundred Jews jump to their deaths after the torture and execution of the scribes (ll. 713–14);[12] the unborn child of a woman is ejected over the walls after the mother's belly is struck by a missile (ll. 829–32), and, in the most notorious instance of violence, the starvation of the Jewish defenders of Jerusalem leads one citizen, a certain Mary, to devour part of her own child and offer the remains to looters (ll. 1081–96).[13] Rather than merely revealing a penchant for violence, which could be as easily attributed to the literary traditions of popular romance as to reaction to the brutal realities of siege warfare,[14] the narrator of the poem unsettles

contemporary criticism by going to great lengths to link the violence
against the citizens of Jerusalem with Christ, thereby presumably stamping
the activities with divine authorization. The Roman management of the
action is undermined by the narrative project of presenting the invasion as
Christ's for-forty-years-delayed vengeance upon the Jews: after a bloody
depiction of Christ's beating and crucifixion (ll. 9–18), the narrator notes
that Christ did not hasten such "vyleny to venge" [to avenge such cru-
elty] on those that his "veynys brosten" [burst his veins], but rather waited,
allowing Jews forty years' time to "tourne" [convert] (ll. 21–24). That the
time for conversion here appears to be passed ensures that the future invasion be seen as purely vindictive, with the Roman soldiers read as Christ's
"knyghts" to "kepe" [protect] (l. 612)[15] enacting vengeance on those such
as Caiphas and his clerks, whom the narrator accuses of having wrought
"tresoun and trey" [treason and pain] against Christ (ll. 725–27).

By foregrounding Titus's hijacking of the Roman invasion, originally
meant to ensure tribute-payment crucial to the maintenance of empire, the
Siege-poet uses the overdetermined mindset of the recent convert to highlight the arbitrariness of military exercises. After Nathan, a merchant sent to
report Jerusalem's withholding of tribute to their imperial overlords, locates
a Titus ailing from a "canker vnclene" [malignant cancer] (ll. 30–32), he proceeds to tell him of the miracles and death of Christ (ll. 101–72). The clearly
moved Titus expresses contempt for Rome, calling the "Cesar" who had
given power to Pilate a "synful wrecche" [sinful wretch] (ll. 168–72), finding
himself healed, even as he speaks these "wordes" [words] of contempt for
Rome. Titus's criticism of Roman imperial policy and introduction to the
story of Christ thus accomplish what no "leche" [physician] had been able
to do (l. 41), linking his rejection of civic identity with healing, as he goes
on to take up the transnational name of the Christian seeking vengeance
on the "deueles" [devils] of Jerusalem (l. 190). The absence of any hint that
any of Titus's soldiers has joined the general in baptism and zealous conversion to holy warrior acts to undermine the theological authorization of the
narrative, rendering ambivalent the participation of Roman forces pressed
into service for a cause tied to their commander's personal medical history.
Indeed, the arbitrariness of the commanders' motives is further enhanced
by the parallel story of the healing of Titus's father, Vespasian, who suffers
from the more "ferly" [wondrous] malady of a "bikere of waspen bees" that
"bredde in his nose" [a hive of wasps that bred on his nose] (l. 34). Vespasian
is also cured in his transition from secular to religious identity, for, after
the "pope" applies Veronica's veil to his body, the object's touch makes the
"waspys" go "away," along with all the related "wo" [pain] (ll. 253–56). The
very excess of Titus's reaction to Nathan's story, along with the exaggerated,
if not absurd, ailment suffered by the preconversion Vespasian serves to

highlight the private desires coopting a military war machine whose only relation to religious inspiration is a product of the combination of military command structure and the shared interest in plunder that the sacking of Jerusalem promises.

Ambivalent Agents: Jerusalem's Others as Moving Targets

How to theorize the violence of the *Siege* must be at the center of any critical approach to the poem, addressing the problem, in Christine Chism's apt phrasing, of a poem "perplexed by an enjoyment" of the "unflinching acknowledgement of Christian violence."[16] The "enjoyment" of such violence is not something I would ask us to ignore—for it feeds audience delight in violence pure and simple, for romance audiences clearly enjoyed hearing of brains spilling all over the place, be they Christian or Saracen.[17] Rather than reading such grotesque violence merely as endorsement of such activity, then recoiling into the self-righteous posture of a morally modern judge of anti-Semitism, we might ask if the poet stokes such feelings in order to align the audience with a Roman invading force so brutal as to vitiate any pretension to sacrality, interpellating consumers of such visceral imagery into virtual participation in the Roman's lengthy, difficult, and finally, totally destructive and mercenary siege of "our" foes.[18] Indeed, the poet may well be channeling such enjoyment into self-reflection on violence in the current empire still being forged at the cost of British blood. Considering L.O. Aranye Fradenburg's incisive interconnection of the stakes of enjoyment with the construction of knowledge, we might well expect that the problem of the audience appetite for images of violence against Jews should inform us about modern critical dispositions every bit as much as medieval attitudes we might too readily analyze as alien.[19]

In a crucial discussion of the problem of identifying who exactly is intended by the Jews of *The Siege of Jerusalem*, Elisa Narin van Court seeks to counteract what she analyzes as a modern predilection toward "displacement" of the Jews of the *Siege* in arguments that in effect "relocate" the anti-Judaism of the poem to representatives of other groups. Van Court assesses the manner in which, in the case of Mary Hamel's discussion, anti-Saracen sentiment is held to be at the heart of the Jewish figures in the poem, while in the case of Ralph Hanna, even with an insistence on regional anti-Semitism animating the *Siege*, the crucial target intended by the Jews of the *Siege* being marginalized Lollards.[20] The Jews of the *Siege* might well be seen as Jews even as they stand in for a generalized, racialized Other, as Geraldine Heng has shown in her magisterial study of

Richard Coeur de Lion, in the midst of which she contends that Jews and Muslims could easily stand in for one another as spectral figures threatening Christian communal identity well into the late medieval period.[21] Van Court seeks to focus attention on the Jew *as* Jew in *The Siege of Jerusalem*, insisting that a profound ambivalence concerning Jewish identity is at the heart of the *Siege*, which she traces to an Augustinian interest in a relatively tolerant historiography associated with the monastery of Bolton to which she traces the composition of the *Siege*.[22]

We might well see the poet moving away from the emphasis on the theological basis of Jewish difference, by analyzing the editorial decisions made by a compiler who worked carefully in bringing together his sources. In the source the poet is using at the opening, Jacobus de Voragine's *Legenda Aurea*, the messenger who comes to Titus and Vespasian comes with a clearly theological message—to justify the killing of Christ.[23] But in the *Siege*, the poet either changes the reason—or, according to Hanna and Lawton's view of direct use of Josephus's *De bello Iudaico* in this instance[24]—produces a far more secular, far more defiant romance pose. As the Jews defy the Roman empire by refusing to pay tribute, they might readily recall those most famous deniers of Roman imperial demands, King Arthur and his followers, who first challenge Lucius's emissaries in the foundational *History of the Kings of Britain* of Geoffrey of Monmouth, which work R.R. Davies reads as simultaneously a celebration and challenge to English empire by the ethnic other within.[25] In recalling both the killers of Christ and the foundational figures for English imperial identity, the Jews of *The Siege of Jerusalem* evoke something like the ambivalence of English self-identity as analyzed in Kathy Lavezzo's recent study of the profoundly double English self-conception as geographically marginal (inhabiting an extremity on *mappae mundae* with Jerusalem and Rome at the center) and yet geopolitically central.[26]

The Siege of Jerusalem goes beyond mere undercutting of key players to a rendering impossible of any easy reading of ethnic identity, through an emphasis on the politics of place borne by the messenger carrying the message of nontribute to the Romans. From Nathan's enthusiastic description of Christ's activities, it seems clear that he is a convert to Christianity, though the creed from which he has converted is unclear. Identified as "Neymes sone of Grecys" [the son of Nahum of the Greeks], the well-traveled Nathan is sent by Sensteus of Syria to Rome on an "eraunde fram" [errand from] the Jews. Whether Nathan is merely a convenient agent for delivering a message from the Jews or is, as a Jew, one who can deliver that message is left ambiguous, with the possibility of Jewishness marked by his sharing a name with one of Israel's prophets.[27] That Nathan is a traveler also renders ambivalent what location is intended when he states that Christ had come to "our londe" [land] (l. 102), and his close knowledge of the events of Christ's activities leave open the possibility that he is referring to a Palestine occupied by Jews, Romans, and those such as he whose ethnic status is unclear. Indeed, his very ethnic opacity raises the specter of non-Jews living in Jerusalem also suffering from the Christ-endorsed violence of Titus and Vespasian coopted Roman forces, calling into question the easy endorsement of a siege that will bring about the slaughter of numerous innocents.[28]

Unsettling Otherness: Unease with Imperialism Then as Now

Material evidence can help us isolate medieval uneasiness with the crusading aspect of Titus's invasion, as variant reception speaks to more than unproblematic vengeance being narrated in the *Siege*. In three of the manuscripts, including Laud Misc. 656 [L], which is the probably earliest and is typically used as the base text for editions of the poem,[29] Titus is said to have been made a "Cristen kyng that for Crist werred" [Christian king who warred for Christ]; four of the manuscripts [AEDC], perhaps looking forward to such grim details as the plucking of gold coins from the guts of slaughtered citizens of Jerusalem (ll. 1165–72), seem to move to dissociate Titus's military exploits from his newfound Christianity, saying rather that he was made a king who "served" Christ. The L-text emphasizes that the Romans invade Jerusalem during the Jewish holiday of "paske" [Passover], whereas four manuscripts [EDUC] erase this savage tactic. In three manuscripts [LVA], the Jews killed in the initial attack are also "drowen" [drawn], whereas four of the texts [EDCU] remove these acts of mutilation. Even before the prolonged siege begins, the self-styled Christian invading force of *The Siege of Jerusalem* displays a brutality that produces anxiety not only among current critics, but among the poem's medieval redactors.

The manner in which the Jews resist the Roman invasion also contributes indirect criticism of the crusading Romans. In *The Siege of Jerusalem*, we are far from the stereotypical image of Jews as calculating and cowardly, either operating treacherously and invisibly through, say, the poisoning of wells in Middle English Mary romances or in the attacks on defenseless children featured in the blood libels and martyrdom tales such as those connected to Hugh of Lincoln[30]—not far from Clifford's Tower, in York, site of an 1190 massacre of Jewish citizens besieged by a mob.[31] The Jews of the *Siege* consistently refuse to talk terms with the Romans, hold their ground in open combat, and prove to be skilled defenders in the art of siege warfare. As Titus explains in a Roman council called to deal with the difficult campaign, the

Jews are "felle of defence, ferce men and noble" [intense in defense, fierce
and noble men] and their town is "tenful to wynne" [difficult to conquer]
(ll. 871–72). Indeed, the Jews of the *Siege*—whose initial response to the
demands of the invading armies at their gates is to cut off the beards of the
diplomats and send them back to the Romans naked and bound—have a
kind of swagger that readily recalls the boisterous, posturing Arthurians who
defy Roman tribute-demands on England, also undiplomatically threatening messengers and, for good diplomatic show, beheading a key diplomat,
as does the Gawain of the Alliterative *Morte Arthure*.[32] The Jews' message to
Titus—that they will ignore his requests and do not "dreden" his "dome"
[fear his judgment], and that they have indeed "atled" [intended] his death
to be determined on the "felde" [field of battle] (ll. 369–72)—presents an
image of Jews as warriors every bit as brash and boastful as the Britons of
Arthurian literary history. That the Romans, faced with such stiff resistance, only succeed in taking the city after adopting the strategy of starving
out the Jews—to "honte" [hunt] them with "hunger" (ll. 877–82)—hardly
presents the Roman army in a glorious light, calling attention to the civilian
suffering of siege warfare, while also rendering unclear the reasons why an
army supported by Christ would need to resort to such cruel and dehu-
manizing tactics.

Learning from the Conquered: The Medicinal Other in the Time of *Siege*

If manuscript variation and Jewish valor indeed indicate anxiety about
Titus's first act as a Christian being his assemblage of an army bent on
plundering Jerusalem and massacring its inhabitants, the poet's manipulation of source material shows even more clearly a systematic, though
indirect criticism of the imperial invasion. Recalling Christine Chism's
powerful linkage of enjoyment and violence in a *Siege of Jerusalem*'s read
as a "foundation for Christian imperialism,"[33] we might well consider
whether enjoyment of violence is intended by the poet ultimately to
turn such dark entertainment against itself, channeling its energies into
a criticism of the unethical deployment of military force for what is only
nominally a Christian project. The poet's use of sources allow us to trace
a steady foregrounding of the atrocities committed by the Roman legions
upon a Jewish population, with images that depart radically from ste-
reotypically anti-Semitic medieval depictions of Jews. As Bonnie Millar
demonstrates very clearly in her material analysis of texts of the *Siege*, the
poet made extensive use of three principal sources (the *Vindicta Salvatoris*,
Ranulf Higden's *Polychronicon*, and Roger d'Argenteuil's *Bible en francois*),
occasionally supplementing the work with original material and with

extracts from *The Legenda Aurea*.[34] The poet's reworking of his sources is so well documented as to allow deviations from his sources to repay close analysis. While the atrocities of the Romans often derive from details drawn from sources, we can see the poet exacerbating the viciousness of the Roman army by his setting of the time of the initial assault on Jerusalem as the holiday of Passover, the sanctity of which celebration is violated not just by the slaughter of numerous worshippers, but by the added detail of their being "drowen" [drawn] (ll. 321–24).[35]

It is in his interpolation of the story of Josephus's healing of Titus that the poet presents the clearest evidence for a systematic criticism of the crusading pretensions of the Roman invaders, allowing the vilified Other to offer instruction concerning ethical behavior consistent with the Christianity the generals have only recently adopted. For the story of the second healing of Titus (who, in a scene of excess we might also see as comically ambivalent, falls sick with joy after hearing that Vespasian has been named emperor), the poet makes a rare turn to a the *Legenda Aurea* attributed to Jacobus de Voragine.[36] The only suitable physician that can be found for Titus is Josephus, who, besides being the orchestrator of Jewish resistance, is also an esteemed "surgyan" [surgeon].[37] Asking that safe-conduct be allowed for someone to come from behind the besieged walls of Jerusalem, Josephus sets up a cure based upon Titus coming face-to-face with his Other—for it is Titus's bitter "enemy" whom Josephus summons from the city suffering from Titus's relentless siege. After initial rage at the sight of his enemy, Titus suddenly finds that his blood begins to flow normally again, and he soon regains his color and is brought back to himself (ll. 1049–54). Josephus then explains his medicinal use of the Other, urging Titus to grant his enemy "grace" and become friends with his "foman" [enemy], for his enemy has him "holpyn" [helped] and was his "bote" [cure]—and Titus indeed "satles" [makes peace] with his former foe (ll. 1057–61). Titus, overjoyed with his regained health, has jewels, broaches, and rings brought for Josephus; but Josephus, in a detail apparently original to the poet, "forsakeþ" [refuses] all reward, choosing instead to return behind the besieged walls of Jerusalem, where the citizens continue to experience the "hard hunger and hote" [difficult and intense hunger] that Titus continues to cause (ll. 1065–68).

As Christine Chism has shown, it is not a citizen of Jerusalem, but rather one of Titus's slaves who is used by Josephus for the cure in the *Legenda Aurea*.[38] By choosing to have Titus's healing enemy be an inhabitant of the very city the Romans are besieging—by having Titus be healed *by* a Jew and *through* a Jew—the poet presents the possibility that Titus might learn a lesson about mercy and call off his brutal siege. The pressure of history, of course, works against such an outcome, and Titus appears to see no irony in his having been healed by one of the very "devils" upon whom he has come to exact Christian vengeance. Titus's later refusal to grant mercy to the Jews who plead that it is "paske-euene" [Passover-eve], appealing to the religious sensibilities Titus putatively espouses—the very same Jews to whom Titus had offered peace when it seemed pragmatic, days earlier—suggests further and fundamental criticism of the theological justification of the brutal Roman force that becomes momentarily the receiver of Josephus's ethical instruction.

The added detail of Josephus's refusal of payment for his healing of Titus allows us to see that the violence over which, according to critics, the poet seems to salivate, may actually serve to criticize the violence of imperialism—for Josephus's lessons of mercy, forgiveness, and disdain for worldly wealth surely reverberate for readers as the Romans soon run rampant in the city, sacking and plundering Jerusalem in a destruction both violent and total. Here, *The Siege of Jerusalem* proves to offer an uneasy look at the shaky foundations of a militaristic culture that unquestioningly assumes the divine warrant of its actions. For the *Siege* shows that the objects of a veritable Crusade, who themselves as subjects believe fervently, indeed religiously in the rightness of their actions, have much to teach a Western Christian juggernaut largely blind to the ethical import of its expansion.

The Siege of Jerusalem, apparently originating in western Yorkshire, speaks more to the destruction of raids and sieges enacted by both Scots and English in the bloody process of forming the borders of Britain—and perhaps also to the regional trauma of the 1190 massacre of Jews in the siege of Clifford's Tower in York[39]—than it does to the abstract theological interests that need to be foregrounded in order to see the text as of fundamentally anti-Semitic intent. By presenting the Jews of Jerusalem as resolute soldiers and figuring their military leader Josephus as an ethical instructor to a brutal and morally ambiguous imperial army, *The Siege of Jerusalem* produces a fundamentally ambivalent interrelation of Jew and Christian on a battlefield largely emptied of theological significance. Though *The Siege of Jerusalem*, as Ralph Hanna cogently argues, may well speak to the regional traumas of the 1190 siege of Clifford's Tower and other twelfth-century atrocities in northern England, the focus on Jews as primarily brash defenders and as victims of the cruelties of medieval siege warfare allows the text to recall just as readily the ghosts of Scots, English, and Welsh foot-soldiers fighting the nation-building wars on the borders of an expanding late medieval England. Through its sympathetic portrayal of Jews decimated by an army that proves to behave in ways incompatible with the Christianity its leaders claim to uphold, *The Siege of Jerusalem* would seem to find affiliation with alliterative works interested in undermining the legitimacy of brutal, military expansionism, such as the Alliterative *Morte Arthure*, which attributes King Arthur's violent felling by the Wheel of Fortune as judgment due to his aggressive expansionism.[40] But *The Siege of Jerusalem* would also link up with the literary figure with which we began. Just as Langland's Wit depends upon a simultaneous repulsion and admiration of Jews in order to urge contemporaries to revise their own civic behavior, so does the poet of the *Siege* stoke anti-Semitic tendencies at the same time as he presents Jews in secularized terms as bold, but broken victims of unrestrained militarism.

Notes

1. William Langland, *The Vision of Piers Plowman*, rev. ed., ed. A.V.C. Schmidt (London: J.M. Dent, 1995), l. IX.82–86. All citations from *Piers Plowman* are from Schmidt's edition; bracketed translations are my own based on Schmidt's glosses.

2. The date of composition of *The Siege of Jerusalem* is uncertain, with little internal evidence leading to speculation on borrowing from *The Destruction of Troy*. In their critical edition, Ralph Hanna and David Lawton discuss the problems involved in dating *The Siege of Jerusalem*, suggesting the most probable date would be some years before 1385–86, *The Siege of Jerusalem* (*E.E.T.S.* o.s. 320, 2003), xxv–xxxvii; Michael Livingston concurs with Hanna and Lawton in his edition, situating the poem "sometime in the 1370s or 1380s," *The Siege of Jerusalem* (Kalamazoo: Medieval Institute Publications), 12–13. In their 1932 edition, Mabel Day and E. Kölbing, basing their findings on the presumption of borrowing from *The Gest Hystoriale of Destruction of Troy* (a relationship of debt that Hanna and Lawton reverse), date the poem to 1390–1400 (*E.E.T.S.* o.s. 188), xxix.

3. See Bhabha's analysis of stereotyping as a function of desire, in which "by acceding to the wildest fantasies" of the "colonizer, the stereotyped Other reveals something of the 'fantasy' (as desire, defence) of that position of mastery" (117), in Homi K. Bhabha, *The Location of Culture* (New York and London: Routledge, 1994), 94–120.

4. See Walter Benjamin, "Critique of Violence," in *Reflections*, ed. Peter Demetz, trans. Edmund Jephcott (New York: Schocken, 1978), 294–94 [277–300]. Benjamin's insistence that divine violence has to do with power, not with law, might well derive from a fourteenth-century perspective disillusioned by centuries of church-endorsed Crusading military activities, linking a transnational war-weariness with regional concerns about militarism in the more immediate region of the English North.

5. For analysis of the sociological and economic impact of warfare in the northern regions of England fueled by Anglo-Scottish conflict and by recruitment for military activities in the Hundred Years War and elsewhere, see Anthony Tuck, "War and Society in the Medieval North," *Northern History* 21 (1985): 33–52. For a broad-ranging survey of military recruitment in the Northwest Midlands, both near to Yorkshire and also the site of much alliterative composition, see Michael J. Bennett, *Community, Class and Careerism: Cheshire and Lancashire Society in the Age*

of "Sir Gawain and the Green Knight" (Cambridge: Cambridge University Press, 1983).

6. Northern England and Scotland were the sites of circulation of a number of alliterative works interested in undermining the legitimacy of brutal, military expansionism, such as *The Awntyrs off Arthure*, *The Alliterative Morte Arthure*, and *Gologras and Gawane*. Patricia Clare Ingham offers a magisterial analysis of the ambivalent use of fantastic Arthurian narratives in the shaping of English historical identity, in *Sovereign Fantasies: Arthurian Romance and the Making of Britain* (Philadelphia: University of Pennsylvania Press, 2001), 1–17. See also William Matthews, *The Tragedy of Arthur: A Study of the "Alliterative Morte Arthure"* (Berkeley and Los Angeles: University of California Press, 1960), which offers a thoroughgoing analysis of regional malaise concerning the hypermilitarism of northern England. For R.R. Davies, the ambivalent use of the figure of Arthur in English mythology offers special access to the Anglocentric nature of medieval attempts at forging an imperial Britain, in *The First English Empire: Power and Identities in the British Isles, 1093–1343* (Oxford: Oxford University Press, 2000), 1–3.

7. Hanna and Lawton argue that the dialect of the poet of *The Siege of Jerusalem* is of the Barnoldswick-Earby area of the West Riding of Yorkshire, and thus from its very origin in the northerly regions of England, most affected by the oft-militarized Anglo-Scottish frontier. Hanna and Lawton, eds., *Siege*, xxvii–xxxv.

8. For an exhaustive discussion of the manuscripts in which *The Siege of Jerusalem* is attested, see Bonnie Millar, *"The Siege of Jerusalem" in Its Physical, Literary and Historical Contexts* (Dublin: Four Courts Press, 2000), 15–41, as well as the introduction to Ralph Hanna and David Lawton's 2003 edition of the *Siege of Jerusalem* (*E.E.T.S.* o.s. 320), xiii–xxvii, lv–lxix.

9. Ralph Hanna, "Contextualizing *The Siege of Jerusalem*," *Yearbook of Langland Studies* 6 (1992): 109 [109–17].

10. Thorlac Turville-Petre, *The Alliterative Revival* (Cambridge: D.S. Brewer, 1977), 35; David Lawton, "Titus Goes Hunting and Hawking: The Poetics of Recreation and Revenge in *The Siege of Jerusalem*," in *Individuality and Achievement in Middle English Poetry*, ed. O.S. Pickering (Cambridge: D.S. Brewer, 1997), 105 [105–17]. For further analysis of the critical reception of the poem, along with an engaging revision of attempts to reduce the Siege to an exercise in anti-Semitism, see Roger Nicholson, "Haunted Itineraries: Reading *The Siege of Jerusalem*," *Exemplaria* 14 (2002): 447–84.

11. Hanna, "Contextualizing," 110 [109–17]. For a stimulating discussion of methods of marginalization of Lollards in the late medieval period, see Carolyn Dinshaw, *Getting Medieval: Sexualities and Communities, Pre- and Postmodern* (Durham and London: Duke University Press, 1999), 55–99.

12. All references to *The Siege of Jerusalem* are to Hanna and Lawton's 2003 edition; all bracketed translations are my own, based on Hanna and Lawton's glosses.

13. Elisa Narin van Court contends that the scene of cannibalization, when compared to instances in sources that clearly tie the action to anti-Judaic sentiments, should be seen as part of a largely sympathetic portrayal of Jews—which sympathy she traces to "Augustinian" modes of historiography informing the text. See Elisa Narin van Court, "*The Siege of Jerusalem* and Augustinian Historians: Writing about Jews in Fourteenth-Century England," *Chaucer Review* 29 (1995): 234–35 [227–48].

14. Michael Livingston attributes much of the violence so shocking to contemporary critics of the poem in part to the basic realities of siege warfare, both as understood in crusading romances and in the poet's own sources, in Livingston, ed., *Siege*, 17–18.

15. Suzanne M. Yeager offers a valuable analysis of the ambiguous nature of the Roman presence in *The Siege of Jerusalem*, emphasizing the manner in which the Romans are viewed alternately as holy warriors and as overly brutal military agents, in "*The Siege of Jerusalem* and Biblical Exegesis: Writing and Romans in Fourteenth-Century England," *Chaucer Review* 39.1 (2004): 70–102. On the powerful role played by Rome in shaping English notions of empire, see Davies, *The First English Empire*, 35–38.

16. Christine Chism, *Alliterative Revivals* (Philadelphia: University of Pennsylvania Press, 2002), 155. Chism situates her incisive analysis in the context of relational "identities of east and west," reading Christian anxiety about its debt to Judaic culture as generative of much anti-Semitism in the period (188). Chism shares my emphasis on the undermining of the Romans' roles as "sympathetic Christian heroes" through the foregrounding of the "suffering of Jews" (180), as well as my focus on the instructive nature of Josephus's role (184–85) in her rich treatment of the *Siege*, to which this work is deeply indebted, as it is to Chism's earlier analysis in "*The Siege of Jerusalem*: Liquidating Assets," *Journal of Medieval and Early Modern Studies* 28 (1998): 309–40.

17. For a valuable analysis of bodily humor as grotesque, producing precisely the kind of ambivalent imagery brought about by images teetering in the "ambiguous" zone "between pleasure and disgust" (88), see Andrew Stott's study of the grotesque in his survey of bodily humor, in *Comedy* (New York and London: Routledge, 2005), 87–92. For a discussion linking violence with audience focused on medieval romances, see James Simpson's comparison of *Gamelyn* with *Sir Gawain and the Green Knight* in *Reform and Cultural Revolution* (Oxford: Oxford University Press, 2002), 276–83. Simpson's discussion would lead us to conclude that, as with *Gamelyn*, an "aggressive gentry society" (277) may well have been a key target for manuscripts of *The Siege of Jerusalem*.

18. Besides frequently referring to the Jews through terms of otherness, calling them "fals" (e.g., ll. 539, 555), "heþen" [heathen] (l. 561), and servants of the "fende" [Devil] (l. 838), the narrator finds an even more subtle way to render the Jews other and link the audience with the Roman armies, bidding "now blesse vs our lorde" after describing Titus and his ally Sabine's armed forces (ll. 433–45).

19. See Fradenburg's study of the interrelation of desire and discipline in *Sacrifice Your Love: Psychoanalysis, Historicism, Chaucer* (Minneapolis: University of Minnesota Press, 2002), 1–41. See also Fradenburg's caution against conceiving of anti-Semitic conventions as purely "medieval," for such alteritist attitudes blind criticism to the "competing representations of reality" embedded in literary texts, in "Criticism, Anti-Semitism, and *The Prioress's Tale*," *Exemplaria* 1 (1989): 76. Jerold C. Frakes provides a powerful antidote to reductivism among medievalists in locating modern complexities of meaning in medieval texts, in *Brides and Doom: Gender, Property, and Power in Medieval German Women's Epic* (Philadelphia: University of Pennsylvania Press, 1994), 6–7.

20. Van Court, 227–29. Van Court refers to the powerful precedents of "displacement" set by Mary Hamel, "*The Siege of Jerusalem* as a Crusading Poem," in *Journeys Toward God: Pilgrimage and Crusade*, ed. Barbara N. Sargent-Baur (Kalamazoo: Medieval Institute Publications, 1992), 177–94, and by Ralph Hanna, "Contextualizing *The Siege of Jerusalem*," *Yearbook of Langland Studies* 6 (1992): 9–17. Suzanne Conklin Akbari, in the midst of an essay theorizing a radically variable Jew that can take on the characteristics of Muslim and Christian as readily as the Jew in *The Siege of Jerusalem*, offers a thought-provoking discussion of the interwoven history of Jew and Muslim in the Western imagination, in "Placing the Jews in Late Medieval English Literature," in *Orientalism and the Jews*, ed. Ivan Davidson Kalmar and Derek J. Penslar (Hanover: Brandeis University Press, 2004), 32–34 [29–50].

21. Geraldine Heng, *Empire of Magic: Medieval Romance and the Politics of Cultural Fantasy* (New York: Columbia University Press, 2003), 78–91. For analysis of the monstrous forms in which Saracens were racialized in the late medieval period, with such ambivalently attractive and yet repulsive images capable of being attributed to Jews as marginal figures, see Jeffrey Jerome Cohen, "On Saracen Enjoyment: Some Fantasies of Race in Late Medieval France and England," *Journal of Medieval and Early Modern Studies* 31.1 [Ed. Thomas Hahn] (2001): 119–21 [113–46]. For further analysis of the critical problem of figuring the Jew, see David Lawton's discussion of the predilection to theorize disembodied Jews in the theorization of post-Expulsion England, in "Sacrilege and Theatricality: The Croxton *Play of the Sacrament*," *Journal of Medieval and Early Modern Studies* 32.3 (2003): 289–93 [281–309]. In "Postcolonial Chaucer and the Virtual Jew," Sylvia Tomasch argues that post-Expulsion Jews in medieval England, while effectively absent, disclose crucial aspects of contemporary mind-sets, in *The Postcolonial Middle Ages*, ed. Jeffrey Jerome Cohen (New York: St. Martin's Press, 2000), 254–55 [243–60]. For evidence of post-Expulsion Jews in late medieval England, see Henry Asgard Kelly, "Jews and Saracens in Chaucer's England: A Review of the Evidence," *Studies in the Age of Chaucer* 27 (2005): 129–69.

22. Van Court, 240–43. Van Court's article has been recently republished in Sheila Delany's valuable collection of articles assessing fourteenth-century

English attitudes concerning Jews, *Chaucer and the Jews*, ed. Sheila Delany (New York and London: Routledge, 2002), 165–84. See also van Court's recent discussion of the upsurge in revisionary activity concerning the previously marginalized *Siege of Jerusalem*, in "*The Siege of Jerusalem* and Recuperative Readings," in *Pulp Fictions of Medieval England: Essays in Popular Romance*, ed. Nicola McDonald (Manchester: Manchester University Press, 2004), 151–552 [151–70]. Hanna and Lawton also trace *The Siege of Jerusalem* to Bolton; see *Siege*, lii–lv.

23. See the story of Saint James the Less, in Jacobus de Voragine, *The Golden Legend*, ed. and trans. Granger Ryan and Helmut Ripperger (New York: Arno Press, 1969), 265 [261–69].

24. Hanna and Lawton contend, as against previous editors of the poem, that the poet of the *Siege* had access to a Latin translation of Josephus's *The Jewish Wars*. For Hanna and Lawton's ample and convincing evidence for this case, see their edition of the *Siege*, xl–lii.

25. See Davies, *The First English Empire*, 39–48. For the scene in Geoffrey, see Geoffrey of Monmouth, *History of the Kings of Britain*, ed. and trans. Lewis Thorpe (London: Penguin, 1996), 230–36. The Arthurian refusal of tribute is crucial to the opening of another alliterative work critical of militaristic attitudes, the Alliterative *Morte Arthure*, ed. Valerie Krishna (New York: Burt Franklin, 1976), ll. 78–487.

26. Kathy Lavezzo, *Angels on the Edge of the World: Geography, Literature, and English Community, 1000–1534* (Ithaca and London: Cornell University Press, 2006), 1–26.

27. See Michael Livingston's discussion of possible links with the prophet Nathan in his edition of the *Siege*, p.86n.

28. For valuable surveys of the problems involved in theorizing racial identity in the medieval period, see Thomas Hahn's introduction to his special-edition volume, "The Difference That Race Makes: Color and Race before the Modern World," *Journal of Medieval and Early Modern Studies* 31.1 (2002): 1–37; see also Lisa Lampert, "Race, Periodicity, and the (Neo-) Middle Ages," *Modern Language Quarterly* 65.3 (2004): 391–421; and see also Jeffrey Jerome Cohen, *Hybridity, Identity and Monstrosity in Medieval Britain* (New York: Palgrave Macmillan, 2006), 1–10. Much recent work on race depends upon Robert Bartlett's emphasis on the cultural, rather than biological reality of racial identity in the Middle Ages; a recent presentation of this position is presented in Robert Bartlett, "Medieval and Modern Concepts of Race and Ethnicity," *Journal of Medieval and Early Modern Studies* 31.1 (2001 [Ed. Thomas Hahn]): 39–56.

29. Day and Kölbing use MS Laud Misc. 656 as the base text for their 1932 edition, as do Hanna and Lawton in their 2003 text. Livingston also bases his text on L, with special consultation of two other manuscript texts for emendation, *The Siege of Jerusalem* (36–38).

30. For analysis of stereotypes of Jews current in late medieval England, see Anthony Bale, *The Jew in the Medieval Book: English Antisemitisms, 1350–1500* (Cambridge: Cambridge University Press, 2007). For the

broader European context of stereotypical presentations of Jews, see Miri Rubin, *Gentile Tales: The Narrative Assault on Late Medieval Jews* (New Haven, CT: Yale University Press, 1999), and see also Steven F. Kruger, *The Spectral Jew: Conversion and Embodiment in Medieval Europe* (Minneapolis: University of Minnesota Press, 2006). For primary source material related to medieval conceptions of Jews, see Alan Dundes, ed., *The Blood Libel Legend: A Casebook in Anti-Semitism Folklore* (Madison: University of Wisconsin Press, 1991). Joshua Trachtenberg provides a wealth of images and documents of medieval stereotypes of Jews in *The Devil and the Jews: The Medieval Conception of the Jew and Its Relation to Modern Anti-Semitism* (1943; Philadelphia and Jerusalem: The Jewish Publication Society, 1983).

31. On March 16–17, 1190, a mass of citizens of York, many of them in debt to Jews and so with an economic interest in stoking discord, slaughtered much of the city's Jews, who had taken refuge after the storming of the house of the survivors of Benedict of York, who was himself the victim of the anti-Semitic riots that took place in 1189 due to rumors of Jewish conspiracies following the coronation of Richard I. For discussion and excerpts from chronicle sources of both these incidents, see Jacob R. Marcus, ed., *The Jew in the Medieval World: A Source Book, 315–1791* (New York: Atheneum, 1981), 131–36. See also R.B. Dobson, *The Jews of Medieval York and the Massacre of March 1190*, University of York Bothwick Papers 45 (1974, rev. 1996). Ralph Hanna links the violent anti-Judaic past of the Yorkshire region with the later reception of *The Siege of Jerusalem*, in "Contextualizing," 110–11 [109–21].

32. Krishna, ed., *Morte*, ll. 1352–55.

33. Chism, *Alliterative*, 185.

34. For detailed treatments of the use of sources in *The Siege of Jerusalem*, see Millar, *Siege*, 42–75, and Hanna and Lawton, eds., *Siege*, xxxv–lv.

35. Lines 265–324 of the poem cannot be conclusively tied to any of the poet's known sources; before and after this section, the text otherwise closely follows Roger d'Argenteuil's *Bible en francois*. Hanna and Lawton argue that much of this material comes from Josephus, who indeed names Passover as the time of the arrival of the invading armies into Jerusalem, after having ravaged their way there following an initial landing in Syria. Whether Josephan in origin or not, the addition of details of atrocities—the killing and torture of citizens engaged in religious worship—is clearly important enough for the poet to move away from the source with which he is working in order to interweave key material. For the *Siege*-poet's use of Josephus, see Hanna and Lawton, eds., *Siege*, xlii–lii. Phyllis Moe establishes the *Siege*'s debt to d'Argenteuil in lines 201–724 in "The French Source of the Alliterative *Siege of Jerusalem*," *Medium Aevum* 39 (1970): 147–55. For further discussion of the *Siege*'s use of integration of material from Roger d'Argenteuil's *Bible*, see Millar, *Siege*, 56–60, and Hanna and Lawton, eds., *Siege*, xxxix–xl.

36. For discussions of the *Siege*-poet's use of the *Legenda Aurea*, see Millar, *Siege*, 72, and see also Hanna and Lawton, eds., *Siege*, xxxviii–xxxix.

37. Hans Lewy, in "Josephus the Physician," analyzes the medical profession was one avenue for marginalized Jews to improve their social status in the medieval period, *Journal of the Warburg Institute* 1 (1937–38): 241–44. Lewy notes that Josephus, in the thirteenth-century German law-code known as the *Sachenspiegel* of Eike von Repgow (III.7.3), is said to have won the "King's peace" through his healing of Titus (221). Were such cultural negotiations present to the mind of the *Siege*-poet, it makes all the more powerful Christine Chism's contention that Josephus's healing of Titus, concludes that Josephus's ethical actions intimate "possibilities of paternal respect, gratitude, and even love," in *Alliterative Revivals*, 183–85.

38. In the *Legenda Aurea*, Josephus chooses a "servus adeo Titus molestus" [a slave who annoyed Titus], *Jacobi a Voragine Legenda Aurea*, ed. T. Graesse (1846; Osnabrück: Otto Zeller Verlag, 1999), 301. For an English translation of the scene, see Jacobus de Voragine, *Legend*, ed. and trans. Ryan and Ripperger, 267–68.

39. Hanna, "Contextualizing," 109–17.

40. *Morte*, ed. Krishna, ll. 3394–3407.

CHAPTER 8

SUBVERSIVE HISTORIES:
STRATEGIES OF IDENTITY IN
SCOTTISH HISTORIOGRAPHY

Katherine H. Terrell

> *Flickering between contact and avoidance, interaction and interdiction, border lines produce spaces "in between," gaps or middle places symbolizing exchange and encounter. As such, they are the areas wherein identity and sovereignty are negotiated, imaginatively and discursively, in relation to the necessary other.*

> —Michael Uebel, *Ecstatic Transformation: On the Uses of Alterity in the Middle Ages*, 14.

*T*his chapter examines Scottish historiographical responses to Geoffrey of Monmouth's myth of Brutus, finding that even as Scottish chroniclers challenge this myth and the English claims of hegemony that it comes to represent, their persistently dialogic engagement with Geoffrey's text reveals the hybridity underlying their constructions of identity.

In the second book of John of Fordun's fourteenth-century *Chronica Gentis Scotorum*, the chronicler turns his attention to the hermeneutical significance of the Anglo-Scottish border. Describing the island, he concludes that at its narrowest point, "[a]s a result of this flowing in of great rivers from both sides, even though they do not touch each other, some historians have written that the country is practically divided into two islands" (2.1.25–28).[1] In attempting rhetorically to bifurcate the island, Fordun suggests a potent fantasy of a clearly delineated border, an unmistakable demarcation that starkly contrasts with the reality of shifting allegiances and permeable boundaries that historically characterized

Anglo-Scottish relations. Yet even as it suggests a vision of a wholly auton-omous Scottish identity, Fordun's narrative reveals the traces of a more authentic complexity. Modeled on a lengthy tradition of topographic *descriptio* going back to Gildas and Bede, the geographical sketch inevitably calls to mind recollections of Fordun's more recent sources, including the English chronicler Ranulph Higden and Geoffrey of Monmouth, whose revisionist challenge to anglocentric history had itself been coopted by the English.[2] And perhaps more significantly, it leads Fordun to confront the narrative that until this point has been the unwritten subtext of his chronicle: Geoffrey's account of the Trojan origins of Britain.

This moment exemplifies a recurrent paradox of nationalist Scottish historiography: texts that are written for the explicit purpose of delimiting Scotland's geographical and cultural boundaries nevertheless inevitably expose the vexed "middle places" of Anglo-Scottish relations. The per-sistent threat of English imperialism from the late thirteenth century onward has a marked effect on representations of Scottish identity. Scottish historians turn to the distant past in order to stake out a territory that is at once literal and literary; in so doing, they necessarily engage the sources, particularly Geoffrey of Monmouth's *Historia Regum Britannie*, that were invoked to support English hegemony. Yet the inherently dia-logic structure of Scottish historiography is seldom purely oppositional: rather, Scottish historians create hybrid histories characterized by both appropriation and defiance. Although, like Fordun, historians regularly disavow this hybridity—instead insisting on a natural and autonomous Scottish identity—the subversive potential in Scottish historiography lies precisely in its ability to redeploy English structures for ostenta-tiously Scottish ends. I would argue that far from being complicit in what R.R. Davies calls the "Anglicization of the British Isles," the dia-logic nature of these Scottish writings enables a kind of writing back to England that becomes indistinguishable from the nationalist project of writing Scotland.[3]

As a source text employed to legitimize English ambitions in Scotland, Geoffrey of Monmouth's twelfth-century *Historia Regum Britannie* under-lies much of medieval Scottish history-writing. In this masterwork of legendary history, Geoffrey tells of how Brutus, great-grandson of the Trojan Aeneas, comes to be the eponymous founder of Britain. After driving out the giants from the otherwise uninhabited island, "Brutus then called the island Britain from his own name, and his companions he called Britons."[4] He later divides the island among his three sons: Locrinus and Kamber inherit England and Wales, respectively, while "Albanactus, the youngest, took the region which is nowadays called Scotland in our language. He called it Albany, after his own name."[5]

However, Albanactus is later killed during an invasion by Humber, the king of the Huns, who is in turn defeated by Locrinus. After this point, Geoffrey is unclear as to whether Locrinus and his descendants continue to rule Albany, or whether its own kingship is reestablished. But the ideological thrust of the tale is clear: Brutus establishes his territorial rights through both primacy and conquest, and passes the land down in perpetuity to his descendants. As Francis Ingledew has noted, by filling the empty stretches of history with invented tales, "the *Historia* takes possession of time as the basis for ideology."[6] The authority to narrate time in turn justifies the domination of land, in a mutually reinforcing system of temporal and physical conquest.

This apparently simple tale was already weighted with ideological significance when Geoffrey adopted it, and his retelling only expanded its possible range of meaning. Geoffrey likely drew his version of the legend from the ninth-century *Historia Brittonum*, traditionally attributed to Nennius. Nennius took his own cue from the Franks, who had originated the legend of Trojan descent by the mid-seventh century; for them, the myth had primarily served to explain military prowess and justify cultural dominance by asserting an equal relationship to Rome—a relationship of competition rather than descent.[7] In redeploying this myth on behalf of the Britons, by this time a politically and culturally marginalized group known as the Welsh within a country colonized first by Angles, Saxons, and Danes, and now dominated by the Normans, Geoffrey crucially altered its possible range of signification. The myth no longer functioned exclusively to serve the interests of the ruling elite. Instead, by "transform[ing] the indigenous displaced into the invading displacers," Geoffrey provided the Welsh with their own claim to an illustrious cultural history, a potentially subversive maneuver that was complicated by this multivalent text's ability to bear a precisely opposite interpretation.[8] Indeed, Patricia Ingham has suggested that "the popularity and cultural usefulness of Monmouth's fantasy of the Britons involves its ability to accommodate diverse uses...serving both the pleasures of parvenu Anglo-Norman aristocrats and their Welsh resisters," both of whom could trace their ancestry to the Britons.[9]

However, the very qualities that made Geoffrey's text attractive to a Welsh resistance made it problematic for Scots similarly faced with English aggression. In particular, the myth of Brutus, which the Welsh could interpret to signify their own inherited right to Britain, offered no such reassurances to Scots who traced their lineage elsewhere. Nor was it sufficient for Scottish historiographers merely to follow William of Newburgh in accusing Geoffrey of having propagated "a laughable web of fiction."[10] For Scottish historiographers, disputing Geoffrey's claims was

not simply a matter of professional pride; tales told about the distant past
could have real political consequences, and in English hands Geoffrey's
narrative of origins served imperialist ambitions. English hegemonic
claims based on Brutus's primacy bookend the fourteenth century, with
Edward I's 1301 demand for Scottish homage being repeated precisely
one hundred years later by Henry IV.[11] One of the chief fascinations
of Geoffrey's narrative is its proffering of "a lost yet promised figure
of insular wholeness," one that, Ingham reminds us, "alludes to ancient
British days while it also encodes massive political, geographic, and
military losses for England, Scotland, and Wales."[12] In supplying the historical basis for the fantasy of a united Britain, Geoffrey also supplied a
ready authorization for later English attempts to turn fantasy into reality
through conquest.

Thus, while Edward I has been called the "midwife" of Scottish historiography, Geoffrey had a role to play in its conception, a conception that
was bound up in the politics of a colonization that stretched backward
into the distant past, even as it endeavored to extend its reach into the
future.[13] Scottish historiography came into its own as a direct result of
the colonial crisis precipitated by a disputed succession in 1290. By this
point, "there seems little doubt that…the Scots already saw themselves
as an established nation, entitled to their separate identity in a defined
territory which they collectively embodied as a sovereign nation-state."[14]
Yet when the Scottish King Alexander III and his only direct heir—
his granddaughter Margaret, known as the "Maid of Norway"—died
one after the other, Edward I stepped in to arbitrate among the throne's
various claimants, with the underlying motive of imposing his authority
as Scotland's overlord.[15] Edward decided upon John Balliol in 1292, but
was soon disappointed when his chosen king began to chafe at his deter-
mination to have a hand in Scottish affairs. Edward accordingly invaded
Scotland and deposed Balliol only four years after setting him on the
throne, thereafter assuming direct rule of Scotland and setting in motion
the lengthy Wars of Scottish Independence.

Geoffrey's narrative first appears as a basis for political conflict
in 1301, as a result of Pope Boniface VIII's attempt to intervene in
Scotland's defense. Claiming that he knew of no basis for Edward's claim
to Scotland—and that Scotland "belonged rightfully…to the Roman
church"—Boniface invited him to submit evidence to the papal court.[16]
Edward, unsurprisingly, responded with a letter asserting that "our predecessors and progenitors, the kings of England, by right of lordship and
dominion, possessed, from the most ancient times, the suzerainty of the
realm of Scotland and its kings."[17] As proof of this contention, he offered
a lengthy historical narrative, beginning with the legendary history

of Brutus drawn from Geoffrey of Monmouth's *Historia*.[18] Within this account, Geoffrey's vision of primal unity legitimizes Edward's attempt to dismantle Britain's boundaries.

In rehearsing Geoffrey's story of Brutus, Edward makes two significant embellishments in order to enhance the legal validity of his case. First, he stipulates that Brutus divided his lands with "the royal dignity being reserved for Locrine, the eldest," thus clarifying that Brutus never intended to create three separate and sovereign kingdoms.[19] More importantly, Edward concludes his account by insisting that after the death of Albanactus, "Albany reverted to Locrine."[20] This addition establishes, in place of Geoffrey's ambiguity, a clear precedent for English assumption of authority over Scotland at the death of a Scottish ruler— the exact maneuver that Edward himself was trying to accomplish. The precision of Edward's language, together with what James Goldstein ironically calls the "remarkable correspondence between Trojan and Anglo-Norman law," suggests a deliberate attempt to heighten the political value of the myth.[21] Elevating the importance of the distant past by invoking it as a valued precedent capable of establishing his right to a kingdom, and thereby forcing a Scottish response on similar grounds, Edward unwittingly inaugurated a tradition of Scottish historical writing that would last for centuries.

However, the Scots were relative latecomers to the high-stakes game of colonizing the distant past. While English historiography burgeoned in the twelfth and thirteenth centuries, a comprehensive account of Scottish history had yet to be written when Edward submitted his letter to the papal court.[22] This task fell, initially, on Baldred Bisset, the Scots' chief representative in Rome.[23] Yet both Bisset and subsequent historians found their task complicated by the fact that, by the fourteenth century, the past was already crowded with the writings of a hostile nation. The most authoritative accounts of the island's earliest days, like Geoffrey's, tended to provide rationales for disenfranchising the Scots; yet these accounts became impossible to ignore, either as literary models or as historical precedents. Faced with this weight of authority, Scottish historiographers seeking to (re)script the past were left with a limited range of options: they could directly challenge the English version, or they could exploit the gaps and ambiguities of English historical accounts, anchoring their narratives in the interstices of English history.[24]

Bisset employs both of these strategies, disputing Edward's narrative of Brutus as "specious and mutilated history" (11.49.23) while furnishing an alternative account "in order to provide fuller knowledge of the story" (11.49.30–31). In doing so, he deploys many of the same manipulations of which he accuses Edward. On the one hand, Bisset takes Edward to task for his self-serving manipulation of the historical record, and charges him with basing his case on "unproven fictions about an obsolete distant past" (9.48.44). Yet in claiming a more authentic knowledge of Brutus's actions—accepting, for example, Brutus's division of his kingdom among his sons, while denying "that Albanactus held his kingdom in fee from Locrinus" (11.61.32–33)—Bisset implicitly accepts the relevance of the distant past; as he goes on to flesh out history, this supposedly obsolete antiquity becomes the foundation of Scotland's freedoms. Goldstein has suggested that we regard this seeming contradiction as "a form of adversarial gamesmanship rather than as a serious betrayal of hermeneutical principles," and indeed, the Scots had little choice at this point but to play Edward's game.[25] Once the intimate link between historical and political authority had been established, contesting its legitimacy was insufficient; only a counterlegend would do.

Happily, Bisset had an origin myth at hand, one that was readily adaptable to counter Edward's strategic deployment of Geoffrey's narrative. The version of the myth that Bisset ultimately presented to the papal court runs as follows:

> a daughter of Pharaoh king of Egypt landed in Ireland with an armed force and a very large fleet of ships. Then after taking on board some Irishmen, she sailed to Scotland...She conquered and overthrew the Picts, and took over that kingdom. And from this Scota the Scots and Scotland take their name...These Scots are known to have retained the name and country to the present day. Therefore the Scots and Scotland are no concern of the king of England; and the English could have claimed no more of a right to the kingdom of Scotland than the Egyptians. (11.62.1–13)

Bisset's direct source for this legend is unknown, but versions of it had been around for centuries; curiously, one of the earliest references to the Egyptian origin of the Scots occurs in the same chronicle attributed to Nennius that provided Geoffrey's probable source for the tale of Brutus.[26] This common ancestry makes the clash of the English and Scottish legends at the papal court all the more striking: lavishly embellished and invested with political weight, the two myths that once existed comfortably side by side have been transformed into conflicting ideological weapons.

In relating his alternative vision of history, Bisset attempts to shore up the boundaries between kingdoms and peoples that Edward has systematically tried to break down; yet his very enforcement of these boundaries relies upon strategies of argument drawn from Geoffrey's *Historia*. For Bisset, as for Geoffrey, the most fundamental boundaries are enforced by conquest and borne out through the culture of a people. Thus he portrays the Scots' banishment of the Britons as absolute: "The place of the name Albany was taken by the new name Scotland along with the new people, the Scots, with their rites, language and customs—regarding which the Scots have nothing in common with the Britons" (11.49.62–65). Just as Brutus's successful conquest led to the "eponymic fusion of names, land, and language" that indelibly marked the island and its people as his legacy, so the Scots' conquest entirely supplants previous history.[27] Bisset explicitly draws this comparison, claiming that the Scots possess Scotland "by the same right and title as that by which Brutus had earlier occupied the whole of Britain" (11.49.54–55). Seemingly unaware of the irony involved in citing Brutus as a precedent for the rights of conquerors at the same time that he dismisses English claims based on that precedent, Bisset creates a totalizing discourse that is absolute in its commitment to Anglo-Scottish difference.

Using similar reasoning, Bisset attempts to divorce the English from their own supposed history, in the process bolstering the authenticity of his own origin myth. Following the logic that conquest fundamentally alters the character of a kingdom, he asserts that Edward has no more to do with Brutus than do the Scots. In a strategy that would be used repeatedly by Scottish chroniclers to emphasize the Anglo-Scottish divide, Bisset stresses the ruptured lineage of the English monarchy. Even accepting the fact of Brutus's conquest, he points out, does not necessarily help Edward's case. For at that time, "all the inhabitants of the kingdom of England were Britons, who were afterwards overthrown by the Saxons, the Saxons by the Danes, and again the Danes by the Saxons, and the Saxons themselves by the Normans...from whom (not from the Britons) this king is known to have descended" (11.61.40–44). Revealing Edward's bias, Bisset demolishes his claim to have inherited a kingdom from a man who, if he ever existed, was no ancestor of Edward's. In so doing, he exposes a vulnerability that could be something of a sore spot for the descendants of William the Conqueror; indeed, the popularity of Geoffrey's *Historia* has been partly explained by its ability to "legitimate and naturalize the Norman occupation of England by linking it to Britain's earliest prehistory."[28] Bisset counters this legitimizing function of the narrative by rendering the seams of English identity visible, insisting on the alterations wrought by successive waves of conquest. This fracturing of the English past, in contrast with the relative stability of the Scottish monarchy, guarantees the efficacy of the Scottish origin myth.

Not content merely to cordon off English from Scottish history as a means of securing the Scots' possession of temporal and territorial rights, Bisset also emphasizes the physical and cultural boundaries between the two kingdoms. His vision of radical alterity extends well beyond the political realm of Edward's investment; while Edward's interests are best served by minimizing cultural and genealogical difference and stressing the feudal and familial ties between the two realms, in Bisset's writings, the political border emerges as the inevitable consequence of a legion of other more fundamental boundaries. Thus, Hadrian's Wall provides evidence of an ancient physical separation, but is also a marker of culture. Built by the Romans so that "the Scots and Picts should not be able to make raids into Loegria against the Britons, nor harm them in their usual way" (11.49.88–89), this border comes to signify a more intrinsic difference marked by a casually customary antagonism: from its beginning, Scotland is "always hostile to the kingdom of England" [semper infestum regno Anglie] (11.50.59). Safely bounded by this wall, secure in their perpetual hostility toward England and their consequent autonomy from all things English, the Scottish land and its people emerge in Bisset's writings as whole, complete, and independent, unlike the English with their fragmented identity. Geoffrey's fantasy of a united Britain has been supplanted by an equally potent fantasy of an island perpetually divided.

Yet the very nature of a border implies a relationship between sides; borders are points of interaction as well as separation, and the genesis of Bisset's narrative—created in response to Edward's aggression and modeled on Geoffrey's myth—belies his absolutist claims of English alterity and Scottish autonomy. The paradox involved in Bisset's basing his counterdiscourse on his enemy's foundational text suggests the complexities endemic to Scottish historiography. Writing of a similar predicament faced by Welsh poets, Ingham usefully proposes that "such poignant complications suggest not a complicity with conquest that must be deplored, but the difficulty of oppositional strategies."[29] The persistence of Geoffrey of Monmouth's role as both antagonist and model for Scottish chroniclers attests to this difficulty, as well as to the creative possibilities engendered by such a paradox.

When John of Fordun, chantry priest of Aberdeen, set out in the mid-fourteenth century to compose a comprehensive chronicle of the Scottish people from their mythical origins to his present day, he was attempting a project unprecedented in scale, yet one that clearly followed in the tradition inaugurated by Bisset.[30] Like his predecessor, Fordun was alert to the political implications of history; he aimed to fill the need for an authoritative version of the distant past that could rally nationalist sentiment and actually help to preserve Scotland's liberty and integrity in future conflicts. Accordingly, in the early portions of his *Chronica Gentis Scotorum* he develops and expands Bisset's origin myth, solidifying the Scots' temporal and territorial claims. Fordun, like Bisset, takes Geoffrey's *Historia* for his model, more effectively exploiting its subversive potential while deepening Bisset's critique of Geoffrey's methods. Yet unlike Bisset, Fordun appears ambivalent about employing Geoffrey's strategies of fabrication; whereas Bisset follows Geoffrey in confidently forging a streamlined history out of the murky depths of time, Fordun reluctantly admits to the constructedness of history in a way that ultimately threatens historiography's claim to accurately represent the past. However, even while revealing the seams of history he promotes a different version of historical truth, one that attempts to circumvent the awkwardness of hybridity by finding verification in contemporary identity.

The Anglo-Scottish border looms large in Fordun's *Chronica* as a site of contested political dominance, one whose significance is determined as much by textual incarnation as by military possession; thus Geoffrey's *Historia* becomes critical to Fordun's account of Scotland's earliest days. Yet I would argue that Fordun manages to turn the subversive element in Geoffrey's mythmaking to his own ends, and so the relationship of Fordun's *Chronica* to Geoffrey's *Historia* is far more complex than the unambiguous hostility that has sometimes been claimed.[31] Geoffrey provides Fordun with a successful model for writing the history of a people regarded as uncivilized barbarians by the possessors of more sophisticated historical traditions, and for inserting legendary history into the scheme of established historical narrative.[32] Yet while Geoffrey expands the possibilities of English historical narrative from within, Fordun takes the rebellious energy of Geoffrey's myth and directs it outward, to compete with Geoffrey's own vision of history. In so doing, Fordun heightens the competitive function of national mythmaking, not merely claiming equality with England but insisting upon superiority.

In elaborating the myth of Scottish origins and embellishing it from disparate sources, Fordun develops it into a worthy opponent of Geoffrey's legend. According to Fordun, the history of the Scots begins in the time of Moses, when Gaythelos, the son of a Greek king, leaves his father's kingdom and travels with a band of followers to Egypt. There he marries Scota, the daughter of Pharaoh. After Moses's exodus, the couple leave Egypt and "for the forty years during which the children of Israel lived in the wilderness under the leadership of Moses, Gaythelos also wandered with his people through many lands with frequent changes of direction" (1.13.7–10). Eventually they land in Spain, and after successfully battling the inhabitants they found a city, where Gaythelos teaches his people laws derived from those of the Greeks and Egyptians. However, troubled by the continued attacks of the Spaniards, he sends out ships to search for uninhabited territory, and they discover Ireland. In a rousing deathbed speech, Gaythelos instructs his sons to take possession of this land,

and successive waves of Scots accordingly settle in Ireland. When the Picts arrive on their shores seeking a place to live, the Scots suggest the "northern limits of Albion, hitherto uninhabited" (1.30.13); they also provide the Picts with Scottish wives, and other Scots follow these first settlers. However, soon the Picts ungenerously turn against the Scots in their midst, prompting the Scottish king Fergus Ferard to come to their rescue; he becomes the first king of the Scots to reign in Scotland. This is the basic story as related by Fordun, but the way in which he tells it is far from simple.

Throughout his recitation of this legend, Fordun implicitly relies upon Geoffrey's mythologizing while suppressing any mention of Brutus, whose legend his own so patently contradicts. Instead, in the early portions of his narrative he concerns himself with the assertion of a more implicit superiority: inserting the Scots into both classical history through their Greek descent, and biblical history through their relations with the Egyptians, he establishes their origins as doubly illustrious. The historical one-upmanship at work in the legend manifests itself even in the choice of Greece rather than Troy as an ancestral homeland—a sly dig at the prestige of a Trojan ancestry, as Virgil's *Aeneid* (the underlying text of the Trojan narrative) opens with the Trojans fleeing the ruins of a city decimated by the Greeks. Yet the correspondences between Geoffrey's narrative and Fordun's illustrate the appeal of certain aspects of the myth across the board, including an illustrious classical ancestry; the exile of the hero from his homeland; an eponymous founder; extensive wanderings; and an initial, failed, attempt to settle in an occupied region followed by the successful foundation of a realm in a largely uninhabited land.[33] Like Geoffrey's narrative, Fordun's depicts its protagonists as bearers of culture, responsible for translating the classical civilization to a barren landscape where it develops its own traditions parallel to and in defiance of the classical world.

Of course, the main target of Fordun's defiance is England itself, and delaying his discussion of the Brutus myth allows him to plant doubts about Geoffrey's credibility before taking on the central issue. The English and Scottish myths clash even before the Scots land on Scottish soil, with the arrival in Ireland of a massive wave of Scottish immigrants, led by their king Partholomus. In his first direct challenge to Geoffrey, Fordun dwells upon a major discrepancy between his and Geoffrey's versions of history: Geoffrey claims that an English king granted Ireland to Partholomus, while Fordun asserts that, as an earlier wave of Scots had already colonized Ireland, it "had been inhabited before the arrival of Partholomus and was not empty, nor had it been received as the gift of a foreign king" (1.24.3–4). Instead, Fordun frees the Scots from the political implications of this narrative by suggesting that Geoffrey has mixed up the arrival of the Scots with the arrival of the Picts: a serious error in chronology. "Unless I am mistaken," he says condescendingly, "this story about the Picts given above in Geoffrey's version has been described as being about the Scots through the fault of the narrator [*vicio relatoris*]" (1.25.7–9). If Geoffrey is capable of such a basic error, he implies, who knows what else he might have gotten wrong? Fordun reaches new rhetorical heights as he scornfully dismisses Geoffrey's account once and for all: "This is the basis for the claim that Ireland had been given to the Scots by the gift of their own king, invented by the idle chatter of the people, who took excessive pride in such a chance piece of advice" (1.25.11–14). Fordun implies that Geoffrey should take his job as a historian more seriously, as he is doubly to blame: first for listening to the "popularis inepta loquacitas," instead of taking his information from more reliable sources, and then for passing on this mistaken information in his history.

This clear disdain for Geoffrey's methods is reflected in Fordun's ambivalence toward his own mythmaking—an ambivalence that manifests itself in his fragmented presentation of the Scottish origin myth. Throughout the first eight chapters of the first book of his *Chronica*, in which Fordun informs his readers about world geography and briefly rehearses the events of the first six ages of the world, he appears to be fully in control of his material. The narrative voice is unobtrusive, and a casual reader would find it difficult to determine whether Fordun is drawing on one source or several, so seamlessly are they integrated into a single narrative; citations to other works are limited to a quotation from Ptolomy, a brief review of opinions on the authorship of the Book of Wisdom (conclusively deciding on Solomon), and a few unattributed lines of poetry. However, this style of narration abruptly changes when Fordun arrives at the chapter entitled "The first move in the origin of the Scots and their first king Gaythelos" (1.9). In this chapter, following a brief introduction, he quotes a passage from "alia cronica" followed immediately by a longer passage from the "legenda Sancti Brendani," and then by another passage from "alia cronica." Returning to his own narration, he cites the *Historia Scholastica* and Methodius as his sources, before concluding with a long quotation from Methodius; this patchwork style of narration continues throughout much of the first book.

The abruptness of this change in narrative technique is striking, particularly because the chronicles that Fordun quotes disagree with one another about important facts. For example, was Gaythelos a dutiful son sent by his father to aid Pharaoh, or an aspiring tyrant exiled for leading a failed rebellion? Did the Scots leave Egypt when all of its nobles were driven out by a peasant uprising; or were only the Scots expelled, due to the Egyptians' fear of foreign domination; or did the Scots leave in fear of divine wrath? The contradictions multiply as Fordun proceeds further into the story. Gaythelos initially intends to "seize a kingdom and territory from other peoples to be inhabited for ever by force of arms" (1.12.9–10), but he later regrets having abandoned his supposedly original plan to settle only in an uninhabited region (1.16). The status of Ireland upon the arrival of the Scots varies wildly: although the Scottish sailors kill some islanders with their oars, the territory is soon after praised for being "devoid of inhabitants" (1.17.19); or perhaps it is inhabited by giants; or else the Scots "killed some of the few inhabitants...and enslaved the rest" (1.18.24–25). The list could easily be extended, but this should suffice to give a sense of the continuity errors from which this section suffers. Fordun makes no comment; he merely sets the opposing sources side by side, and lets the readers judge for themselves.[34]

The difficulty lies not in Fordun's narrative technique itself, but in its difference from other portions of his narrative. The typical position of the medieval historian was that of the *compilator*, who was expected to record the opinions of others, not necessarily to make critical judgments about the soundness of those opinions. This was not the only model of medieval historiography, as Geoffrey's narrative demonstrates—his primary citation being to a "very ancient book" that may well be his own invention.[35] Yet it was an influential one, employed among others by Fordun's source Ranulph Higden, whose narrative style—described by Antonia Gransden as "almost entirely a compilation, made up of borrowings from ancient and more recent authorities"—Fordun's resembles here.[36] However, this historiographical model seems insufficient to explain why the origin myth is the only portion of Fordun's *Chronica* to assume this appearance of bricolage, with its assembly of incongruous sources seemingly outside of the narrator's control. Fordun is clearly on shakier ground here than usual, and although not every chapter in this section suffers from these discrepancies, still it stands out as by far the least assured in the chronicle. Once Fordun moves beyond the earliest period in Scottish history, he resumes a style much closer to the seamless narration with which he began. He will sometimes cite sources or quote directly, occasionally even at some length, but it becomes rarer for his sources to be in contradiction, and the narrative never again assumes the patchwork effect of the chapters that deal with the origin myth. In a text that elsewhere seems so concerned to establish historical precedent, it seems particularly odd that Fordun makes no attempt to disguise these contradictions or present a more coherent, streamlined version that would raise fewer doubts as to its authenticity and thus be better suited to his ideological goals.

In so openly forging a national identity out of the contradictory chronicles of an uncertain past, Fordun exposes the fundamental constructedness of history itself, thereby potentially drawing into question the basis of the very national identity that he writes to support. And to a certain extent Fordun appears to be aware that he risks losing his audience's confidence. In the midst of this section he suddenly steps back from his narration and turns his attention to the wider issue of why authorities often disagree, in a chapter entitled, "How the chronicle justifies the discrepancies of histories" (1.26). He bases his explanation on the pervasiveness of contradictions among historical narratives, apparently missing the irony of his reassurance that "historians are seen to disagree in many of their writings every day" (1.26.3–4). He goes on to cite Isidore's opinion that "we ought not to condemn as ignorant historians or commentators or rather writers of fiction [*comentatores vel comentores*] who give different versions, because the mistake originated with antiquity itself" (1.26.19–22). Fordun himself inserts the phrase "vel comentores" [or rather writers of fiction], perhaps as a dig at Geoffrey's propensity for substituting imaginative narrative for demonstrable fact. Yet the passage can also be read as placing fiction on a par with fact, equating the *comentatores* with the *comentores*. In either case, this justification insufficiently accounts for the discrepancies of Fordun's own narrative, and in one sense seems an odd philosophy for a history writer to hold. Far from boosting the truth-value of Fordun's own sources, the pervasiveness of disagreement among chronicles seems to draw the very possibility of truthful historical narrative into question. In Fordun's hands, the passage comes close to reducing all history to the status of fiction and giving up on any claim to veracity about the distant past.

However, viewed from another perspective, the blending of fact and fiction may even be seen to support Fordun's ideological perspective: for if history is merely fiction, then surely fiction may also be history. Seeking documentary evidence for his historical narration, Fordun cannot help but notice that his sources sometimes disagree; yet Fordun's *Chronica* ultimately espouses an alternate view of historical truth, one that takes up Geoffrey's genealogical vision of history while avoiding the complications endemic to a genealogy that must support the interests of both colonizers and colonized. While Geoffrey's narrative "must constantly strike a balance between continuity and discontinuity, center and periphery, endogamy and exogamy, genealogy and filiation," Fordun is able to follow Bisset's relatively unproblematic tying of the Scots to their first ancestors by an unbroken lineage.[37] Genealogy substitutes for textuality, as the living descendants of the Scots' eponymous founders themselves come to signify the truth of Fordun's narrative. The ideals of contemporary Scots are strengthened and confirmed through being rooted in ancient history, but this process also works in reverse, finding its proof in the continuity of the bloodline across time: the ancestors of the Scots must have held certain values, because their descendants do. Thus the mythic utility of Fordun's narrative is scarcely damaged by the discrepancies among his sources, the proliferation of which, when seen in this light, lends credence to the myth's antiquity and prevalence rather than detracting from its integrity.

Fourteenth-century Scottish nationalism itself comes to seem hearteningly atavistic, largely due to Fordun's own imaginative additions to his sources. Gaythelos's deathbed speech exhorting his sons to conquer Ireland, for example, strikes a tone reminiscent of the 1320 *Declaration of Arbroath*, a patriotic assertion of Scottish independence that, Alexander Grant has argued, was itself "an attempt to articulate a theory in order to account for and justify events which had already taken place during the last thirty years" of the Wars of Independence.[38] The speech, equally applicable to Gaythelos's immediate audience and to Fordun's fourteenth-century readers, introduces themes that will occur throughout the *Chronica*: the idea that the Scots possess their lands by divine right; the value of freedom; the ideal of self-sacrifice; and the exclusive power of the Scottish monarch:

> So now, my sons, receive with gratitude the gifts of the gods offered to you, and go without delay to the island ready and waiting for you, where you will be able to live noble and free, since it is the highest nobility known to man and the joy most desired in the world to all the noblest hearts, or rather it is the precious gem rightly to be preferred to all the jewels in the world, to refuse to endure the rule of any foreign domination, but to accept willingly the hereditary power of one's own nation only. (1.17.24–36)

In placing these words in the mouth of his founding hero, Fordun establishes these principles as having been central to the Scottish nation from the beginning, and thus frees them from the taint of English influence. Just as the Scots possessed their land prior to any English claim, so did they possess the principle of freedom prior to any thought of English aggression. In reality, the Scots had not given much thought to their independence until it was threatened, yet although Fordun's rhetoric here—like the *Declaration of Arbroath*—may be part of a theoretical justification for events that had already transpired, he prefers to establish the principle of independence as an integral part of a preexisting identity. Fordun thus strengthens both the appeal of that independence and the completeness of a Scottish identity that thereby appears self-sufficient, no longer part of a dialogic relationship with England.

This attempt to disavow both his own history's hybridity and the heterogeneity of Scottish identity is analogous to the fantasy of geographical separateness with which I began; before striking at Geoffrey's myth of Brutus, Fordun undermines Geoffrey's credibility and shores up Scotland's autonomy on every front. In so doing, he acknowledges the power of the myth that has been the unwritten subtext of his *Chronica* all along: as I have tried to demonstrate, Fordun implicitly relies on Geoffrey's successful pattern of mythologizing and employs his strategy of genealogical argumentation, even as he challenges Geoffrey's authority. Yet Fordun not only delays this final, pivotal confrontation to the second book of his *Chronica*, after he has thoroughly laid out his own countermyth, but also subordinates it within a discussion of geographical nomenclature, as if to deny its prominence as the established touchstone of English imperialist rhetoric.

Yet by the same token, Fordun recognizes that geographical nomenclature is frequently regarded as coterminous with political authority; unable to ignore the fact that in common parlance the island once known as Albion is frequently referred to as "Britain," Fordun challenges the anglocentric slippage of terminology by which "Britain" becomes synonymous with "England." Correctly speaking, he says, Albion "gave up its first name after the time of the giants and as a consequence acquired two names, Britain and Scotland," corresponding to its natural topographical divisions (2.1.30–32). The "primitive and ancient distinction between these kingdoms" is thus inscribed in the land itself, and reflected in terminology of ancient origin (2.2.1). He accrues an impressive range of evidence—largely from Geoffrey of Monmouth himself—in support of this usage before turning to a chapter entitled, "Passages from the same authors maintaining the opposite point of view" (2.4).

Here, at last, Fordun tackles Geoffrey's narrative head-on; but significantly, he counters it not by challenging Geoffrey himself, but by casting aspersions on nationalistically inflected processes of textual transmission. Fordun directly quotes the most damning passage from Geoffrey's tale of Brutus: "'Albanactus son of Brutus gained possession of the land which in our day is called Scotland. He gave it the name Albany after his own name'" (2.4.16–18). Yet he then steps back in order to draw attention to the discrepancies within chronicles, as he has previously discussed the contradictions between them:

> although frequent discrepancy of this kind has been found in the chronicles,
> it must not in the least be held against the writers [*auctoribus*] who were

experts in their field, or rather saints, and wrote their histories carefully according to the truth, altering nothing that they found in their sources, but rather it is the transcribers [*scribis*] of an antagonistic nation who must be blamed. Through their malice certain chronicles have been turned upside down, degraded and abused in order to weaken the authority of neighboring kingdoms, and often changed so indiscriminately that the purport of one chapter completely cancels out that of the next one. But no matter what difference of opinion of this kind concerning the boundary of Britain is found in the chronicles through the inadequacy of the writers [*scriptorum*], the commonly held opinion at the present time is that the whole of Albion was called Britain from the name of Brutus, who had settled none of it except for its southern regions. (2.4.18–37)

Fordun goes even further than Bisset in disputing the accuracy of the Brutus myth. While Bisset had accepted that one of the three portions of Brutus's kingdom corresponded to modern Scotland and disputed only the relevance of that primeval division within contemporary law, Fordun denies that Brutus's authority ever extended over the entire island. Moreover, Fordun here broadens his critique of Geoffrey into an indictment of the entire English system of textual production. Distinguishing between *auctores* and *scribi*, the writers of the histories and the scribes who copied and transmitted them, Fordun explains away Geoffrey's narrative of Brutus's division of the kingdom by denying it even the dubious authority he had previously accorded to Geoffrey's history. Whereas Geoffrey's mistake about Partholomus was the result of his careless confusion of two widely separate events, the basis of England's claim to Scotland derives from the deliberately fraudulent terminology of self-serving scribes.

Again, Fordun calls into question the possibility of truthful historical narration—for even when the original authors are credited with good intentions, their works are prone to alteration by deceitful scribes for nationalistic purposes. The ease with which Fordun assumes the plausibility of a historical conspiracy in which "the transcribers of an antagonistic nation" pervert the historical record demonstrates the degree to which he envisions history as contested political ground. Yet in condemning the falseness of these scribes, he also exposes the extent to which any historical record is open to interpretation, for he does not explain why he identifies these passages—and not the others that support his view—as the deceptions. Once more privileging genealogical intuition over textual transmission, Fordun suggests that truth is not to be found in historical records unless one already knows what to look for. If the written record may be manipulated for selfish goals, then only a historical perspective that is guided by the intangible insights of myth will be able to negotiate complex historical terrain to arrive at truth.

Ultimately, Fordun's development of the Scottish origin myth represents an attempt to do for the historical landscape what his dream of a clearly delineated border does for Scotland itself: to establish it as the inviolable possession of the Scottish people. Origin myths, like borderlines, attempt to forge clarity out of ambiguity, purity out of hybridity; they seek to form orderly narratives and clear demarcations out of fragmented pasts and rugged terrain. Yet just as the starkness of cartographic boundaries conceals their actual permeability, so the ostensible exclusionary force of myths masks their status as spaces of encounter, wherein identity is negotiated through discursive contact with alternative visions of history. Thus while Fordun's elevation of a genealogical mythos drawn from Geoffrey's *Historia* may compromise his assertion of Scottish textual and national autonomy, the hybridity of his history also enables its subversive potential by helping to produce a discursive space in which to cultivate Scottish identity.

Notes

1. Citations of Fordun's *Chronica* refer to Walter Bower, *Scotichronicon*, ed. and trans. D.E.R. Watt, 9 vols. (Aberdeen and Edinburgh: Aberdeen University Press and Mercat Press, 1987–95). Bower, writing in the fifteenth century, incorporated Fordun's *Chronica* into his own work; Watt's edition, which carefully distinguishes between Fordun's text and Bower's additions, has largely supplanted William Skene's edition: *Johannis de Fordun: Chronica Gentis Scotorum*, Historians of Scotland, vol. I (Edinburgh: Edmonston and Douglas, 1871).

2. Monika Otter discusses the *descriptio* tradition in *Inventiones: Fiction and Referentiality in Twelfth-Century English Historical Writing* (Chapel Hill: University of North Carolina Press, 1996), 71–73; also see Michelle Warren, *History on the Edge: Excalibur and the Borders of Britain, 1100–1300*, Medieval Cultures 22 (Minneapolis: University of Minnesota Press, 2000), 3–9. Fordun's description particularly recalls that of Higden, who finds Scotland to be a "promunctorium et borealis pars Brittaniæ majoris, marinis braciis ab ea separata versus austrum;" in Trevisa's translation, "an out strecching…departed in þe south side from Bretayne wiþ armes of þe see." However, neither Higden (whom Fordun does not cite as a source here) nor any of the corroborating authorities whom he does mention comes close to Fordun's assertion that Scotland is "in duabus quasi divisam insulis." Ranulph Higden, *Polychronicon, Together with the English Translations of John Trevisa and of an Unknown Writer of the Fifteenth Century*, ed. Churchill Babington and Joseph Lumby. 9 vols. Rolls Series 41 (London: Her Majesty's Stationary Office, 1865–86), 282–83.

3. R.R. Davies, *The First English Empire: Power and Identity in the British Isles 1093–1343* (Oxford: Oxford University Press, 2000), 142–71.

4. Geoffrey of Monmouth, *The History of the Kings of Britain*, trans. Lewis Thorpe (London: Penguin: 1966), 72.

5. Geoffrey of Monmouth, *History*, 75.

6. Francis Ingledew, "The Book of Troy and the Genealogical Construction of History: The Case of Geoffrey of Monmouth's *Historia Regum Britanniae*," *Speculum* 69 (1994): 680 [665–704]. On Geoffrey's symbolic appropriation of space and time, also see Otter, *Inventiones*, 69–84.

7. Richard Waswo, "Our Ancestors, the Trojans: Inventing Cultural Identity in the Middle Ages," *Exemplaria* 7 (1995): 272 [269–90].

8. Waswo, "Our Ancestors," 283–84.

9. Patricia Clare Ingham, *Sovereign Fantasies: Arthurian Romance and the Making of Britain* (Philadelphia: University of Pennsylvania Press, 2001), 15. See 42–43 for discussion of the Britons as a "doubled people," belonging to both Wales and Normandy.

10. William of Newburgh, *The History of English Affairs: Book I*, ed. and trans. P.G. Walsh and M.J. Kennedy (Warminster: Aris and Phillips, 1988), 29.

11. E.L.G. Stones, *Anglo-Scottish Relations 1174–1328: Some Selected Documents* (1965; Oxford: Clarendon Press, 1970), 192–219 and 346–65.

12. Ingham, *Sovereign Fantasies*, 10.

13. R. James Goldstein, *The Matter of Scotland: Historical Narrative in Medieval Scotland* (Lincoln: University of Nebraska Press, 1993), 119.

14. Keith Stringer, "The Emergence of a Nation-State, 1100–1300," in *Scotland: A History*, ed. Jenny Wormald (Oxford: Oxford University Press, 2005), 75 [39–76]. This collective identity developed in spite of the ethnic and cultural diversity of Scotland's peoples characterized in twelfth-century charters as "English, French, Flemings, Scots, Welsh (Britons), and Gallovidians" (74). For a comparative account of the consolidation and differentiation of English and Scottish political and cultural identities, see Davies, *The First English Empire*, 54–88.

15. Goldstein gives a full account of this episode in *The Matter of Scotland*, 57–78. For a more extended account of Edward's actions in Scotland, see Fiona Watson, *Under the Hammer: Edward I and Scotland 1286–1307* (East Lothian: Tuckwell Press, 1998).

16. Stones, *Anglo-Scottish Relations*, 163.

17. Stones, *Anglo-Scottish Relations*, 193.

18. For a balanced assessment of the validity of Edward's case, see William Ferguson, *The Identity of the Scottish Nation* (Edinburgh: Edinburgh University Press, 1998), 28–33.

19. Stones, *Anglo-Scottish Relations*, 195.

20. Stones, *Anglo-Scottish Relations*, 197.

21. Goldstein, *The Matter of Scotland*, 64.

22. This is not to say that Scottish history was a blank slate; yet compared with the English historiographical tradition, the Scottish tradition was sparse, and generally not focused on narrating the history of Scotland per se; for example, one of the main sources Scottish legendary history, the *Lebor Gabála*, or *Book of the Taking of Ireland*, primarily concerns the Irish

prehistory of the Scots. Other influential sources, including early saints' lives, discuss Scottish history as incidental to their main narratives.

23. Bisset's case survives in two documents: a probable rough draft known as the *Instructiones*, and a more polished document referred to as the *Processus*; both are preserved in Walter Bower's *Scotichronicon*, and citations refer to Watt's edition. Although the *Processus* seems the more likely to have been presented to the papal court, a report on the contents of the *Instructiones* also seems to have reached Edward: see the "Report to King Edward I from the papal court" in Stones, *Anglo-Scottish Relations*, 220–35.

24. Ironically, these are the very strategies that Geoffrey of Monmouth himself employs toward earlier English chronicles. Jeffrey Jerome Cohen, in *Hybridity, Identity and Monstrosity in Medieval Britain: On Difficult Middles* (New York: Palgrave Macmillan, 2006), describes the effect of Geoffrey's revisionist history: "It was as if someone had hurled a Molotov cocktail against the histories of Bede and William of Malmesbury, challenging their seemingly imperturbable authority through the time-changing power of a prequel" (65).

25. Goldstein, *The Matter of Scotland*, 73.

26. For the early history of the Scottish origin-myth, see Dauvit Broun, "The Birth of Scottish History," *Scottish Historical Review* 76 (1997): 4–22; Dauvit Broun, *The Irish Identity of the Kingdom of the Scots in the Twelfth and Thirteenth Centuries*, Studies in Celtic History 18 (Woodbridge: Boydell Press, 1999); Edward J. Cowan, "Myth and Identity in Early Medieval Scotland," *Scottish Historical Review* 63 (1984): 111–35; Goldstein, *The Matter of Scotland*, 104–32; and John and Winifred MacQueen, "Introduction to Books I and II," *Scotichronicon*, xiii–xxxiii, who conclude that the legend had assumed its basic shape by the thirteenth century.

27. R. Howard Bloch, *Etymologies and Genealogies: A Literary Anthropology of the French Middle Ages* (Chicago: University of Chicago Press, 1983), 81.

28. Laurie A. Finke and Martin B. Shichtman, *King Arthur and the Myth of History* (Gainesville: University Press of Florida, 2004), 45.

29. Ingham, *Sovereign Fantasies*, 39.

30. Fordun completed his *Chronica* through the 1153, and at the time of his death in 1385 had made notes—now referred to as the *Gesta Annalia*—through the year 1384.

31. See, for example, Marjorie Drexler, "Fluid Prejudice: Scottish Origin Myths in the Later Middle Ages," in *People, Politics, and Community in the Later Middle Ages*, ed. Joel Rosenthal and Colin Richmond (New York: St. Martin's Press, 1987), 60–76; William Ferguson, *The Identity of the Scottish Nation* (Edinburgh: Edinburgh University Press, 1998); Roger A. Mason, "'Scotching the Brut': The Early History of Britain," in *Scotland Revisited*, ed. Jenny Wormald (London: Collins and Brown, 1991), 49–60; Hans Utz, "Traces of Nationalism in Fordun's 'Chronicle,'" in *Scottish Studies 4, Scottish Language and Literature, Medieval and Renaissance: Fourth International Conference Proceedings, 1984*, ed. Dietrich Strauss and Horst W. Drescher (Frankfurt am Main: Verlag Peter Lang, 1986),

139–49; and Bruce Webster, "John of Fordun and the Independent Identity of the Scots," in *Medieval Europeans: Studies in Ethnic Identity and National Perspectives in Medieval Europe*, ed. Alfred P. Smyth (New York: St. Martin's Press, 1998), 85–102. For a view that stresses the existence of more congenial Scottish attitudes toward British ancestry, see Steve Boardman, "Late Medieval Scotland and the Matter of Britain," in *Scottish History: The Power of the Past*, ed. Edward J. Cowan and Richard J. Finlay (Edinburgh: Edinburgh University Press, 2002), 47–72.

32. See Nancy F. Partner, *Serious Entertainments: The Writing of History in Twelfth-Century England* (Chicago: University of Chicago Press, 1977), 64–65, and Waswo, "Our Ancestors," 284–85 for arguments that the Britons were considered to be uncivilized. For the English "monsterization of the Celtic fringe," see Cohen, *Hybridity, Identity and Monstrosity*, 35–36.

33. Waswo, "Our Ancestors," 287. On the common characteristics of origin myths, also see Susan Reynolds, "Medieval *Origines Gentium* and the Community of the Realm," *History* 68 (1983): 375–90.

34. Goldstein carefully unravels the story of Fordun's sources (109–121), observing that he draws on "several conflicting traditions" in which Gaythelos is by turns an "aggressive or rebellious hero" and "a passive victim," and supplements these with his own additions (114).

35. Geoffrey of Monmouth, *History*, 51.

36. Antonia Gransden, *Historical Writing in England, vol. ii: c. 1307 to the Early Sixteenth Century* (Ithaca: Cornell University Press, 1982), 47.

37. Finke and Shichtman, *King Arthur*, 54.

38. Alexander Grant, "Aspects of National Consciousness in Medieval Scotland," in *Nations, Nationalism and Patriotism in the European Past*, ed. Claus Bjørn, Alexander Grant, and Keith J. Stringer (Copenhagen: Academic Press, 1994), 88 [68–95].

CHAPTER 9

SLEEPING WITH AN ELEPHANT: WALES AND ENGLAND IN THE *MABINOGION*

Jon Kenneth Williams

*T*his chapter proposes that several prose tales of the Mabinogion acknowledge
*English military and political supremacy over Wales during the centuries that
followed the Edwardian conquest. Such a recognition of English might enable
Welsh literature to exhort its audience to a mutually profitable complicity with the
English, one of the goals of which was the perpetuation of the Welsh language.*

When thinking of the position of Wales in the Middle Ages one might
well be put in mind of one of Canadian statesman Pierre Elliot Trudeau's
more memorable *bons mots*. While speaking at the National Press Club in
Washington in 1969 he likened living next to an economic and cultural
superpower to "sleeping with an elephant; no matter how friendly and
even-tempered is the beast, one is affected by every twitch and grunt."[1]
Within the framework of the theme of this volume, the matter of the
British Isles, Trudeau's analogy provides a convenient lens through which
to view England and its insular neighbors in the Middle Ages. Wales
especially was aware that the British archipelago was no longer British
in the ancient sense but was becoming English—or, at the very least,
was becoming British in a new, reoriented sense of the term. Medieval
England, at least from a Welsh perspective, was elephantine if not always
friendly and even-tempered, and its twitches and grunts must have been
felt in all aspects of Welsh life, even—and perhaps especially—in its
vernacular literature.[2]

By the thirteenth and fourteenth centuries, when England began to
turn its attention in earnest to its smaller neighbor, the Welsh-speaking

people had already come to define themselves as Welsh rather than British. For centuries the British/Welsh people had inhabited the region today known as Wales, and for just as long the English, first under their Anglo-Saxon kings and then under their Anglo-Norman and Angevin ones, had referred to them as *Welsh*, a term derived from the Anglo-Saxon *wealh*, alternately a foreigner, stranger, slave, or other such shameless person.[3] This terminology of Wales and the Welsh first appears in the late seventh-century laws of Ine; by the middle of the twelfth century such language was the norm.[4]

Accompanying this renaming of the Welsh people was their redefinition as inhabitants of the rocky central-western region of Britain rather than the displaced rulers of the whole island. The Anglo-Norman and then English encroachments into Wales from the eleventh to the fourteenth centuries may then be viewed as a second, distinct wave of attacks on the Welsh-speaking Celts that occurred some centuries after the initial Saxon invasions of Britain. As R.R. Davies poignantly notes, one eleventh-century Welsh annalist passed over the year 1066 in silence but saw fit to describe 1093 in almost apocalyptic terms: the so-called French invaded Wales, bringing on a "litany of deaths which constitute the staple diet of Welsh and Irish annalists."[5] Attempts at absolute subjugation by the English were to become facts of life for the Welsh until the late thirteenth century, when any sense of Welsh sovereignty or independence would be extinguished in 1282 with the death of Llewellyn ap Gruffydd.

To modern eyes, and quite possibly to medieval ones as well, the conquest of Wales by England was inevitable. England, unified and centralized, could boast a population anywhere between eight and thirteen times the size of that of Wales, a small and fractious place that only too late realized the value of political consolidation.[6] Indeed, to refer to Wales in the singular prior to the Edwardian conquest is to adopt a convenient but misleading shorthand: Wales was "hardly...more than a geographical expression" in the Middle Ages.[7] By the time Wales belatedly began to imagine itself as a unitary state the English had already arrived, and the threat of conquest that had been omnipresent since the Norman Conquest was realized. The year 1282 settled, finally, an issue whose outcome had been suspected for two hundred years.

Given the momentous political realignment that overtook Wales between the twelfth and fifteenth centuries, if there is but one historical resonance to be seen in the literature of the period it must that of the occupation that left Wales beholden to a foreign power. More than any of its Celtic neighbors, Wales had reason to reconsider its national status—as an independent polity, as a collection of regions bound by a common language, as a unique appurtenance of a larger island unit—during the period in which its independence was questioned and finally extinguished. Middle Welsh prose, especially the *Mabinogion*, is complicit in this rethinking of the Welsh relationship to the whole of the British Isles, ultimately marking its native audience as inhabitants of a circumscribed part of Britain rather than as the inheritors to the whole of the island.

In making this argument I build on work by scholars such as Andrew Welsh and Catherine A. McKenna that seeks to read Middle Welsh literature in a historical rather than folkloric or mythological context. Both Welsh and McKenna argue that much modern scholarship of Welsh literature tends to fall into two critical camps: the diachonric one, which reads into medieval Welsh literature glimpses of lost but potentially recoverable whole epic bodies, and the synchronic one, for which surviving medieval Welsh texts are as much—or are at least as much—about the age in which they were produced as they are about prior eras.[8] Welsh and McKenna identify these critical groupings in relation to the four branches of the *Mabinogi*, whose sometimes oblique relatedness leads diachronic readers to argue that they are decayed remnants of a prehistoric ur-text that can be glimpsed behind or under the medieval texts that are our branches of the *Mabinogi*. McKenna puts the diachronic case most eloquently when she writes that it "sees the *Mabinogi*, or at least each of its Branches, as a unified whole of which we see but a distorted shadow on the wall of the cave."[9] Diachronic thought would therefore look backward through various *Mabinogion* texts toward, in the case of the four branches, some kind of mythological or historical entirety, and in the case of the independent native tales and the romances, toward ancient and folkloric rather than contemporary resonances.

A synchronic reading, on the other hand, considers each tale of the *Mabinogion* "not an accidental product but an intentional one…a work of medieval literature."[10] Hence a synchronic reader of Middle Welsh literature would be concerned less with reconstructing an ancient or classical past to which a tale might relate than in situating it in its particular historical and contextual moment. It seems right to say of the redactors of the *Mabinogion* that they mixed memory and desire and were adept enough at their craft to refer to Welsh and British antiquity at the same time as they reflected on the age in which they lived. Given the momentous nature of the historical period in which the manuscripts of the *Mabinogion* were produced, ascribing to the *Mabinogion*, like other medieval texts, at least some contemporary political sensibilities is reasonable.

I read two of the *Mabinogion*'s so-called independent native tales, *Culhwch and Olwen* and *The Dream of Macsen Wledig* in a synchronic way. In these two texts, the former the oldest of the *Mabinogion* tales and the latter a historical narrative, I identify parallel political reasoning; both tales reorient Welsh historical lore to accommodate contemporary medieval political realities. In so doing, these texts accept English political domination by advocating Welsh complicity in order to ensure the survival of native culture and the vernacular. *Culhwch and Olwen* deflates the notion of a primeval Arthurian polity by referring to pre-Arthurian British histories, and *Macsen Wledig* defines Wales's glorious past in a Roman rather than British time. These textual movements redefine the British occupation of the island as historical epoch rather than originary moment, and in so doing they condition a Welsh audience to admit the political fact of Welsh political marginalization.

Reimagining the Origin Myth: *Culhwch and Olwen*

Central to the reconsideration of the relationship of Wales to the rest of the British Isles in the Middle Ages is the reevaluation of Welsh/British origin myths. That the Welsh considered themselves the heirs to the ancient Britons was a medieval commonplace, but that they would eventually effect a reconquest of the island was far less certain. Even Gerald of Wales, whose loyalties and sympathies were understandably divided, could not bring himself to imagine that the Welsh would ever effect a reconquest of Britain, although he did allow to them the possibility that they might retain Wales for themselves.[11] To Anglo-Norman and English eyes, Welsh pretensions to the mastery of the whole island were safely of the past, powerful but superceded, potentially dangerous only if deployed as a living Welsh nationalism.

Buried in the center of *Culhwch and Olwen*, the oldest Arthurian narrative, is a native Welsh sense that a unified, primeval, Welsh-speaking British polity never really existed, and that any language of reconquest is inherently flawed. This reconsideration of the bedrock of Welsh national mythology occurs when members of Arthur's retinue parlay with a group of talking animals in an effort to locate Mabon, the son of Modron, whose presence they require. The talking animals question Arthur's entitlement to Britain by speaking to his retinue in an aboriginal language that is unknown to them. They must rely on Gwrhyr the Interpreter, whose abilities extend to speaking the language of animals, to solicit information about Mabon from a series of geriatric creatures—a blackbird, a stag, an owl, an eagle, and a salmon—each of which is older than the last.

A salient point about these chatty, informative animals is that they are neither supernatural nor particularly magical by nature but are simply old, well connected, and open to inquiries. The Blackbird, the *Mwyalch Gilgwri*, establishes a language of deferral that successive animals use to redirect their human petitioners to yet older animals when he tells

Gwrhyr, "Kenedlaeth vileit yssyd gynt rithwys Duw no mi" [There is a type of creature God made before (he made) me].[12] Similar language is used by the Stag, the Owl, and the Eagle. This language of redirection is language of appeal to the authority of age, and it marks the animals in *Culhwch and Olwen* as sources to which the comparably far younger humans must turn for information. That Arthur's retinue must seek information from their elders the animals suggests a submerged, chthonic realm unknown to the humans of Arthur's world but recalled by the Oldest Animals.

The animals are eventually able to lead Arthur's retinue to the one of their number—the ancient Salmon of Llyn Llyw—that knows where Mabon is hidden away. But as the various animals defer to other, older authorities, a world of former epochs is evoked. The Blackbird recalls an anvil that it has ground down to nothing over the years by pecking at it with its beak. The Stag tells of an oak tree that he knew in his youth, which same tree he watched go from sapling to tall tree to red stump. The Owl situates the valley in which he lives in both geological and anthropological history by telling of its past as a succession of forests sometimes inhabited by older races of men. Finally, the Eagle remembers a giant stone on which he used to perch that by Arthur's time has been eroded to a hand's breadth in size.

By virtue of their age the Oldest Animals are able to represent themselves as authorities that greatly predate Arthur's kingdom: they are individually older than the humans who live in Britain, and their memories are longer than those of the people with whom they share the island. By virtue of their animality these creatures mark for themselves a place of privilege in the landscape of Britain. They are not quite coextensive with the land, but as undomesticated "wild" animals they are viscerally *of* it in a way that humans are not. By suggesting a tangible native history of which Arthur's retinue is unaware, the animals identify the Arthurian polity as one that is a successor to other, prior ones. The narrative of the Owl in particular conjures a sense of cyclical time, of recurring epochs, and hints that Arthurian Britain may be only the latest in a series of distinct Britains. The Owl says that when he was first in his valley it was a wooded glen: "y cwm mawr a welwch glynn coet oed," he says, continuing that "y deuth kenedlaeth o dynyon idaw, ac y diuawyt, ac y tyuwys yr eil coet yndaw," which is to say that there came a race of men [to that glen], and that it was laid waste, and then there was a second growth of trees. "A'r trydyd coet yw hwnn" [this is the third such wood], the Owl adds. The current occupants of the island of Britain are ignorant of their predecessors, and the prior ages recounted by the Owl are not marked as Arthurian prehistories, as ages awaiting fulfillment in the coming of

Arthur, but instead as other, distinct times. Arthur's polity, by implication, might one day fade into memory.

The animals' language also connects them to a prehistoric or
aboriginal insular past. The five animals encountered by Gwrhyr and
company appear to speak the same language. The Eagle of Gwernabwy
recounts having communicated with fish representatives of the Salmon of
Llyn Llyw after a comic episode in which the Eagle attempted to eat the
Salmon, only to be injured himself. In the presence of Gwrhyr the Eagle
at one point speaks directly to the Salmon, and the Salmon replies in
turn; the animals are depicted as speaking a kind of unified native animal
vernacular as opposed to eagle-speak, fish-speak, and so forth. Whatever
kind of aboriginal language this is, it is tied to ancient Britain in a way
that the human vernacular, Welsh, is not.

But what relevance might this supposed submerged polity, as embodied
in the ageing animals, have? As the Owl indicates, he has lived through
the coming of three forests and has witnessed the invasion of at least one
race of men and the plunder and deforestation that accompanied that
invasion. The Owl's account takes the form of native commentary on
centuries of invasions, marking Arthur and his people neither as originary Britons nor as the embodiments of a romanticized origin myth.
Instead, the members of Arthur's retinue are a people divorced from the
native traditions and language of the land that they inhabit and who
are dependent upon truly native intermediaries to negotiate that land's
secrets, one of which is the whereabouts of Mabon.

Mabon, like the Oldest Animals, is a figure deeply anchored in the
physical landscape of the island of Britain. His presence in the fifty-second
of the Welsh triads marks him as one of the Three Exalted Prisoners
of the Island of Britain, a man who is viscerally of the island.[13] Hence
"Mabon is not only the Great Prisoner, he was also the Immemorial
Prisoner—the Great Son who has been lost for aeons and is at last
found."[14] Ysbadadden Chief Giant takes it for granted that Culhwch
will be unable to locate Mabon, and without Gwrhyr and the Oldest
Animals Ysbadadden might well have been right. Mabon, although a
human figure, is unknown to the Arthurian regime; Mabon and the
Oldest Animals make clear to Arthur that he may inhabit the land but
he is not of it.

When the Oldest Animals question the originality of the Arthurian
polity in Britain they essentially question the mythological foundation
of what we might call early medieval Welsh national definition. As
R.R. Davies notes of Welsh self-identification with the ancient Britons,
it "was...a profound historical, political, and prophetic statement.
Historically it proclaimed that the Britons were the aboriginal and still

authentically the only true proprietors of the Island of Britain."[15] But the Britain that the Oldest Animals bring to mind is a nation whose quintessential ancient king, Arthur, is nothing but another occupier. Arthurian Britain, potentially essential for the purposes of creating a medieval Welsh national mythology, is here far from an idealized Welsh past.

The Oldest Animals act as a prism through which the Welsh imagination of Arthurian Britain ought to be viewed. Brynley F. Roberts explains Arthur's presence by arguing that the "Arthurian scene—king, companions, an acknowledged legend of exploits and death—was so well defined that Arthur could not be less than central in any narrative in which he appeared. His presence in any story was overpowering and could brook no competition."[16] This Arthur is a warlord monarch, the legend and personality of whom are of such a great magnitude that the tale must become an Arthurian one. The animals reflect back at this regime, this impressive "Arthurian scene," a seemingly unfeigned loyalty that is at once both genuine and politely restrained. The animals, after all, have seen other eras and possibly other kings before, and it may well be that they will see yet more.

There is a telling ambivalence in the animals' interactions with Arthur's men. The animals recognize Arthur's authority—the Blackbird makes that clear when he offers to lead Gwrhyr and company to an older animal. "Peth yssyd iawn, hagen, a dylyet ym i y wneuthur y gennadeu Arthur, mi a'e gwnaf" [That which is proper, my duty to Arthur's messengers, I shall do], he says. The animals' knowledge of the Arthurian government is deep enough that they recognize his deputies. Nevertheless, they act more as authorities of the natural world than they do subjects of a political regime. Their age and their memories afford them a somewhat indefinite position in the Arthurian polity, a peripheral yet deeply rooted position, in that polity and yet not of it. Whereas Arthur is accustomed to being a figure from whom boons and favors are asked, here his men must take on supplicating roles on his behalf.

In proposing that *Culhwch and Olwen*'s animal figures act as embodiments or mementoes of an extinguished aboriginal British state I also suggest that they evoke an implicitly transitory Arthurian polity, one that has been preceded in its geographical site and that, by extension, might itself be succeeded. Such speculation about the nature and duration of empires in Britain would have been of obvious interest to the audiences of *Culhwch and Olwen*. The tale—whether it dates to the last decades of the eleventh century, as Bromwich and Evans suggest in their edition, or to the middle or end of the twelfth century, as Simon Rodway has recently argued—is one that can be dated to a period that followed both numerous Anglo-Saxon invasions and the Norman Conquest.[17] Jeffrey Jerome Cohen formulates the twelfth-century policy of the Normans toward Wales as one that "employed multifarious strategies to annex those territories that dared to stand so invitingly at their borders," and this formulation—of Wales or Britain as always a vulnerable territory prone to consecutive invasions, as seductively ripe for repeated conquest—is palpable in the prehistoric Britain that the animals evoke.[18] *Culhwch and Olwen* looks skeptically in two ways, backward and forward, first by questioning the fixity of a British, Arthurian polity, and then by questioning the permanence of *all* British polities, including, by extension, those such as the English one that sought to conquer Wales.

Joan N. Radner, in her study of irony in *Culhwch and Olwen*, characterizes the national consciousness of the text as a "double" one, noting that during "an era in which Welshmen allied with strangers against Welshmen, and the territories defended by the historical Arthur had long since been lost to the English, literary portrayal of native warrior champions must inevitably have carried an ironic double consciousness."[19] The animals' representations of this double consciousness fluctuate between nostalgia for a Britain gone by and their constructive engagement with Gwrhyr and the rest of Arthur's men. To return to Radner, "to treat native Welsh tradition ironically in *Culhwch ac Olwen* was neither to exclude the outsiders and innovators nor to offend the traditionalists, but to share a sly wink with both, and to leave the interpretation of that wink quite open."[20] In other words, the ambivalence that I ascribe to *Culhwch and Olwen*'s treatment of the Arthurian polity ought to be read as an awareness of the inevitability of the endless invasions and migrations that defined the island of Britain from its prehistory. Although cold comfort, the possibility is held out that the nascent English empire might also fade after it too has had its epoch.

The Welsh origin myth, then, the dream of entitlement to the whole of the island of Britain, is both neutralized and reoriented such that the fixed memory of a Welsh-speaking Britain is demoted from historical centrality and instead cast as one of many British pasts. That this reconsideration comes as it does in the mist of a narrative in which King Arthur is one of the central figures is all the more telling: Arthur, stripped of the mythological baggage that would later be ascribed to him, exists in *Culhwch and Olwen* quite comfortably alongside other figures whose memories predate him and his government. This is a textually savvy move: in the presence of Arthur, *Culhwch and Olwen*'s audience is reminded that "their" island is prone to repeated conquests. The English, then, might be viewed as Arthur the warlord's inheritors, another race of men come to Britain to fell the woods and assume mastery of the island.

Complicity and Gain: *The Dream of Macsen Wledig*

The possibility that a foreign prince might occupy the Arthurian role is present in Middle Welsh prose from its earliest Arthurian narrative. It is for another *Mabinogion* tale, however, to explore the possibilities open to Wales that might result from a foreign occupation. *The Dream of Macsen Wledig* imagines an invasion of ancient Britain by a Roman emperor, Macsen Wledig, and then lays out a design of native complicity by which, as the tale illustrates, the Welsh-speaking peoples might carve out a miniature empire for themselves by creating a role for their province in the larger imperial unit of which they find themselves a part. Although the conquest effected in *Macsen Wledig* is Roman, the colonial aggression faced by its audience was English, suggesting a contemporary relevance for *Macsen Wledig*'s rhetoric of complicity.

Macsen Wledig is a narrative of desire. It is not, however, a narrative in which only the desires of the colonizer are realized. Instead it is a text that is primarily concerned with defining the agency of the colonized, with determining how and in what way a colonized space, a province, can exert influence on an empire as a whole. Likewise at hand is the crucial question of what benefit a province can derive from its domination by or integration into an empire. The tale begins, as many tales of conquest do, with a vision of desire. Emperor Macsen's is for Elen, a woman of whom he dreams while he naps during an afternoon of hunting outside of Rome: "Morwyn a welei yn eisted rac e vron e mewn cadeir o rudeur nyt oet haws edrech arnei na disgwyl noc ar er heul pan vyd taeraf a thecaf rac y theket hitheu" [He (then) saw a maiden sitting before him in a chair of red gold. It was no easier to look upon her because of her beauty than to look upon the sun when it is the most fierce].[21] So far so good: Macsen dreams of a woman who is the figuration of a land that will become a part of his empire. This vision so stimulates Macsen that he sends a deputation to Wales and then invades; the seductive nature of Wales is both literal and unstoppable.

Next, *Macsen Wledig* advocates a savvy, almost Machiavellian political strategy for conquered lands when Elen and her brothers engage with Macsen. After Elen surrenders her body to Macsen she demands her maiden price [*hagwedi*], and at this moment the roles are reversed and Macsen, who has taken Elen's body, is in a position not to make demands but to fulfill them. Elen seizes personal and national agency for herself; after Macsen lays claim to her body she lays almost reciprocal claim to the accoutrements of civilization that Macsen can provide. She demands roads and castles, defensive fortifications against future invaders and insular rivals, and she has her father made viceroy of Britain, Macsen's under-king there. The native

Britons adopt a policy of happy complicity rather than forlorn resistance in response to Macsen's conquest; they eagerly and quickly respond to his amorous and martial desires with demands of their own.

The national agency that the Britons have is apparent from the outset of Macsen's interest in Elen. After having dreamt of her, Macsen sends a deputation to Britain to find this woman of his dreams. His nobles locate and approach Elen, who, keenly aware that the ball is in her court, tells the nobles that while she does not doubt their claims—that she is the beloved of the Emperor of Rome—she does not overmuch believe them, either, saying: "Namen os mivi a gar er amperauder, deuet hyt eman e'm ol" [If, therefore, I am the love of the emperor, then let him come here after me].[22] Although it could be said that Elen is merely being coy or playing hard to get, Elen's refusal to go to Rome—and her demand that Macsen come to Britain—shifts the locus of imperial power to Britain, enabling its fortification and the propulsion of her family to its lordship.

The native Britons are certainly ready for Macsen when he arrives to claim his empress. Elen's brothers, Cynon and Gadeon, kill time while awaiting him by playing *gwydbuyll*, surely plotting their next moves all the while, and their father sits nearby, carving *gwydbuyll* pieces as Elen sits in her throne, seemingly awaiting her destiny.[23] Cynon and Gadeon bide their time after Macsen arrives and begins to rule, with Elen, from Britain. Elen's family strategize over the *gwydbuyll* board for years as Macsen has Roman soil [gweryt Ruvein] brought from Italy so that he can graft a little bit of home on to the ground of his new province. Elen's male relatives lurk in the background of Macsen's polity for seven years until they are able to be of use to their new lord.

The emperor's Roman cronies have a custom amongst them that any emperor who has gone missing for seven years is automatically dethroned and replaced, and after Macsen has kept house with Elen and been absent from Rome for that long his erstwhile lieges send him word of his deposition. At this development Macsen invades the continent, but he finds himself stymied at the gates of Rome. For all his martial prowess in the provinces, Macsen gets nowhere besieging his home city, and the stalemate drags on for a whole year. After this fruitless year Elen's brothers seize the opportunity to display to their colonial master the usefulness of his new subjects. This they do when they realize that Macsen, probably dethroned because of Roman fears that he had gone native during his seven years in Wales, has deviated not one bit from Roman culinary customs. This is to say that both the Romans and Macsen's party stop fighting when they break for lunch. Such niceties are as eminently polite as they are eminently ineffective as a war strategy. This seems obvious only to the Britons, who vow to fight in a wiser way [nini a geisswn ymlad a'r gaer yn gallach no hyn].[24] The strategic innovation proposed by the Britons is remarkably successful: they drink all morning, and then, in high spirits (they are *brwysc*, or drunk), they scale the walls of Rome with ladders, thereby recapturing for Macsen his throne. Such tactics hardly amount to high chivalry, but they do work.

The small band of provincials that so easily overcomes the imperial defense force is a testament to the importance of injecting fresh blood into a seemingly sclerotic body politic. Macsen brought the Britons roads and castles, the trappings of civilization, and in return they lent him their might as mercenaries. The stereotype of the eternally abused colonial subject falls away here, and instead we see a complimentary relationship between, as it were, junior and senior partners. Yet another stereotype that falls away is that of the rustic, clueless Welshman, the depiction so common to romance. These Welshmen are canny, tactical, and shrewd. Their presence is not only useful but also integral to Macsen's designs and to the tale's resolution.

Why, then, is *Macsen Wledig*'s depiction of Welsh interaction with Roman imperial power one that encourages eager complicity? Certainly the ancient rhetoric of Welsh entitlement to the whole of Britain was no longer suited to political realities. *Macsen Wledig* recognizes this as well as the need to craft a new British position for Wales. *Macsen Wledig* mines native historical and mythological lore for a memorial antecedent to the English occupation, and it does so by rediscovering the Roman occupation. Just as Huw Pryce has argued that the replacement of the terminology of "Briton" and "British" with that of "Welsh" and "Wales" does not indicate Welsh fatalism but adaptability to circumstance and necessity, so too do I argue that this narrative's exhortation of the useful-ness of empire reflects pragmatic post-Norman Welsh sensibilities about the possibility of belonging—or belonging again—to an empire.

In *Macsen Wledig* the medieval Welsh state—or, perhaps more correctly, the Welsh-speaking part of Britain—articulates a strategy more politically efficacious than that of resistance born of proud if outmoded mythology. Wales in the Middle Ages could gaze across the Marches at a country that had valiantly and vainly attempted to halt an invasion force. The failure of this attempt resulted in the wholesale mauling of the local vernacular, the slaughter of most of the native nobles, and the eventual reorganization of the polity along foreign lines. Such a sea change in England must have caused ripples in Wales, and by the mid-thirteenth century, when Welsh eyes had seen the Anglo-Saxons become Anglo-Normans, the results of a full-scale cultural and political invasion must have been obvious. With the English steadily asserting their power not only in the Marches but also in the heart of Wales after the late thirteenth century, Welsh minds would quite logically have concerned themselves with making the best of a bad situation. To quote Patrick Sims-Williams, "It is a commonplace of modern anthropology that origin stories are influenced by current realities."[25] I would add that the political preoccupations of this text, a tale of the origins of Wales as a colony, ought to be viewed as the political preoccupations of the culture that produced it.

The abiding concern of *Macsen Wledig*, the goal of the Welsh complicity that I am identifying, is the preservation of the Welsh language. The Britons' reward for recapturing Macsen's throne is Brittany. The Brittany of *Macsen Wledig* is not another Celtic nation that might someday ally itself with the Welsh to retake Britain. *This* Brittany is full of men who need to be slaughtered and women who need to have their tongues cut out so that British speech—Welsh, that is—will not be corrupted by the native language. Here is the fruit of Welsh cooperation with Romans: their language is allowed to survive unscathed. Roman imperial authority, backed by Welsh military force, allows the Welsh a free hand in Brittany and the power to maintain their culture.

At the center of the positioning of medieval political sensibilities as classical history is the sense that the redactors of this tale were well aware of contemporary political developments and were concerned with how best to grapple with them and to incorporate them into the corpus of native Welsh literature. *Macsen Wledig* demonstrates for its audience that cooperating with an occupying power and maintaining the integrity of Welsh culture and the Welsh language are by no means mutually exclusive. In fact, the skilful manipulation of foreign perceptions of Wales is crucial to the perpetuation of Welsh identity. Such a claim is hardly revolutionary. I point again to Huw Pryce, who argues that a similar process informed the shift in the terminology the Welsh people used to refer to themselves in the Middle Ages. He writes that to "adopt names such as *Wallia* and *Walenses* did not mean that the Welsh rejected their British inheritance, still less that they ceased to think of themselves and their country as *Cymry*."[26] Just as it was politically expedient in the twelfth century for Welsh writers to adopt a foreign term for their country while retaining, amongst themselves, the native term, so too was it politically expedient a few centuries later to propose that accommodating the desires of an occupying power might well result in the fulfillment of native ambitions—in this case, the maintenance of the vernacular. The message here is clear: be useful to the occupiers and they will leave us alone, or at least leave us unmolested.[27] The text's decision to include the detail that Macsen drove the prior king of Britain, Beli, into the sea is a reminder of the consequences of adhering to a different strategy.

Into England, Into Britain

Where, then, do these and similar readings situate Wales in relation to the wider British archipelago? Most broadly, they craft for Wales a role in the margin of a larger neighbor. In *Culhwch and Olwen* and *The Dream of Macsen Wledig*, Wales is growing used to the dimensions of the geographical space it inhabited in the Middle Ages and continues to inhabit today. By relinquishing memories of the supposed Welsh dominion over all Britain the medieval contours of Wales are normalized, and Wales becomes its own, entire space rather than the remnant of an ancient and divided whole. These tales gently remind their audience that it would be incorrect to think of Britain as *no longer* a unified, Welsh-speaking state. Instead, Britain was *never really* or *never only* a unified, Welsh-speaking state.

Such a revised formulation disputes the view that Welsh political actors in the Middle Ages seriously looked back at a unitary Britain with an eye toward recreating it in their own time. Although medieval Wales was certainly aware of the physical bounds of the island of Britain, it would be a mistake to conflate geographical awareness with a political ambition. To assert, as R.R. Davies does, that the idea of Britain "presented a prospect of unity and simplicity in what was a fragmented and fissile world" lends too much credence to a historically questionable, mythic British state. Likewise, that the Anglo-Saxon kings of England occasionally took to referring to themselves as masters of Britain does not necessarily indicate that the "rulership of Britain was clearly part and parcel of [the] ambitions and vanities" of the English.[28] Might it not be that such titular pretensions of the Anglo-Saxon kings might have been intended for domestic consumption? Only after Athelstan "had *recovered* York in 927" (italics mine) did he purport to the title *rex totius Britanniae* by inscribing it on his coinage. We should not read too far into such acts, nor should we be quick ascribe to such boasts implications more suitable for later periods: the propaganda of Edward I differs from the affectations of Athelstan, who was almost certainly more bent on bringing the Vikings to heel in England than he was on conquering his Briton neighbors. There certainly was an "idea of Britain" in medieval England and Wales, but it was not always of an ancient unitary polity.

The geographical recentering that the *Mabinogion* undertakes through distancing itself from a mythic past leaves us with a text that is very much of its period, and one that is profoundly medieval. To conclude such a synchronic reading, I wish to direct my gaze to a vision in the *Mabinogion* not of history but of contemporary life, of the world that the

Mabinogion's audience would have known. It is a vision of Hereford, a symbolic limit of England, beyond which lies the great expanse of Wales. Hereford is where Manawydan and Pryderi go to earn livings in the third branch of the *Mabinogi*, and *Manawydan*'s depictions of this border city are exactly what we might expect of a medieval English city with a bustling market: artisans fashion and sell their wares, compete for business and profit, and labor ceaselessly to drive under their competitors. Manawydan and Pryderi enter this mercantile world by becoming saddlers, and they become so successful at their new venture that they threaten to drive their English competition out of business. The other saddlers of Hereford, no doubt irate that upstart aliens are stealing their customers, choose to meet the threat to their prosperity head-on, and they conspire to kill the Welshmen. Thus are Manawydan and Pryderi forced to flee Hereford and to ambulate through the border towns of England, plying a new trade in each city. They are so successful at each new venture they undertake that they have to escape envious English rival artisans routinely, and only after they debase themselves completely by becoming shoemakers do they give up and return to Wales: "Nac ef," says Manawydan, "gwnawn grydyaeth; ny byd o galhon gan grydyon nac ymlad a ni nac ymwarauun [We shall take to shoemaking; shoemakers lack the courage to fight or to hinder us],"[29] he says, mistaken in this case, as they are soon forced to leave the England for good and return to Wales.

The language of *Manawydan* delights in exploring the vivid world of English commerce. Manawydan and Pryderi make shoes from fine cordwain [*cordwal*] they purchase ready-made from the tanners and use tougher, less expensive leather for the soles: "And then he began to buy the fairest cordwain he found in town. And no other leather than that did he buy except the leather of the soles" [Ac yna dechreu prynu y cordwal teccaf a gauas yn y dref. Ac amgen ledyr no hwnnw ny phrynei ef eithyr lledyr guadneu].[30] Once they have made their shoes they adorn them with fine golden buckles they have learnt from the town's goldsmiths how to make. The Welsh language easily accommodates an array of specific commodity and market-related terms, happily importing those it lacks.[31] Exploring the developing market economy next door is eminently possible for a Middle Welsh text, and *Manawydan* playfully satirizes the differences between England and Wales by marking England as a nation in which people work for livings, manufacture crafts, and trade with one another. Wales, on the other hand, is a realm whose residents are sometimes turned into mice by malevolent sorcerers. *Manawydan*'s synchronic gesture, then, is to indicate that Wales, for all its proud mythology and supposed otherness, is well able not only to operate in but also to succeed in a transnational medieval market economy.

So too might Wales succeed in existing next to England, the proverbial elephant, and so too might the Welsh language be perpetuated thereby. *Manawydan*'s playful vision of Welsh ability is striking in both its optimism and its pragmatism. Welsh people are described as just as economically canny and artistically gifted as their English neighbors— more so, in fact. Richly implicit in *Manawydan* is the prospect that Welsh people might replicate the economic vitality of Hereford and the border towns in their own land. Taken together, the various strands of political counsel that I identify in the *Mabinogion* reveal a medieval Wales that is actively fashioning for itself a role in a reoriented British archipelago even as the *Mabinogion* itself advances its own objective of perpetuating its language of composition—and ensuring itself a future audience.

Notes

1. Ivan L. Head and Pierre Elliot Trudeau, *The Canadian Way: Shaping Canada's Foreign Policy, 1968–1984* (Toronto: McLellan & Stewart, 1995), 179.

2. Patricia Clare Ingham puts the point similarly in "Marking Time: *Branwen, Daughter of Llyr* and the Colonial Refrain." "When viewed from the perspective of England's colonial aggressions vis-à-vis the so-called Celtic Fringe," she writes, "the 'Red Book' manuscript becomes politically provocative." Patricia Clare Ingham, "Marking Time: *Branwen, Daughter of Llyr* and the Colonial Refrain," in *The Postcolonial Middle Ages*, ed. Jeffrey Jerome Cohen (New York: Palgrave Macmillan), 179.

3. From *The Oxford English Dictionary* and *A Concise Anglo-Saxon Dictionary*, ed. J.R. Clark Hall (Toronto: University of Toronto Press, 1960). See also David A. E. Pelteret, *Slavery in Early Mediaeval England: From the Reign of Alfred until the Twelfth Century* (Woodbridge: Boydell Press, 1995), which contains an excellent appendix on *wealh*.

4. Huw Pryce, "British or Welsh? National Identity in Twelfth-Century Wales," in *English Historical Review* 116 (2001): 780 [774–801].

5. R.R. Davies, *The First English Empire: Power and Identities in the British Isles 1093–1343* (Oxford: Oxford University Press, 2000), 4.

6. The population of Wales in the early fourteenth century can be reckoned at about 300,000, while the population of England at the same period, just prior to the coming of the Black Death, can be estimated at anywhere between two-and-a-half and four million. John Davies, *A History of Wales* (London: Allen Lane, Penguin Press, 1993), 186–87 and May McKisack, *The Oxford History of England: The Fourteenth Century, 1307–1399* (Oxford: Clarendon Press, 1959), 312–13.

7. R.R. Davies, *The Revolt of Owain Glyn Dwr* (Oxford: Oxford University Press, 1995), 23.

8. See Andrew Welsh, "'*Manwaydan fab Llyr*: Wales, England, and the New Man" and Catherine A. McKenna, "The Theme of Sovereignty

in *Pywll*," in *The Mabinogi: A Book of Essays*, ed. C.W. Sullivan III (New York: Garland, 1996), 121–41 and 303–30.

9. McKenna, "The Theme of Sovereignty," 303.

10. Welsh, "*Manawydan fab Llyr*," 126.

11. Gerald of Wales, *The Journey Through Wales and The Description of Wales*, 265–74.

12. *Culhwch and Olwen: An Edition and Study of the Oldest Arthurian Tale*, eds. Rachel Bromwich and D. Simon Evans (Cardiff: University of Wales Press, 1992). All of my citations of *Culhwch and Olwen* are to this edition. The Oldest Animals sequence runs between lines 839 and 919 on pp. 31–33.

13. *Trioedd Ynys Prydein*, 3rd edn. ed. Rachel Bromwich (Cardiff: University of Wales Press, 2006), 146–49.

14. W.J. Gruffydd, "Mabon vab Modron," in *Y Cymmrodor*, XLII:142 [129–47].

15. Davies, *The First English Empire*, 44.

16. Brynley F. Roberts, "*Culhwch and Olwen*, the Triads, Saints' Lives," in *The Arthur of the Welsh*, ed. Rachel Bromwich, A.O.H. Jarman, and Brynley F. Roberts (Cardiff: University of Wales Press, 1991), 79.

17. *Culhwch and Olwen*, ed., Bromwich and Evans, lxxxi, and Simon Rodway, "The Date and Authorship of *Culhwch and Olwen*: A Reassessment," in *Cambrian Medieval Celtic Studies* 49 (Summer 2005): 21–44.

18. Jeffrey Jerome Cohen, "Hybrids, Monsters, and Borderlands: The Bodies of Gerald of Wales," in *The Postcolonial Middle Ages*, ed. Jeffrey Jerome Cohen (New York: Palgrave, 2000), 86.

19. Joan N. Radner, "Interpreting Irony in Medieval Celtic Narrative: The Case of *Culhwch and Olwen*," *Cambridge Medieval Celtic Studies* 16 (Winter 1988): 56 [41–60].

20. Radner, "Interpreting Irony," 56.

21. *Breudwyt Maxen Wledic*, ed. Brynley F. Roberts (Dublin: Dublin Institute for Advanced Studies, 2005), ll. 67–69, p. 3. All my citations of *Macsen Wledig* are to this edition.

22. *Breudwyt Maxen Wledic*, ll. 195–96, p. 7.

23. *Gwydbuyll* is the Modern Welsh word for chess; in the Middle Ages it was a similar game of strategy in which a piece that represented a king was defended from attack by other game-pieces.

24. *Breudwyt Maxen Wledic*, l. 274, p. 9.

25. Patrick Sims-Williams, "Some Functions of Origin Stories in Early Medieval Wales," in *History and Heroic Tale: A Symposium*, ed. Tore Nyberg, Iørn Piø, Preben Meulengracht Sørensen, and Aage Trommer (Odense: Odense University Press, 1985), 103.

26. Pryce, "British or Welsh?" 799.

27. See Davies, *The First English Empire*, esp. 142–71.

28. Davies, *The First English Empire*, 36–37.

29. *Manawydan fab Llyr*, ed. Patrick K. Ford (Belmont: Ford and Bailie, 2000), ll. 146–47, p. 4.

30. *Manawydan fab Llyr*, ed. Ford, ll. 151–54, p. 5.

31. The term *hossan*, defined in the glossary as a "protective leg covering, reaching down to the foot or covering the top part of the foot," is an example. *Hossan* might be glossed merely as hose, but it clearly carries a weightier and more specific connotation. A Germanic term, its Welsh and Cornish forms are loan-words from English (OED).

CHAPTER 10

CHAUCER AND THE WAR
OF THE MAIDENS

John M. Ganim

The legendary history of the origin of the Czech dynasty, with its account of a matriarchal founder and Amazonian rebels, probably accompanied Anne of Bohemia to England, where she became Richard II's Queen. These legends may underlie the alternation of agency and compliance found in the female characters in Chaucer's works traditionally associated with Anne.

This chapter has a relatively simple thesis, but since this thesis is developed by a circumstantial route, it would be best to state it at the beginning. That is, the treatment of the Amazons in Chaucer's Knight's Tale is informed by accounts of the legendary origins of Bohemia in a female leader who surrenders her authority at the same time that a concomitant Amazon-like insurrection of maidens who refuse to so surrender is suppressed. Given the association of so many of Chaucer's works with Anne of Bohemia, who becomes the queen of Richard II, I conjecture that Chaucer might well have known of this legendary history. Such a legend, however, would have been relatively inflammatory, adding to the paranoia about Anne's foreign origins and Richard's purported alternations of vacillation and rashness. Whether coincidental or intentional, instead of any direct reference, the rhythms of the legendary history of Bohemia are dispersed through certain of Chaucer's works, becoming part of their political unconscious.

Prologue: Islands upon the Land

In a still influential book, *Southern California Country: An Island on the Land*, the journalist Carey McWilliams, writing in the 1930s, captured

the urban contradictions of the region in the language of his subtitle.[1]
McWilliams was alluding to a famous legend apparently grounded in
Garcí Rodriguez Ordóñez de Montalvo's sequel to the popular chivalric
romance, *Amadis of Gaul*, first printed in 1508 by Montalvo himself, *Las
Sergas de Esplandían* [The Adventures of Esplandian], printed in 1510:
"On the right hand of the Indies, there is an island called California, very
close to the side of the Terrestrial Paradise, and it was peopled by black
women, without any man among them, for they lived in the fashion of
Amazons."[2] These women feed their male children and captured males
to griffins:

> They were of strong and hardy bodies, of ardent courage and great force.
> Their island was the strongest in all the world, with its steep cliffs and
> rocky shores. Their arms were all of gold, and so was the harness of the
> wild beasts which they tamed and rode. For, in the whole island, there was
> no metal but gold. They lived in caves wrought out of the rock with much
> labor. They had many ships with which they sailed out to other countries
> to obtain booty...In this island...there were many griffins, on account of
> the great ruggedness of the country, and its infinite host of wild beasts,
> such as never were seen in any other part of the world. And when these
> griffins were yet small, the women went out with traps to take them.
> They covered themselves over with very thick hides, and when they had
> caught the little griffins, they took them to their caves, and brought them
> up there. And being themselves quite a match for the griffins, they fed
> them with the men whom they took prisoners, and with the boys to whom
> they gave birth...Every man who landed on the island was immediately
> devoured by these griffins; and although they had had enough, none the
> less would they seize them and carry them high up in the air, in their
> flight, and when they were tired of carrying them, would let them fall
> anywhere as soon as they died.[3]

Eventually, Califia finds her way to Europe, takes part in both the attack
and defense of Constantinople, and is involved with both Amadis of Gaul
and Esplandian. California, it is suspected by some, got its name because
Cortez had read The Adventures of Esplandian. This at any rate, was the
argument of the American writer Edward Everett Hale, who translated
part of the novel and published it in *The Atlantic Monthly* in 1864, as the
Civil War was ending and only a bit more than a decade since California
became part of the United States.[4] McWilliams was probably pointing to
some of the themes in his own history of California, one of them being
its troubled history of racial and ethnic tension.

Such a connection between legend and material reality may well
be unsurprising to medievalists familiar with national origin myths.

According to the California African-American Heritage Preservation and Restoration Society, "Queen Califia is common knowledge among professors of medieval literature."[5] In my casual queries of colleagues, it turns out to be an obscure reference even among them, but it used to be a sort of secret code among poets and sexual rebels, at least until the secret went public in 2001 during the renovation of Disneyland. At the annex to Disneyland, called "California Adventure," there is a theater decorated with a mural depicting Califia. Inside, there is a brief wide-screen film called Golden Dreams directed by Agnieszka Holland, with the voice of Whoopi Goldberg as Califia, the queen of California. One of Niki de Saint Phalle's last projects was "Queen Califia's Magical Circle" in Escondido, California. Califia emerges from the cultural underground to be a spokeswoman for a newly multicultural California.

As Patrick Geary has demonstrated, the presence of females as a necessary element in the founding of a people in origin myths is often followed by the disappearance or the subjugation of women in the longer narrative of such a history. Sometimes these founding mothers are Amazons, sometimes prophetesses or seers, and sometimes significant political movers and shakers. But as Geary notes, the crucial question in such narratives is the uses and purposes of the narration itself, rather than the recovery or dismissal of a legendary past.[6] Califia is a good example of how variously these legends can be employed.

The story of Califia will immediately recall the fantastic accounts of the settlement of Britain that accreted around the Brut legend. Some prequels to Geoffrey of Monmouth's account of the founding of Britain, specifically the Anglo-Norman *Des Grantz Geanz*, the *Anonymous Riming Chronicle*, and the *Prose Brut*, tell an alternative female origin story.[7] Albina and her many sisters plot to murder their husbands. The plot is leaked by the youngest sister and the women escape by sea to an island that Albina names after herself, hence Albion. They cohabit with a devil, giving birth to the giants who inhabit Britain until the coming of Brutus, who defeats the giants. There was also a female origin myth, told and retold in different versions that traced the origin of Scotland back to one Scotia, a daughter of the Pharaoh of Egypt, who flees the plagues during the time of Moses. In an influential version propounded by Hector Boece in his history of Scotland, her husband is a Greek named Gathelus, who serves the Pharaoh's armies under Moses and succeeds him as commander.[8] The legend of Scotia functions as an anti-Brut, even to the point of providing a positive female point of origin. And it is possible that the Albina myth was propounded as a response to the Scotia legend, framing female origins as monstrously unstable rather than foundationally sound.

Magic Prague

Of the various origin myths of European nations, early Czech, especially Bohemian, history was most closely associated with a spectacular story of female origin with Amazonian overtones. According to the medieval historian of Bohemia, Cosmas of Prague, the area is settled by one Boemus, who initiates a communal paradise for many generations, in which women hunt and arm themselves like Amazons and where men and women dress alike. Prague itself is founded by Libuše, one of the three daughters of a wise chief of the people called Crocco. Despite her abilities, she is pressured by her subjects to choose a husband, so that the land can become as virile and severe as other nations. She warns against the oppression that can result from such a change, but uses her visionary powers to identify a future husband, one Přemysl, a sort of Cincinnatus, who is to be found plowing his lands on the banks of the river Bila with two oxen. Meanwhile, we are told, the young women of Bohemia are founding their own city of virgins and refuse to submit to this new patriarchal order. The young men of the region, unable to take the city by force, enter under false pretenses and carry off and rape the young women, destroying the city.

Cosmas' rhetoric is striking in the verbal power it accords to Libuše. Here is her speech agreeing to be married, but warning about the consequences of a male Duke to whom the people of Bohemia would now have to submit:

> O most pitiable people, who are ignorant of their freedom, which no good man gives up except with his life. You flee that freedom and willingly submit to a servitude you have never known. Alas, in vain you will lament it later, just as the frogs lamented making the snake their king, when he began killing them. If you are ignorant of the legal power of a duke, I will try to tell you briefly. It is easy to put a leader in power, but it is difficult to remove him. For he who is now under your power, whether or not you constitute him as a duke, when you do so appoint him, you and all that is yours will be under his power. Your knees will knock in his presence and your silent tongue will adhere to your dry mouth. You will quake when you hear his voice, answering only with "Yes, lord, yes lord," because without your preknowledge and by his order alone, he can condemn one person and execute another, send one to prison and hang another. He will make you and yours as he pleases some into servants, others into peasants, some into taxpayers, or others into tax collectors, some into torturers, others into public criers, others into cooks, bakers and millers. He will set up tribunes, centurions, villagers, cultivators of vines and reapers of fields, makers of arms, shoemakers of different hides and leathers. He will take your sons and daughters to be under him, and the best of your horses

and mares and cows and oxen. All that now belongs to you, whatever he prefers, of town and farm, of field, of vineyard, of meadow, he will take by force and bring back for his own use.[9]

Cosmas' account of Libuše's speech is quite extraordinary for its time, although Cosmas chronicle coincides roughly with the Peace of God, with its strong condemnation of feudal violence. Libuše also directs the founding of the city of Prague through a vision. Her followers are to follow the river until they come to a man putting up a doorway to a house in the middle of a forest, and because even a great lord must bow his head to enter a doorway (playing on the pun of the Czech word for "threshold" and Praha), they are to build their city there. Interestingly, Libuše, having agreed to marry, chooses, or rather prophetizes, her own future lord and bridegroom. She sends her followers to a bend in a small river where the future king, Přemysl, is ploughing his field with two oxen. Přemysl's dynasty rules the Bohemians through the early fourteenth century.

The legends of Libuše and the origin of Prague are put to many different uses in later accounts. An example from the early fourteenth century is called the Dalimil Chronicle. It retells the legend as a call to resist Germanization, giving Libuše's speech a new emphasis on independence and sovereignty.[10] There is some disagreement as to whether the Dalimil chronicle reflects the antifeminism of late medieval Czech culture. Alfred Thomas, for instance, has described in detail the Dalimil chronicle, where the same events are renarrated to justify the rape of the Bohemian virgins, who are described as insidious and treacherous, and in Thomas' analysis, Dalimil defends the rights of the lower nobility, and a Czech identity symbolized by their masculinity, over and against a larger imperial and multinational notion of Czech identity.[11] Conversely, John Klassen reads Dalimil as one of the wide range of late medieval Czech works that provided models of active and independent behavior for women of the time, noting that Dalimil protests against foreign royal marriages.[12] What does seem to be clear is that the War of the Maidens was subject to different and conflicting interpretations, not only in contemporary scholarship, but in the fourteenth century.[13] This is important because during Chaucer's lifetime, and partly with his admittedly minor assistance, Anne of Bohemia becomes the Queen of England.

A Scandal in Bohemia

Richard II married Anne of Bohemia in 1382, though the negotiations went on for some time before that and Anne had arrived in England in 1381. The consensus is that the "Knight's Tale" dates from about 1386.

There is a long tradition of scholarship that seeks to attempt to connect the tale with the occasion of Richard's marriage, especially since Chaucer, as a courtier and a diplomat, had been involved in negotiations of this and previous possible marriages for Richard.[14] Richard himself was deeply in love with Anne, and when she died in the 1390s, he had their castle at Shene burned to the ground in an extravagant act of mourning. Traditionally viewed as a passive and decorative queen, recent studies have instead pointed to her literacy, her cultivation, her diplomatic sophistication, and her willingness to intercede in affairs of state. While older biographical accounts of Chaucer's development often emphasized the actual or fictional importance of Anne as a patron, they tended to reflect the anti-Ricardian tone of many of the chronicles and assumed that Chaucer condescended to the Queen's taste or resented the conventionality of her commissions. Exceptions to this earlier consensus began appearing in the 1980s, when, for instance, Donald R. Howard's biography of Chaucer read Richard's marriage negotiations and Chaucer's involvement with them as one of the primary motivations of much of Chaucer's work from *The House of Fame* to *The Parliament of Foules*.[15] Indeed, the importance of Anne of Bohemia in the development of Chaucer as a poet has been one of the most interesting strains in recent Chaucer scholarship. Chief among these contributions have been David Wallace's argument that Anne and her cultural cultivation allowed Chaucer to synchronize his interests in French courtly style and Italian humanist thought, and that her death caused him to abandon the political integrity he had thus achieved.[16] Wallace was expanding upon Paul Strohm's classic account of Anne's difficult political position and the relative agency she demonstrated in the strictures of the highly ritualized intercessionary gestures expected of queens that in fact only allowed male rulers to exercise their own options, rather than forcing them to reconsider their own policy.[17] Andrew Taylor has detailed the literary sophistication of Anne's court.[18] Carolyn Collette has tried to redefine Anne's role and Chaucer's analogue to it as more seriously advisory than previous accounts.[19] Arrestingly, Nancy Bradbury Warren, without mentioning the Bohemian materials, noted the strong emphasis on Amazon themes in works by Chaucer associated with Anne.[20] The tremendous explosion of Lollard studies over the past few decades have alerted us to the intense traffic between Wycliffite circles in England and Hussite developments in Bohemia. As the daughter of Charles IV, King of Bohemia and Holy Roman Emperor, and half sister of the present King of Bohemia, her status was significant, especially as it played into shifting English and French papal machinations. At the same time, however, the marriage of Richard and Anne was met by highly negative comments from some directions. The Westminster Chronicle complains about a dowry exorbitant "pro tantilla carnis porcine."[21] Elsewhere, her attractiveness is impugned and predictably xenophobic rants blamed her for introducing outlandish Bohemian fashions. While England cements its connections with Rome over the next few decades as part of an anti-French policy, anxieties remain over a marriage to a daughter of a Holy Roman Emperor.

We do know something about Richard II's books, and about Anne's probable reading.[22] There is no evidence that any of the Czech chronicles found their way to England with her. Given the difficult position that foreign queens found themselves in, one would doubt whether Anne and her courtiers would bring along with them a history of Bohemia, and, certainly not one with the implications of the chronicles containing the War of the Maidens. Still, Chaucer, even if he had not read Cosmas of Prague, would likely have known something about the remarkable myths surrounding the foundation of Bohemia, even if he would have been skeptical about them, as he seemed to have been about the legendary history of Britain, to which he alludes to only ironically or indirectly.[23]

Feminine Masquerade

If Chaucer did know of the legendary history of the Czechs, what are the implications for our understanding of his works? Why, for instance, would Chaucer never mention the legend directly? While Libuše and her legend were still common knowledge among fourteenth-century Bohemians, versions of the story such as the Dalimil Chronicle emphasized a strong anti-German, xenophobic, regional, and proto-nationalist slant at odds with the international claims of the Holy Roman Empire ruled by Anne's family. Moreover, with anxiety already high about Richard's rule and his foreign queen, it may not have been politic to advertise a heritage of armed female separatists and influential prophetesses. Chaucer, with his famous caution, may not have found it appropriate to mention the legends directly. At the same time, the legends of Libuše and the maidens also provided images that would have allayed these anxieties. The defeat of the maidens, at least according to Cosmas of Prague, resulted in the subservience of Bohemian women to their husbands. Libuše's willingness to accede to the demands of her people and marry, but, unlike Walter in the Clerk's Tale, also to give up her leadership role and to assume the role of wise adviser and guide, provided a model of how to acquire influence by giving up power. The pattern of the opening of the Knight's Tale, when we meet the defeated Amazons as highly feminine figures and often assuming poses of supplication, replicates the overall corresponding pattern of some versions of the legendary history of Bohemia. The

Amazonian materials acquired a new and unstable charge with the arrival and marriage of Anne of Bohemia to Richard II.

In the opening of the "Knight's Tale," the first of Chaucer's *Canterbury Tales*, Duke Theseus is returning from his conquest of the "land of Feminye," located in Scythia, where he has defeated the Amazons and taken their Queen, Hyppolita, as his captive bride. Accompanying them is her beautiful younger sister Emilye. Emilye's first extended description in the "Knight's Tale" presents her as an embodiment of womanly perfection, perfectly natural in her unselfconscious grace: "She walketh up and doun, and as hire liste/She gadereth floures, party white and rede,/To make a subtil gerland for hire hede;/And as an angel hevenyshly she soong" (I:1033–1055).[24] This description associates Emilye with the flowers she is gathering, with the sense of youth implicit in the morning and with spring. As natural as the scene may be, it is also a highly ritualized activity. Susan Crane has noted that Emilye is in effect gathering flowers as if for a Maying.[25] Presented as an innocent activity, and perhaps understood by Emilye as a return to her earlier state of freedom and ease with the wild, it nevertheless becomes the focus of the gaze of Palomon and Arcite from their prison cell. Her apparently innocent beauty triggers their ferocious internecine struggle. Yet only in the most indirect ways are we made aware of Emilye's subjectivity.

Turning to parallel scenes in Boccaccio's *Teseide*, however, makes us aware of how radically Chaucer has limited our access to Emilye's subjectivity. Chaucer presents Emilye as well-nigh perfect, but that perfection is not so much a perfection of character as it as a fulfillment of a feminine ideal extolled time and again in medieval romance and lyric poetry. Such an ideal, by the fourteenth century, was peculiarly abstract, removed from specific portraiture. For Chaucer to foreground that perfect female essence, however, requires the suppression of Emilye's identity as found in his sources, which is to say her previous life as an Amazon. Such a suppression requires Chaucer's minimization of female agency and power. In Boccaccio, however, the power of the feminine is represented as a vital point of origin for everything that happens in the subsequent plot.

By making his Emilia passionate and aware, Boccaccio emphasizes a major motif of the *Teseide*, which is that the characters and actions are driven by sexual and generative energies. In contrast to the unreal quality of Chaucer's Emilye in the scene described above, Boccaccio's Emilia first appears to the two knights in a different guise. Barefoot, she is dressed in a shift, and is described as being artless in her gestures (III:8).[26] She is apparently aware of the two knight's interest in her, while Chaucer's Emilye seems to be oblivious to Palomon and Arcite. Later, when the two knights are fighting in the forest, it is Emilia, rather than Teseo, who discovers them. In that scene, she is dressed in a hunting costume in the fashion of Diana, with a bow and arrow, recalling her Amazon origins. In the tournament scenes, Emilye waits patiently for whatever fate has in store, while Boccaccio's Emilia is enthusiastic about the victor and about victory in general. Emilia's relative sensuality and relative awareness projects a subjectivity that in Chaucer's Emilye remains opaque. In Chaucer's "Knight's Tale," the meaning of life is addressed by the thoughts of male characters such as Arcite, Theseus, and Egeus. In Boccaccio, it is Emilia (XI:290–95) who phrases those metaphysical questions.

Most puzzlingly, Chaucer virtually ignores the first two books of Boccaccio's *Teseide*, with their rich and exciting account of the war against the Amazons. Boccaccio annotated his own manuscript and his notes imply that he considered these two books to be only a preamble to his major focus, which was the love triangle. Chaucer's "Knight's Tale," however, reduced these two extensive books to a brief allusion. Chaucer follows Statius' Thebeid in so doing, as he also follows Statius' emphasis on Theseus, rather than the three lovers, as the central organizing focus of his work. The alignment of the Knight, Theseus, and the First Mover described in the tale's philosophical and theological meditations, is in fact a truism of Chaucer criticism. In Boccaccio's *Teseide*, however, Teseo's role, at least in the first two books, is balanced against Ippolita. She is nearly his equal as a warrior and a leader, and at some points seems to more than match him.

Teseo's character in Boccaccio's *Teseide* also differs somewhat from Chaucer's Theseus. Theseus in Chaucer's "Knight's Tale" is capable of abrupt shifts in plan, largely by tempering his initial authoritarian rigidity thanks to the imprecations of female supplicants. Yet he retains a certain distance and objectivity from the action, perhaps as a result of his obvious parallel to Chaucer's Knight himself, the presumed narrator of the story. Boccaccio's Teseo is much more likely to be moved and involved emotionally, most obviously by battle, but also by love. In this regard, Teseo is more typical of romance heroes, and Theseus something of an exception in his philosophical distance. Boccaccio refers to the fact that Teseo had "ravished" Helen before Paris abducts her to Troy. Teseo was apparently unable to resist Helen's allure, dressed as she was in a tight, soft leather skin suit and oiled with tallow. In the "Knight's Tale," Chaucer briefly mentions that Theseus has had previous romantic experiences. Boccaccio is willing to allow a degree of sensuality and indulgence in his hero. Chaucer, however, emphasizes Theseus public and moral stature. In so doing, he creates a Theseus aware of himself as a duke and as a leader. His strengths and weaknesses are politically significant. In so doing, Chaucer emphasizes the theme of political authority and its attendant concerns.

While Chaucer suppresses or redirects the sexual themes of the narrative, Boccaccio emphasizes the simultaneity of erotic and martial arenas. When Chaucer treats their connection, it is through, for example, the iconography of the temple scenes, when Palomon, Arcite, and Emilye pray to their respective gods. Boccaccio is quite explicit about the actions of the Amazons before their conquest, detailing the facts that the Amazons murdered their husbands and that his Ippolita threatened any man who entered her kingdom with death. Teseo is enraged by this prohibition, since it ostensibly threatens the lives of his subjects. His call to arms (II.4) is in fact filled with expressions of rage. Ippolita, however, lays out her policy and strategy to her followers by appealing to their rational interests. The Amazons are not defeated because the men are better warriors, but because Teseo has taken control of all strategic positions. Only when Ippolita realizes there is no hope for a military victory does she finally surrender. It is at this point that the women express regret for killing their men, but largely because the men may have helped them stave off Teseo's attack.

In Boccaccio, the pairing of Teseo and Ippolita complicates stereotypical masculine and feminine virtues. Teseo fails in a straightforward attack on the Amazonian military positions, and he has to resort to tunneling to breach her lines. Ippolita's military tactics are in contrast more direct and forthright and in some ways more heroic. In her own speech to her army, Ippolita urges her troops to abjure mercy, since mercy is a female virtue used against women. Paradoxically, it is Teseo who is merciful toward the conquered Amazons after the battle. In Books I and II of the *Teseide*, it could be argued that Teseo resorts to insidious trickery, while Ippolita enacts traditional virile virtues. The male figure, in a typical pattern, considers himself justified in resorting to underhanded behavior because the feminine is understood a priori as devious, even when the females upon whom he is acting exhibit no such behavior. Gender attributes are thus reversed in the *Teseide,* with Teseo given some typically feminine responses, whereas the Amazons applaud ruthless rationality and brute force. After Teseo's victory, the Amazons must relearn traditional female roles and Boccaccio describes them sorting out their finery.

Chaucer does recognize the potential of female power in the "Knight's Tale," but it is redirected and sublimated into images. Theseus destroys "the reign of feminye." When the fury emerges to frighten Arcite's horse, the fury is female, but she is invisible. In the *Teseide*, the fury can be seen by the crowd and horrifies them (IX:242). By describing the emergence of the fury and its consequences at length and in great rhetorical detail, Boccaccio makes the action seem less otherworldly than consistent with the values that inhabit his work from the beginning. Chaucer is also cryptic about Emilye's reaction at the end of the battle itself, and he attributes her favorable glance to the fact that women tend to follow Fortune's lead, undercutting the courtliness with which Emilye had been treated up to that point, suggesting, almost, that Emilye's sudden expression of ardor is fatal to the object of her attention. Boccaccio's Emilia's enthusiasm for the winner is described as an explicitly erotic attraction, whereas Chaucer's Emilye's approval of the winner is described in terms of the themes of fate and fortune, coinciding with the fury's appearance. The passive and fickle human female contrasts with the terrifying female fury who emerges from the underworld. In Boccaccio's version of the story, male and female powers struggle with each other. In Chaucer's version, conflict between the sexes is minimized and the poem focuses much more on conflicts between the male characters.

The degree to which Theseus' willingness to change his mind and grant mercy represents a feminization of male heroism has been an ongoing question in criticism of the "Knight's Tale." As Strohm writes, "Yet, not so much in his representation of Hippolyta and Emilye, as in that of Theseus, Chaucer shows his discontent with the whole system of female abjection and male concession. For, unlike the Edward who gives ground only reluctantly and with stubborn reiteration of his original wish, Chaucer's Theseus is permitted to change his mind. In fact, to the considerable extent that pity and mercy are marked in this discourse as distinctly feminine attributes (as opposed, for example, to anger and adamancy), Chaucer may be said to have partially feminized Theseus."[27] Jill Mann has argued that Theseus' compassion "feminises him without rendering him effeminate."[28] Susan Crane responds, however, by pointing out that the final result in Chaucer and in medieval romance is that it is masculinity that is normative and integrative, while similar behavior on the part of female characters is rendered as unnatural or transgressive. For Theseus' "conquering and marrying the Amazon queen is a sexual as well as a political action, one that eroticizes masculine domination and feminine submission. In contrast, taking pity on the widows of Thebes reveals in Theseus a compassion that may seem feminine, complicating his masculinity."[29]

Theseus' instincts, however, tend toward the authoritarian. David Wallace's *Chaucerian Polity*, for instance, read the Knight's Tale as an admonitory essay on the dangers of absolutism. Unallayed by female advice and counsel, the male authoritarian figure could destroy the sometimes fragile allegiances of civil society. The tyranny obvious in Northern Italy, for instance, with its "tyraunts of Lumbardye" (*Legend of Good Women* [G-Text, Prologue 353–55]), loomed as a possibility. Libuše's speech in Cosmas of Prague, with its warning against ducal tyranny, parallels Chaucer's concern. It is especially powerful, not only in describing the economics of feudal lordship from the point of view of an imagined prefeudal voluntary associationism, but in detailing how power creates its own subjects and how these subjects internalize their abjectness. In eloquent terms, Libuše describes the disappearance of eloquence and the silencing effect of the spectacle of power.

Everywhere the "Knight's Tale" seeks to limit the power of females who are not nearly as marginalized in Boccaccio. The tone of the work is infused by a melancholia surrounding patriarchal despair. Its peculiar ending, or endings, reveals a concern with closure without resolution. The Knight and Theseus represent defenses against cthonic forces that are too obviously displacements of a female power threatening even after its defeat. Whatever his ideal presentation in the General Prologue, the Knight constructs a narrative obsessed with masculine control. His female characters are depersonalized relative to his source. Chaucer may have highlighted this patriarchal concern in the Squire's portrait by making a point about the Squire being the son of the Knight, with no mention of a mother. The "Knight's Tale" is elaborately modest in its avoidance of voyeurism, respecting the privacy of Emilye's preparations and censoring Boccaccio's mention of the number of times Palomon and Emilye enjoy themselves on their wedding night. Taken alone, these details are minor, but taken together they suggest a pattern. The very telling of the tale by the Knight repeats Theseus' conquest of his female adversaries. What the "Knight's Tale" seeks to contain is not only the power of his female figures, but the contradictions that arise from their suppression. When we meet Chaucer's Amazons they have already been tamed. Interestingly, their attributes have been dispersed among male characters in the poem and its frame. Strikingly, the Knight in the General Prologue is described as being "as meeke as is a mayde." Such a metaphor is meant to suggest that he maintains the qualities of humility and modesty in his noncombat self-presentation, but it also reminds us of the "feminization" of chivalric culture, wherein feminine attributes are appropriated to suggest interiority and subjectivity in the male courtier. At the same time, he and his alter ego, Duke Theseus, are engaged in censoring the subversive potential of the female characters and erotic drives as found in the plot. The martial qualities of the Amazons, including their scrupulousness and their sternness, are projected on to Duke Theseus and the Knight himself.

The femininity assumed by the conquered Amazons bears a strong resemblance to the behavior Joan LeRiviere called "Womanliness as Masquerade" in her classic essay.[30] Le Riviere noticed an exaggerated, compensatory display of femininity among her women patients who in other respects had displayed the sort of competence and success traditionally expected of men. This donning of femininity as a disguise, she suggests, is an unconscious attempt to forestall a feared punishment for appropriating the castrated penis of the father. The successful woman fears the retribution of men for encroaching on the space of masculinity. "What is the essential nature of fully developed femininity?" she asks. "The conception of womanliness as a mask, behind which man suspects some hidden danger, throws a little light on the enigma." In film theory, thanks to her use by Lacan, Le Riviere's notion has been more widely applied, particularly in terms of films in which females are disguised as men—a not unprecedented theme in medieval and Renaissance romance, one notes—and allowed the freedom and the cultural signification of men.[31] In both Chaucer and Boccaccio, the conquered Amazons assume an almost compensatory femininity, and in both, the threatening power of their former state remains as an undercurrent in the work, though suppressed almost to the point of erasure in Chaucer's version.

This displacement of female prowess and power also occurs in another famous passage from another of Chaucer's works. Chaucer's relation to Anne of Bohemia as a possible patron for the *Legend of Good Women*, and one who might not have approved of everything he wrote, has been widely studied, and it is explicitly articulated in at least one of the two versions of the Prologue to the *Legend of Good Women*. Accused of maligning women in his works, the narrator, identified as the poet, offers a sort of plea bargain. In the face of accusations of heresy against the God of Love, the narrator is helpless. *Troilus and Criseyde* is especially cited: "And of Creseyde thou hast` seyd as the lyste/ That maketh men to wommen lasse triste/ That ben as trewe as ever was any steel" (*Legend of Good Women* (F-Text Prologue 332–35]). But Alceste points to some positive portrayals, one of them being the representation of love in the "Knight's Tale" or an earlier version of it: "And al the love of Palamon and Arcite/ Of Thebes, thogh the storye ys yknowen lyte" (*Legend of Good Women* [F-Text Prologue 421]).

The Legend of Good Women presents Alceste, and the women in the narratives themselves, as both orthodox subjects and as agents that maneuver within the confines of their role. But what is interesting for our purposes here is that, as with the "Knight's Tale," the powers and poses of the female are disaggregated and distributed among the male figures: "And doun on knes anoon-ryght I me sette,/And, as I koude, this fresshe flour I grette,/Knelyng alway, til it unclosed was,/Upon the smale, softe, swote gras" (*Legend of Good Woman*[F-Text Prologue:115–18]). The sensual imagery of the Prologue, with its dense associations of odors and sounds, overcomes the narrator, as does his own sense of mystery at the power the apparently powerless flower holds over him. This reversal of power

comes to life a few lines later, as the daisy is revealed to be Alceste. She
is accompanied by the God of Love, who, while a male figure, acts out
the drama of accusation and threats of punishment traditionally associated with a woman betrayed. The figure of Alceste has noted a curious
duality to her representation, alternately commanding and domineering
on the one hand, and supplicating and moderating on the other. The
women who appear as if in an apocalyptic vision embody their own tales
and supplant the poet who has allegedly defamed their memory. In the
General Prologue, the narrators of the stories that follow are the pilgrims
who are described in detail. In the Prologue to the *Legend of Good Women*,
the characters of the stories that follow themselves appear. By manifesting
both women and fictional subjects, they dramatize the difficulty a male
poet like Chaucer must face in representing women.[32]

Gender positions are both supported and undermined in the ensu-
ing trial. The God of Love takes on the patriarchal voice heard from
Theseus in the "Knight's Tale," and Alceste pleads for mercy, much like
the supplicating women in that tale. The God of Love is implored not
to become like a tyrant. The possibility of tyranny also underlies the
extreme authoritarianism of Theseus' initial responses to crises, which
is deflected by appeal to his sense of pity. The threat of punishment and
rigid enforcement of the law is presented as an attribute of the masculine
God of Love and forgiveness and mercy are presented as attributes of
the female queen. Such a polarization does not bode well for tales that
follow, suggesting that they might present the women in the stories as
passive and helpless victims. At the same time, the quick anger of the
God of Love also resembles the arrogant behavior of the courtly mistress,
such as Guinevere in Chretien's *Lancelot*. The potential power and voice
of the female, which in courtly literature could be assigned to Alceste,
is projected on to the punitive and threatening male. Alceste's tone, for
instance, mirrors the rhetoric of the mirror of princes and advice tradition recently studied by Judith Ferster. Indeed, she is less a submissive
petitioner than an active adviser to princes, and the princely adviser was,
since John of Salisbury, an active figure in political discourse. If Chaucer
did know of the legendary history of Bohemia, he has created an analogue
to the prophetess and judge role of Libuše and to her subsequent role as an
exceptionally adept adviser as described in the Czech chronicles.

Conclusion

My generalizations about possible alternative histories and my technical
observations about Chaucer's "Knight's Tale" and it relation to its source
are connected. In the narratives of the legendary history of Bohemia, the

power of the female guide and founder is circumscribed, but her wisdom and her aura are passed on to the male rulers who succeed her. It is an ambivalent legacy, since she chooses, in a vision, her mate, but it is not necessarily her lineage that inherits her rulership, but a title and a ducal throne that may or may not be dynastically related to her. That is, the virtues and power of Libuše are dispersed into the history of Bohemia itself, at least according to Cosmas. Meanwhile, the truly threatening female potential, represented by the City of Virgins and their refusal to bend to male will as has Libuše, are ruthlessly suppressed. Libuše acquires a certain halfway status between Amazon and compliant supporter of ducal rule. It is possible, even likely, that the stories of the legendary founding of Prague by the prophetic female leader Libuše and by an associated battle against Amazon-like women usually referred to as the War of the Maidens accompanied Anne and her courtiers to England. Anne may have thought of her own role as akin to that of the legendary heroine of her homeland. Traces of the legendary history of Bohemia can be located in the political unconscious of the Knight's Tale and perhaps in Chaucer's famously complex deployment of gender as local topic and as political metaphor. If it is impossible to prove that Chaucer was aware of the cultural freight of the female foundation of Queen Anne's homeland, it is nevertheless possible to point to striking analogues to the ways in which he deploys the powers of his Bohemianized women.

Notes

1. Carey McWilliams, *Southern California: An Island on the Land* (Santa Barbara, CA: Peregrine Smith, 1973).
2. Garci Rodríguez de Montalvo, *Sergas de Esplandián*, ed. Carlos Sainz de la Maza, Clásicos Castalia (Madrid: Editorial Castalia, 2003).
3. Garci Rodríguez de Montalvo, *The Queen of California*, trans. Edward Everett Hale (San Francisco, CA: Colt press, 1945). See the recent full translation, Garci Rodríguez de Montalvo, *The Labors of the Very Brave Knight Esplandián*, trans. William Thomas Little (Binghamton, NY: Center for Medieval and Early Renaissance Studies, 1992).
4. Edward Everett Hale, "The Queen of California," *Atlantic Monthly* (March, 1864): 265–78. Hale had announced his thesis two years earlier.
5. See *The California African-American Heritage Preservation and Restoration Society Home Page*, <http://www.caaahprs.org/site_us/story.htm> accessed March 29, 2007.
6. Patrick J. Geary, *Women at the Beginning: Origin Myths from the Amazons to the Virgin Mary* (Princeton: Princeton University Press, 2006), 5–6.
7. See James P. Carley and Julia Crick, "'Constructing Albion's Past: An Annotated Edition of *De Origine Gigantum*,'" in *Arthurian Literature XIII*

(Woodbridge: D.S. Brewer Rowman and Littlefield, 1981), 31–114; Ruth Evans, "'Gigantic Origins: An Annotated Translation of *De Origine Gigantum*,'" in *Arthurian Literature XVI* (Woodbridge, Suffolk: D.S. Brewer Rowman and Littlefield, 1981), 197–211; Ewald Zettl, *An Anonymous Short English Metrical Chronicle*, ed. Ewald Zettl, Early English Text Society Series (London: Early English Text Society, 1935); Jeffrey Jerome Cohen, *Of Giants: Sex, Monsters, and the Middle Ages*, Medieval Cultures (Minneapolis: University of Minnesota Press, 1999), 47–60.

8. Hector Boece, *A Description of Scotland* (London: John Bellenden, 1587).

9. Cosmas of Prague, *Die Chronik der Böhmen Des Cosmas von Prag*, ed. Bertold Bretholz (Berlin: Weidmannsche Buchhandlung, 1923), I: 5, p. 14. My translation.

10. I have consulted the MHG translation, *Di Tutsch Kronik von Behem Lant*, ed. Josef Jiricek, Fontes Rerum Bohemicarum, Vol. 3 (Prague: Nádaní Františka Palackéo, 1882). In January 2007, the National Library of Prague announced that it had purchased a lavishly illustrated and previously unknown Latin translation of a fragment of the Dalimil Chronicle.

11. Alfred Thomas, *Anne's Bohemia: Czech Literature and Society, 1310–1420*, Medieval Cultures (Minneapolis: University of Minnesota Press, 1998), 50–62.

12. John M. Klassen, *Warring Maidens, Captive Wives and Hussite Queens: Women and Men at War and at Peace in Fifteenth Century Bohemia*, East European Monographs (New York: Columbia University Press, 1999), 14–32.

13. The best account in English of Cosmas' original context is Lisa Wolverton, *Hastening Toward Prague: Power and Society in the Medieval Czech Lands*, Middle Ages Series (Philadelphia: University of Pennsylvania Press, 2001).

14. John Livingston Lowes, "The Tempest at Hir Hoom-Cominge," *Modern Language Notes* 19 (1904): 240–43. Lowes noted that Chaucer adds a "tempest at hir hoom comynge," *KnT* 884, as Hipolyte accompanies Theseus to Athens, which Boccaccio does not mention. Thomas Walsingham mentions a disturbance of water, "*maris commotio*," when Anne of Bohemia landed at Calais, December 18, 1381, and Lowes speculates that Chaucer may have alluded to Anne's arrival in the poem itself.

15. Donald R. Howard, *Chaucer: His Life, His Works, His World* (New York: Dutton, 1987).

16. David Wallace, *Chaucerian Polity: Absolutist Lineages and Associational Forms in England and Italy* (Stanford: Stanford University Press, 1997), esp. 357–78. A case could be made that the Chaucer's "Clerk's Tale" also echoes some of the themes of the legendary history of Bohemia, including the assent of both governed and governor, the limits, or lack of them, of feudal lordship, the frightening and silencing power of the ruler, and the relative activity or passivity of females in a social contract. On the "Clerk's Tale" and Anne of Bohemia, see Michael Hanrahan, "'A Straunge Succesour Sholde Take Youre Heritage': The *Clerk's Tale* and the Crisis of Ricardian Rule," *Chaucer Review* 35 (2001): 335–50.

17. Paul Strohm, *Hochon's Arrow: The Social Imagination of Fourteenth-Century Texts* (Princeton: Princeton University Press, 1992), 96–119.

18. Andrew Taylor, "Anne of Bohemia and the Making of Chaucer," *Studies in the Age of Chaucer* 19 (1997): 95–119.

19. Carolyn P. Collette, *Performing Polity: Women and Agency in the Anglo-French Tradition, 1385–1620*, Medieval Women (Turnhout: Brepols, 2006).

20. Nancy Bradbury Warren, " 'Olde Stories' and Amazons: The *Legend of Good Women*, the 'Knight's Tale,' and Fourteenth Century Political Culture," in *The Legend of Good Women: Context and Reception*, ed. Carolyn P. Collette, Chaucer Studies (Woodbridge: D.S. Brewer, 2006), 83–104. See also the excellent article by Keiko Hamaguchi, "Domesticating Amazons in *The Knight's Tale*," *Studies in the Age of Chaucer* 26 (2004): 331–54.

21. *Westminster Chronicle*, ed. and trans. L.C. Hector and Barbara F. Harvey (Oxford: Clarendon Press, 1982), 24.

22. Edith Rickert, "King Richard II's Books," *Library* 4 (1932): 144–47; Roger Sherman Loomis, "The Library of Richard II," *Studies in Language, Literature and Culture of the Middle Ages and Later*, ed. E. Bagby Atwood and Archibald A. Hill (Austin: University of Texas Press, 1969), 173–78; Richard Firth Green, "King Richard II's Books Revisited," *Library* 31 (1975): 235–39.

23. The possible references in Chaucer to the legendary history of Britain and his limited and probably ironic uses of Arthurian romance have been widely discussed. See, for instance, Sheila Delany, "Geoffrey of Monmouth and Chaucer's 'Legend of Good Women,' " *Chaucer* Review 22 (1987): 170–75; Edward Donald Kennedy, "Gower, Chaucer and French Prose Arthurian Romance," *Mediaevalia* 16 (1993): 55–90; Joerg Fichte, "Images of Arthurian Literature Reflected in Chaucer's Poetry," *Archiv* 230 (1993): 52–61 and Tison Pugh, "Queering Genres, Battering Males: The Wife of Bath's Narrative Violence," *Journal of Narrative Technique* 33 (2003): 115–42.

24. Citations from Chaucer are to L.D. Benson et al., ed. *The Riverside Chaucer,* Third Edition (Boston: Houghton Mifflin, 1987).

25. See Susan Crane, "Medieval Romance and Feminine Difference in *The Knight's Tale*," *Studies in the Age of Chaucer* 12 (1990): 47–64.

26. Giovanni Boccaccio*, Teseida*, ed. G.C. Sansoni (Firenze: Accademia della Crusca, 1938).

27. Strohm, *Huchown's Arrow*, 112.

28. Jill Mann, *Geoffrey Chaucer*, Feminist Readings (Atlantic Highlands: Humanities Press International, 1991), 174. See also Jill Mann, *Feminizing Chaucer*, Chaucer Studies (Woodbridge: D.S. Brewer, 2002).

29. Susan Crane, *Gender and Romance in Chaucer's Canterbury Tales* (Princeton: Princeton University Press, 1994), 16.

30. Joan Le Riviere, "Womanliness as Masquerade," *Formations of Fantasy,* ed. Victor Burgin, James Donald, and Cora Kaplan (London: Metheun, 1986), 35–44 reprinted from the *International Journal of Psychoanalysis* 10 (1929): 303–13.

31. Compare Mary Anne Doane, "Masquerade Reconsidered: Further Thoughts on the Female Spectator," *Discourse* 11 (1988–1989): 42–54, discussing Joan Riviere's theory of masquerade: "Femininity, in this description, is a reaction formation against the illicit assumption of masculinity. Hollow in itself, without substance, femininity can only be sustained by its accoutrements, decorative veils, and inessential gestures" (43).

32. Such reversals are no longer possible to dismiss as irony alone, particularly in light of Elaine Tuttle Hansen's *Chaucer and the Fictions of Gender* (Berkeley: University of California Press, 1991), who argues that the Chaucerian persona, as is typical of the male poet apparently fascinated with female characters, in fact appropriates the slippery signification and relative lack of fixity of the feminine other, the aspects of that projection most useful to poetic discourse. Chaucer presents himself and his project as "feminized" while in fact effacing female subjectivity from the works themselves.

CHAPTER 11

THE SIGNS AND LOCATION OF A
FLIGHT (OR RETURN?) OF TIME: THE
OLD ENGLISH *WONDERS OF THE EAST*
AND THE GUJARAT MASSACRE

Eileen A. Joy

> *For all colonization involves the taming of the beast by bestial methods and hence both the*
> *conversion and projection of the animal and human, difference and identity. On display, the*
> *freak represents the naming of the frontier and the assurance that the wilderness, the outside,*
> *is now territory.*
>
> —Susan Stewart, *On Longing: Narratives of the*
> *Miniature, the Gigantic, the Souvenir, the Collection*

*T*his chapter examines two widely divergent instances of sexualized violence
against women whose bodies have been figured as foreign and barbaric threats
within collective national bodies: the real case of a massacre in the modern state of
Gujarat in southwestern India in 2002 and the imaginative case of Alexander the
Great's massacre of a race of giant women in the fantasized Babilonia of the
Anglo-Saxon Wonders of the East.

The Historian Never Knows Which

In his account of the possession of the Ursuline nuns of Loudon, France
in the 1630s, Michel de Certeau concluded that this possession ultimately
"has no 'true' historical explanation, since it is never possible to know
who is 'possessed' and by whom."[1] However, as an historical and even
socio-psychological *crisis*—for those nuns who believed themselves to

be possessed as well as for their witnesses, intercessors, and judges—the possession revealed "an underground existence, an inner resistance that has never been broken." To the question of whether this possession was "something new, or the repetition of the past," Certeau answered:

> The historian never knows which. For mythologies reappear, providing the eruption of strangeness with forms of expression prepared in advance, as it were, for that sudden inundation. These languages of social anxiety seem to reject both the limits of a present and the real conditions of its future. Like scars that mark for a new illness the spot of an earlier one, they designate in advance the signs and location of a flight (or return?) of time.[2]

In this chapter, I want to examine two widely divergent instances of what I understand to be a sexualized violence against women whose bodies have been figured as foreign (and even, as animal and barbaric) threats within collective national bodies: the real case of a massacre in the modern state of Gujarat in southwestern India in 2002 and the imaginative case of Alexander the Great's massacre of a race of giant women in the fantasized *Babilonia* of the Anglo-Saxon *Wonders of the East*. Both cases reveal, I believe, certain persistent social anxieties about the female body as, in Elizabeth Grosz's terms, "a formlessness that engulfs all form, a disorder that threatens all order," and a "contagion."[3] Out of the horror and disgust that sometimes arises in the encounter with the female body that is perceived as aggressively monstrous, and that is seen to mark, in the words of William Ian Miller, "a recognition of danger to our purity,"[4] we can trace a very ancient and ritualized type of reactionary (riotous, yet also highly controlled) violence that is both morally condemnatory and sublimely (even sexually) ecstatic, and that can be seen, to a greater and more restrained degree, respectively, in the Gujarat genocide and the Old English text.

This is a violence, moreover, that participates in what Dominick LaCapra, writing about the Holocaust, has described as a "deranged sacrificialism in the attempt to get rid of" stranger-Others as "phobic or ritually impure objects that polluted the *Volksgemeinschaft* (community of the people)."[5] And to participate in this "deranged sacrificialism" is, according to LaCapra, to partake in a moment of *Rausch*—an elation, intoxication, delirium, or ecstasy—whereby "an unspeakable rite of passage involving quasi-sacrifice, victimization, and regeneration through violence" is undertaken as a labor of political culture.[6] In the Gujarat massacre, which involved the mass sexual mutilation, torture, and brutal murder of hundreds of Muslim women, we can also glimpse what Certeau terms the "latent *singularity*" that is "revealed in the continuous plurality of events"[7] or what Paul Strohm calls the "traces or residues of an unexhausted past."[8] These are traces that join with the lines of the Old English text that describe Alexander's killing of a race of giant animal-woman hybrids because they were "shameful" [*æwisce*] and "unworthy" [*unweorðe*] "in their bodies" [*on lichoman*].[9] In both instances, the supposedly unruly and shameful bodies of women occasions a trauma in which, as Jeffrey Cohen argues, "[s]exed bodies are materialized along with the past in which they figure," with women representing "the Real in all its inhuman, biological vitalism" and male heroes (who are also the founders of nations) signifying "the structurating principle that overcodes these obscenities of the flesh."[10]

My yoking together of two widely disparate events—one terrifyingly real and the other purely textual, separated by approximately one thousand years and an entire continent—is admittedly somewhat contrived, although I must confess that my scholarly method is indebted to the aesthetic of the novelist W.G. Sebald, who sought in his writing to adhere to an "exact historical perspective" by "patiently engraving and linking together apparently disparate things in the manner of a still-life."[11] In an age that values speed and liquidity and synergistic conflation, it may be that one of the chief values of a medieval studies today would be in its ability to account, in slow and semi-still measure, for the phenomenology of what Cohen has defined as "the localized cultural matrix or meshwork," which includes individual bodies, "within which time moves"[12] and where history is always *becoming, going on*, and *returning*.

I would also like to note here, before this chapter progresses further, that while I agree with Michael Calabrese that "we cannot proceed uncritically in the pursuit of ethics as an attendant aspect of our studies of the medieval," I do not agree that "all such criticism that foregrounds the history of violence and difference in an attempt to practice critical ethics risks reducing the text under study to a type of historical hate crime."[13] I disagree for two important reasons: first, because I understand violence to be a perduring feature of human nature and societies across time, I am not interested in assigning some kind of blame or moral repugnance to either characters *in* or authors and readers *of* medieval texts that represent fear of (and violence against) a particular group of persons, so much as I am interested in tracing circuits of anxieties that have always coalesced and continue to coalesce around the multiple histories of and contestations over becoming-human—the careful delineation of which histories and contestations by medieval and other scholars of premodern periods I see as critical to the future of humanism and the humanities; and second, I don't see how we can possibly maintain what Calabrese terms "Arnoldian

disinterestedness"[14] over contemporary issues out of a fear for how the
so-called corporate university might assimilate our politically sensitive
scholarship in the service of global capitalism. Everything, ultimately, is
up for grabs by global capitalism, including love and death, and while I
agree with Calabrese that we should avoid adopting in our literary scholarship contrived political *affects* that are nothing more than postures, while
also embracing an academic culture that is as open to as many competing
viewpoints as possible, I ultimately concur with Françoise Meltzer that
"the study of culture without politics is an inane undertaking," although
I would substitute "humanism" for her "politics."[15]

Was This the India of My Childhood?
Were These My People?

In the roughly seventy-two hours between February 27 and March 2 of
2002, there was a spectacular eruption of anti-Muslim violence in the
southwestern Indian state of Gujarat that was partly a boiling over of long-
simmering post-Partition tensions between Hindus and Muslims living
there, but was also directly orchestrated by Hindu nationalist groups in
collaboration with local political officials and police authorities.[16] More
specifically, the event was triggered by a fire-bombing on an express train
pulling out of Godhra station on February 27 that was filled with mainly
Hindu passengers returning home from a pilgrimage to Ayodhya, Uttar
Pradesh, the supposed birthplace of the Hindu god Rama, a site that
had become a kind of tinderbox for anti-Muslim sentiment. Fifty-eight
passengers perished in the fire, and to this day it is not certain whether
a Muslim mob throwing rocks at the train as it was departing the station
or Hindu nationalists inside the train were responsible for the flammable
substance that was either thrown into or poured within the car.[17] What
is certain is that in the days following, and partly fueled by local media
and certain political officials allied with the Hindu nationalist right who
sought to link the firebombing incident to Pakistani and international
"Islamic" terrorism,[18] a terrible wave of anti-Muslim violence seized
the state. The attackers were mainly gangs of young men armed with
swords, explosives, chemicals, and *trishuls* (three-pronged spears associated with Hindu mythology), and the intention of the architects of this
violence was clearly to make it appear as if it were the spontaneous riot
of a "mob" of long-suffering "ordinary" Hindus no longer able to contain their rage against Muslim "outsiders."[19] When it was over, approximately two thousand Muslims—men, women, and children, the elderly
and the infirm—were dead, many by being hacked with swords and then
burned alive. Muslim mosques, businesses, vehicles, and homes were also

defaced and destroyed, thereby creating a mass exodus of over a hundred thousand Muslims.

Most shocking of all were the mass rapes and sexual mutilation of the women, often staged in front of children who were made to watch and then killed afterward (or vice versa), in which the "typical tactic was first to rape or gang-rape the woman, then to torture her [primarily by mutilation of the genitals with metallic objects, such as swords, rods, and *trishuls*], and then to set her on fire and kill her."[20] Fetuses were ripped out of the wombs of pregnant women who were often also split down the middle with a sword and then burned. On some occasions, the breasts of the women were cut off; petrol was poured into the mouths of children, who were then exploded with lit matches; heads were cut off and displayed on platters to frighten those still alive; iron rods were used to electrocute children and to pierce young girls' stomachs—to continue rehearsing these details is to risk entering the realm where, as one survivor put it, "I feel like my mind has been destroyed."[21]

Although the violence in Gujarat left almost no Muslim body in the region untouched, the bodies of Muslim women and girls received special attention, and even, special violence. For the authors of the International Initiative for Justice's feminist analysis of the massacres, "Threatened Existence," the "scale and brutality of the sexual violence unleashed upon the women was new, or felt as if it was new,"[22] and Flavia Agnes, a feminist legal activist, testified that the "scale and extent of atrocities perpetrated upon innocent Muslim women during the recent violence, far exceeds any reported sexual crime during any previous riots in the country in the post-independence period."[23] According to the historian Tanika Sarkar, who interviewed many of the eyewitnesses, "[t]he pattern of cruelty suggests three things. One, the woman's body was a site of almost inexhaustible violence, with infinitely plural and innovative forms of torture. Second, their sexual and reproductive organs were attacked with a special savagery. Third, their children, born and unborn, shared the attacks and were killed before their eyes."[24]

It was no accident that the violence in Gujarat reserved a special place for sexual sadism against Muslim women, for, as Martha Nussbaum has written, at the time of the massacres, Muslim female bodies symbolized "a recalcitrant part of the nation, one as yet undominated by Hindu male power," and because the founders of the Hindu right in the 1930s borrowed much of their rhetoric and political culture from National Socialism in Germany and "openly expressed their sympathy with German ideals of racial purity," a "very similar, and similarly paranoid, idea of male purity has taken deep root in the culture of the Hindu right, in a way that is unconnected to authentic Hindu religious and cultural traditions."[25]

The authors of "Threatened Existence" make very clear as well how the Hindu right, prior to the attacks, distributed pamphlets and ran training camps that purposefully promulgated the sexualized and gendered character of the *Hindutva* project, in which male sexual potency and rape are important tools in eliminating the "foreign" Muslims, with the bodily integrity of girls and women as the most special target. For Nussbaum, the critical importance of the operations of disgust in the Gujarat violence—especially in its sexual violence—cannot be underestimated, and also has to be understood in a more global context in which disgust has a long history as "a powerful weapon in social efforts to exclude certain groups and persons," and in which history "the locus classicus of group-projected disgust is the female body." Therefore, "[i]n very many cultures and times, women have been portrayed as dirt and pollution, as sources of a contamination that allures and must somehow...be both kept at bay and punished."[26] And because the woman's body is a *reproducing* body, it occupies a precarious position within any community that considers itself a collective "nation," one in which family is the basal unit.

Although it is clear that part of the campaign of rape of Muslim women was connected, on one level, to the making of "little Hindus" (in other words, to colonizing Muslim women's bodies through impregnation), the Gujarat massacre was unique for the ways in which many of the rapes were inseparable from mutilation and murder (and therefore were decidedly *not* about colonization through impregnation), especially in light of the fact of how many women and girls were penetrated with metal objects and then also set on fire. The bodies of women have always, in the words of Anne McClintock, been "subsumed symbolically into the national body politic as its boundary and metaphoric limit."[27] Nevertheless, there was, in Sarkar's words, a "dark sexual obsession"[28] at work in the Gujarat genocide that could be said to pose an almost debilitating historical moment for global feminism, but also for the idea of a secular and pluralistic India. For Uma Chakravarti, a feminist historian at Delhi University who participated in the International Initiative for Justice in Gujarat, the genocide was a kind of psychic deathblow:

> I was a child of independent India, among the first generation of post independence children who had watched the nation being born on the midnight of August 14, 1947. Even as I grew into a civil rights and women's rights activist I had a strong sense of faith in the ability of "the people" of the country to resist oppression and redress their grievances and fight for justice. Gujarat spelled the collapse of that faith....I despaired as I watched the horror of Gujarat unfold through its various stages....Was this the India of my childhood? Were these my people?[29]

"Was this the India of my childhood?" and "Were these my people?" are laments worth lingering over. They point, I believe, to a moment of personal but also political crisis, as well as to a type of longing for something that has never been and can possibly never be—a polity that could align itself as a collective "body" under a name such as "India," and in which name a radically liberal politics tied to that identity's collective body could be articulated. Chakravarti's plaint also gestures to a hope that a nation of "origin" could be predicated on something other than exclusion and violence. Chakravarti's questions, which insist on one level that there is such a country as an independent India, a unity that could be capable of expressing a collective will and consciousness (implied to be humane, radically liberal, and incapable of violence), also cover over (or refuse to engage) the absence of history—similar to the Hindu right's "pure" India, which they locate in an apocalyptic future tethered to the inheritance and rebirth of an ancient "holy land,"[30] Chakravarti's nation born on the midnight of August 14, 1947 never existed, or has yet to arrive, except as an event-to-come. This is not to say that there is no history in India (although some have claimed so),[31] but rather, that the matter of India having a history as "India," however defined, is always an open question (or wound) that must address itself not only to the context of what Eric Hobsbawm has termed the "exclusively" and "historically recent" nation (or, "modern territorial state"),[32] but also to the context of the premodern world in which ideas of "peoples" [gentes] were always tied to particular physiognomies and geographies, and where, to paraphrase Roger Bacon, place was always the beginning of existence.[33]

A Moment of Unraveling Transference

The tenth-century Old English text, *The Wonders of the East* (British Library, Cotton Vitellius A.xv, fols. 98v–106v),[34] an early pictorial catalog of monstrous bodies and animal and human marvels is not typically considered a romance narrative—indeed, Mary Campbell has argued that the *Wonders* is a text that "records a mass of unsynthesized data shorn of any relation to an experiencing witness."[35] Susan Kim believes that it is "difficult to discern any consistent method behind the organization of the catalog,"[36] and Asa Simon Mittman argues that the text's "accounts of various human, animal and plant oddities are disconnected, discontinuous descriptions" that, extracted from their exemplar's epistolary framework, are "extracted and essentialized"—"little ethnographical and zoological morsels, easily consumable individually or all together."[37] In some respects, the Old English *Wonders*, a text that is derived from Latin and Greek sources on travels to the East that have been filtered through

Continental translations over a period of hundreds of years before being made over into a local vernacular in an Anglo-Saxon manuscript, functions somewhat like a cabinet of curiosities, or more properly, a *collection* that, in Susan Stewart's words, "seeks a form of self-enclosure which is possible because of its ahistoricism. The collection replaces history with classification, with order beyond the realm of temporality."[38]

The *Wonders* then, lacks what could be called a linear or other type of explicit narrative structure—it cannot even, properly speaking, be called an ordered or orderly *series*, progressing, say, from plants to animals to "humans" (in that sense, even if it's a collection, it's an unruly one). Nevertheless, by virtue of Alexander's sudden appearance toward the end of the text as the executioner of a race of thirteen-feet-tall and white marble-bodied "women who have boars' tusks and hair ample to their heels, and ox-tails on their loins," as well as "camel's feet and boar's teeth" (sec. 27, p. 200), I want to suggest that the *Wonders* text is stitched to the one that follows it in the Nowell codex of the Vitellius A.xv manuscript, the Old English *Letter of Alexander to Aristotle*, and therefore the *Wonders* partakes in the long-established corpus of Alexandrian romance. In the Old English *Letter*, Alexander tells his old teacher Aristotle that his "memory" [*gemynd*], which is also his "mind" and his "memorial" in the form of all the letters and monuments he leaves behind, should "stand and loom perpetually as an example for other earthly kings, so that they [will] know very well that my might and my honor were greater than all of the other kings who ever were in the world" (sec. 41, p. 252). In this sense, Alexander's killing of the giant animal-human women in the *Wonders* participates, if even tangentially, in the genre of medieval romance, in which, as Cohen writes, "[t]he defeat of the giant is a social fantasy of the triumph of the corporeal order (in all its various meanings) written as a personal drama, a vindication of the tight channeling of multiple somatic drives into a socially beneficial expression of masculinity."[39]

Although *The Wonders of the East* exists in three manuscripts of medieval English provenance dating from the tenth through twelfth centuries, I am concentrating my analysis primarily on the Vitellius version of *Wonders* as that is the earliest copy in English and also because, in addition to sharing the Nowell codex with the Old English *Letter of Alexander to Aristotle*, it shares that space with *Beowulf*, which follows the *Letter*. Following the thinking of Nicholas Howe, I consider the Nowell codex as a "cultural atlas" that, "by depicting regions in continental Europe, the Middle East, and Asia," may have established for its Anglo-Saxon audience "a vivid, expansive, and sometimes cautionary sense of place."[40] The savvy client-reader of the Anglo-Saxon monastic library would have likely recognized from other manuscripts on the shelves (or from their knowledge of classical literature) many of the marvels recorded in the *Wonders*, such as the men without heads whose eyes and mouths are in their chest (the *Blemmyae*) and the dog-headed men (the *Conopenae*), but by virtue of these marvels' enclosure within the vernacular language and because early medieval maps positioned the British Isles at the furthest margins of the world—often in the same outermost band that contained the monstrous races of Africa—the Anglo-Latin *Wonders* tradition might have constituted an already known but discomforting arrangement, one in which monsters and the English shared an uneasy geography.[41] This discomfort would have been augmented by the illustrations that, "particularly in the Vitellius version," as Kim has argued, "are characterized by their aggressive and persistent movement outside their frames, and even. . .by their invasion of the textual space."[42]

I further agree with Howe that the texts in the cultural atlas of the Nowell codex also "form a *compilatio* in the sense that Martin Irvine uses the term: 'the selection of materials from the cultural library so that the resulting collection forms an *interpretive* arrangement of texts and discourse.' "[43] While we cannot say for certain how the texts in the Nowell codex—none of which are actually set in England—might have functioned as part and parcel of, say, a post-Alfredian program of nation-building, we can certainly identify the social context of the codex's assembly, as Brian McFadden does, as one that was rife with "anxieties caused by tenth- and early-eleventh-century Viking Invasions, the Benedictine Reform, and eschatological concerns provoked by the coming millennium," such that the Old English works gathered together in this *compilatio* could be viewed as highlighting different forms of "resistance of foreign others to containment in either a social or narrative order."[44]

Although Alexander's killing of the giant animal-human women in the *Wonders* can certainly be understood as having participated in a certain romantic (and violent) poetics of nation-building in which, in Cohen's words, "bodies that do not know their proper cultural place because they preexist the masculine 'invention' of place" have to be evacuated,[45] this act of sudden and unanticipated aggression, although it is certainly consistent with Alexander's reputation as a world conqueror, has to also be considered as a somewhat anomalous event within the *Wonders* itself, and even in relation to the text of the *Letter* that follows. In the case of the *Wonders* text, there is, with one other exception (the "barbarous peoples" of sec. 18), almost a complete and total absence of any kind of moral condemnation of the monstrous animals and hybrid creatures and other races, not even where you might expect it most—in the case, say, of the anthrophagic Donestre. These half-human, half-leonine creatures beguile strangers by talking to them in their familiar language and then kill and eat them, except for the heads, over which, afterward, they "sit and weep" (sec. 20, p. 196),[46] an image that could almost be said to construct a moment of pathos for the Donestre who seem caught in an inexorable cycle of consuming their own abject humanness. In addition, the text even praises a group of "benevolent" [fremfulle] people who, "if any man goes to them they give him a woman before they let him go away" (sec. 30, p. 200). This passage is significant because it sets up Alexander's only other interruption of the text as an *active* character: the author tells us that when Alexander visited these people, "he was astonished at their humanity, and he would not kill them nor cause them any injury" (sec. 30, p. 202). The only other mention of Alexander in the text is at the very beginning, where it is mentioned that in the land of Archemedon there are "great monuments" [mycclan mærða] that "the great Macedonian Alexander commanded to be made" (sec. 2, p. 184). From this moment forward, Alexander's presence could be said to hover over the *Wonders* text as an absent yet imposing force who suddenly appears, in a vigorously present past tense, as the executioner of the giant women whom, we are told, he could not capture *alive* [he hi lifiende gefon ne mihte] (sec. 27, p. 200), indicating their position outside any epistemology of knowledge or technique of subjugation: they are "disturbing hybrids whose externally incoherent bodies resist attempts to include them in any systematic structuration."[47] They can be killed, but they cannot be caught (known), which might be another way of saying, they cannot be *penetrated* in the same way that Alexander penetrates, in the *Letter*, the *innanwearde* [innermost part] of India (sec. 9, p. 228). In this respect, it is also worth noting that they apparently live without men.

Although the Alexander of classical and medieval legend, much like the Hercules of the *Liber Monstrorum*, "traveled in battles through almost the entire world, and spattered the earth with so much blood" [paene totum orbem cum bellis peragrasset et terram tanto sanguine maculauisset] (sec. 12, p. 267), the Alexander of the *Letter* seems more intent on "beholding" [sceawigað] the spectacle of "wondrous creatures" [wunderlice wyhta] (sec. 3, p. 226) than he is on killing them, unless they attack first. This is the case when a great multitude of *Cynocephali* (dog-headed men) emerge from the woods with the intent of harming Alexander and his men, to which they respond by shooting them with arrows until they "departed back into the forest" (sec. 29, p. 224). This is not to say that the Alexander of the *Letter* is a somehow gentler, kinder Alexander—far from it. He mentions several battles with foreign armies (there is no kingdom he is not intent on subduing), and he often vents his violent fury at those who serve under his command. After a harrowing night spent at a lake battling hordes of attacking animals, even though he himself had requested that his guides take him by the dangerous and not the safe paths (sec. 9, p. 228), he orders that the guides who led him to such travails be "tied up and their bones and legs broken, so that they would be swallowed in the night by the serpents" (sec. 22, p. 238). But when it comes to certain monstrous "peoples," who are more like local tribes or subpopulations within the kingdoms Alexander is always seeking to topple and absorb as part of his world domination campaign, he seems more intent on what might be called scientific observation than murder and conquest. In the case of the nine-feet-tall naked women and men who are as "shaggy and hairy as wild beasts," and who can snatch whales out of the rivers and eat them, Alexander writes that he wanted to take a closer look and observe them, but they "immediately fled into the water and hid themselves in stony hollows" (sec. 29, p. 242). This Alexander—the explorer and seeker of marvels who desires to *see* the innermost parts of India and who often lets strange creatures run away without pursuing them to the death (and whose narrative persona as a letter writer, in part, is that of the student of a famous teacher)—provides a striking contrast to the Alexander of the *Wonders* who kills the thirteen-foot-tall women "on account of their giant-ness" [for heora micelness],[48] because he could not capture them alive, and because they are "shameful and unworthy in their bodies."

It has to be admitted that the Alexander of the *Wonders* who would kill an entire race because he could not capture one (or more) of them was likely very recognizable to an Anglo-Saxon audience familiar with the Alexander of the Old English *Orosius* who is described there as *se swelgend*—according to Bosworth-Toller, "voracious person" or "glutton," but also, more fittingly in this case, "a place which swallows up, a very deep place, an abyss, a gulf, a whirlpool."[49] In some of the many Continental texts that likely served as exemplars in the transmission of manuscripts leading to the Anglo-Latin *Wonders*, and that still retain something of the original epistolary framework of the *Letter of Pharasmanes* (which pointedly does *not* include mention of the murder of these women, who are described, for all of their animal characteristics, as *specioso corpore* [beautiful in their bodies]), it is remarked that, "The writer desired to look at them, [and] some were killed by three of our comrades because they could not capture them alive." In one manuscript, it indicates that the women fought for a long time and were able to escape.[50] Because the Old English text simply states, in two instances, "hie gefelde wurdon" and "acwealde he hi" [they were killed and he killed them] (sec. 27, p. 200), Alexander therefore killed the entire tribe, or at least whoever of that tribe was visible to him and within reach (although it is amusing to speculate how Alexander killed a entire tribe or race of women whom he supposedly could *not* capture—the implication would seem to be that this tribe of women were such violent fighters that they could not be subdued without retaliatory violence of equal force). In the Latin text included in the Tiberius and Bodleian manuscripts, we are told, "many of them were killed" [multae ex ipsis ceciderunt].[51] Therefore, by the time the *Wonders* text gets transcribed into three early English manuscripts, the number of women killed is either "all" or "many," indicating not the sport of hunting one or two of an exotic species but the wholesale slaughter of a group. Nevertheless, within the created world of the *Wonders* text, which seems mainly constructed around objective and nonjudgmental scenes of fleeting glimpses of foreign Others (and within which scenes, many of the creatures are even described as "shy" or "soft-voiced" or so afraid of intruders they run away when approached), this slaughter is striking in its sudden violence that literally appears from somewhere else (the tradition of Alexandrian romance), and yet could almost be argued to have been called forth by the women's unruly and perhaps too-masculine and hypersexual bodies.

Because we know that there are many bodies in the *Wonders* text that combine human and animal features and that could be thought perverse by an Anglo-Saxon author or reader, yet do not require violent elimination (including the men who give birth in sec. 11), what sets these women apart might be said to be their first-introduced characteristic: they are *wif* [women] first of all, and woman is a term that, historically, has always marked the terrain of the *too queer*. As Elizabeth Grosz writes,

> The metaphorics of uncontrollability, the ambivalence between deep, fatal attraction and strong revulsion, the deep-seated fear of absorption, the association of femininity with contagion and disorder, the undecidability of the limits of the female body…, its powers of cynical seduction and allure are all common themes in literary and cultural representations of women.[52]

The readers of the Old English *Wonders* may very well have been drawn to the image of these women as both frightening and attractive, leading to feelings of both sexual desire (or sexual astonishment), followed by feelings of violent revulsion, the relief of which (through dark enjoyment) might have been provided by Alexander's decisive act of execution. The illustrations in the Vitellius and Tiberius manuscripts bear out the idea that the text was disturbing enough to produce wildly divergent accompanying images. According to Kathryn Powell, whereas the Tiberius illustrator sought to minimize the animal characteristics (the hooves and tusks are present, but quite small) and to emphasize the woman's beautiful and slender naked body (which is modestly covered by her long hair, but revealing enough to be enticing, albeit lacking any hint of breasts and therefore androgynous), the Vitellius illustrator emphasizes a figure "who is only recognizable as a woman by virtue of her partially exposed breasts" and who is thick and muscular and intimidating in her giantness.[53] Further, as Dana Oswald has described the Vitellius illustration, the body parts are "exaggerated": "Her lips are extremely full, and perhaps even red, unlike any other figure in the manuscript. Her breasts are bulbous and reach down to the split of her legs, all of her sexual parts thus seeming to incorporate one another." Conversely, in the Tiberius illustration, the artist "seems to be at pains to simultaneously conceal and reveal this body....Though the woman's chest faces us, she crosses her arms across it, curling her fingers around the locks of hair on either side of her torso." Further, "[t]he hair cascades over her rotated hips, flowing around her exposed buttocks, and between the cross of her legs."[54] Interestingly, the figure judged most "feminine" (Powell) and "delicate" (Oswald) in Tiberius, combines both conventionally feminine (curved hips and buttocks) and conventionally masculine (no breasts, boy-like torso) features—if this woman is attractive, it is partly because her physiognomy is androgynous, or at least bisexed, whereas the woman drawn in the Vitellius manuscript is threatening precisely because the markers of her femaleness (her breasts) are so large, so monstrously out of proportion. In addition, whereas the woman in Tiberius is positioned fully within the frame and turning away to the right (a sign of modesty, perhaps, or some kind of come-on?), the woman in Vitellius is standing with her full body facing forward, her head and hooves extending outside of the frame, and is holding a tri-pointed club (a detail notably absent in the text), making her even more frightening in her imperiousness. To be monstrous in this scenario is not so much to be a mixture of mismatched human and animal body parts (gendered and otherwise) as it is to be *too much* of one thing: *wif*, or woman, while also striking an aggressive pose.

There is something more, too, in both of these illustrations that points to the discomfort both illustrators may have felt when drawing this woman's body: the "ox-tail" [*oxan tægl*], which very clearly, according to the text, is attached "on the loins" [*on lendenum*].[55] As Ann Knock has pointed out, the compiler of the tenth-century *Liber Monstrorum* (believed by both Knock and Andy Orchard to have used the Latin *Wonders* as one of his sources) was squeamish enough about this detail to change *in lumbis* [on the loins] to the euphemistic *in lateribus* [on the side or flank]. Although the Tiberius illustrator had the Latin *in lumbis* and Old English *on lendenum* right in front of him (although, admittedly, he may have been following an exemplar illustration and not the text), he chose to place the tail directly on the woman's left posterior, near the anus, where it is more animal-like and less sexual. In the Vitellius illustration it is difficult to determine at first if the ox-tail is even present, but if you examine the image carefully, it is clear that the tail *is* present, protruding from the woman's right leg, near her hip, and curving downward behind her leg, near the knee, where it joins the long hair flowing behind her back. The outlines of this tail, at the top, stray dangerously close to where the woman's breasts meet her genital area. Because the illustrators for both manuscripts clearly chose to revise the textual directions for the placement of the ox-tail, it would appear they had some anxiety about this feature of the image, and sought to subtly revise it. As Oswald writes, the bodies of these women "imply a kind of action that is far more transgressive than just exceeding human norms. This action is communicated through the possession of a tail, but even more explicitly through the rupture between the artists' rendering of the tail and the writers' words describing it."[56]

The race of women with ox-tails *on lendenum* may have presented, both for the readers of the manuscript as well as for the fictional Alexander and the author who created him in language, an image of a figure too perverse, *too abject*, which, in Kristeva's words, "takes the ego back to its source on the abominable limits from which, in order to be, the ego has broken away."[57] In this scenario, Alexander's murder of the animal-human women would be the natural outcome of Alexander's (and the author's) sudden recognition of the fragility of the subject's "own and clean self,"[58] which would need to be purified by some violent means. That an Anglo-Saxon readership could have understood such a notion is explained by Powell in an analysis of this instance of literary extermination in the *Wonders* text alongside the St. Brice's Day Massacre of 1002, when, as the *Anglo-Saxon Chronicle* records, "the king [Æthelred] commanded that all the Danish men who were among the English be slain...because the king was informed that they wished to ensnare his life, and afterwards all of his counselors, and afterwards have this kingdom."[59] As regards the racialized violence of the attacks (a violence, moreover, that always seeks bodily purity through the elimination of supposedly impure elements), a charter of 1004 from the monastery of St. Frideswide at Oxford records that a certain group of Danes, who had "sprung up" in England like "cockle amongst the wheat," had been forced to flee to the barred church, the doors and bolts of which they broke by force to get inside, and once securely settled there, an angry mob of their neighbors set fire to the church, apparently burning the Danes inside, along with "its ornaments and books."[60] As Powell writes, "The behavior of the Anglo-Saxons on St. Brice's Day suggests that the Danes had become for the English a homogeneous Other who existed solely to deprive them of their every enjoyment—life, land, wealth, and power—and who were unworthy of human sympathy."[61]

We might recall here that in the image of the giant women of the *Wonders* in the Vitellius manuscript, they are holding what looks to be a type of club, an object that would have denoted some type of threatening power for the audience of the manuscript (although no such detail is mentioned in the Old English text). And this threatening strength could have only been complicated by the gender of its wielder, which might have rendered the image both frightening and attractive simultaneously. As Powell explains, the Old English word *æwisce* [shameful], used to describe the women's bodies, "is sometimes used to describe female temptresses, most notably of Eve in *Genesis*, who is called 'ides æwiscmod' [ashamed woman; line 896] after she has enticed Adam to eat the forbidden fruit."[62] The image in the Vitellius manuscript, as well as the Old English text that accompanies it, would appear to work together to construct a moment of "unraveling transference...of love/hatred for the other,"[63] leading to definitive act of "ecstatic destructiveness" that, in the terms set forth by Leo Bersani and Ulysse Dutoit, reading Freud's *Civilization and Its Discontents*, is "ultimately unanalysable":

> It can't be interpretively reduced or reformulated; individual histories are irrelevant to it, as is perhaps history *tout court*....It is postulated as a universal property of the human psyche, something as species-specific as the human aptitude for verbal language....*Jouissance* is without psychological causation; it is the final cause of our desires, the cause (in Lacanian terms) to which no object of our desire ever corresponds.[64]

But if *jouissance*—this dark enjoyment that threatens individuals and whole societies—is a pleasure "beyond pleasure" (in Lacan's terms), can there be a *jouissance* beyond *jouissance*, something that might, in the words of Bersani and Dutoit, "play to the side of it, supplement it with a pleasure at once less intense and more seductive"?[65] The question here would be how to move beyond, or to the side, of the dark poetics of cultural identity in which the figures of unimpregnable and hypersexual female bodies have to be violently evacuated while also being instituted as a sacred-obscene threshold to *natio*, much like the Egyptian Danaïdes of ancient Greek legend whose aggressive refusal to marry their cousins led to their exile in Argos and then their execution, with the eternal punishment of bearing water in jars perforated like sieves to a bottomless cistern.

An Otherness Barely Touched upon and That Already Moves Away

Although we know from both the Latin and Old English texts of the Anglo-Saxon *Wonders* that Alexander "killed" [*ceciderunt* and *acwealde*, past tense] *many* or *all* of the giant women with ox-tails on their loins, this threatening race of women are first introduced to the reader in the present tense—"Then there *are* other women who *have* boar's tusks" [Ðonne *sindon* oðre wif ða *habbað* eoferes tucxas]—and therefore they are always simultaneously killed and still palpably *out there somewhere*, threatening the reader in their monstrous present-ness. Indeed, in all the moments of reading this Old English text, past and present, these women haunt history as *still there*, still too queer, too unsubordinated, and always looming, dangerously, in their unruly sex that threatens to collapse the border between same and different, self and Other. Moreover, these fictional women stand alongside the real women who were mutilated and murdered in Gujarat, where together they mark the place, which is also the boneyard, of something that has always been an ineluctable fact of human existence: the essential volatility of bodies, of biology and culture, and of the fear, loathing, and hatred this impassable condition of history calls forth. And the ethical task that this imposes on us, in Kristeva's formulation, would be to "not seek to solidify, to turn the otherness" of these bodies "into a thing," but to merely "touch it, brush by it, without giving it a permanent structure." This would be the very Otherness that the *Wonders* texts, in its grammar, has already inscribed for us and invites us to marvel at—one that is "barely touched upon and that already moves away."[66]

As Bersani and Dutoit argue, if there is to be "a *jouissance* beyond *jouissance*," we must overcome "the illusion of disconnectedness," an illusion that "makes of the external world...an always potentially dangerous enemy of the self." Since "*jouissance* 'rewards' the illusion of having abolished the distance, and the difference, between the subject and the world," perhaps the alternative "dark enjoyment" would be to allow ourselves to be so "extraordinarily receptive to the being of the world," that even in the midst of war and slaughter itself, in a willed moment of "ontological passivity," of marveling and wondering at the shining strangeness of the world, we could be "shattered by it...shattered in order to be recycled as allness." This shattering might be our "truest human ripeness,"[67] as well as an ecstasy that would lose itself in a marvelous relationality without discernible borders. In this scenario, there would be no city-states, no nations, and no heroic individuals, only wonders.

Notes

The completion of this chapter would not have been possible without the generous assistance of the Newberry Library Center for Renaissance Studies, who funded my travel to the Library in winter 2007 to participate in Susan

Kim's Graduate Consortium Seminar, "Unworthy Bodies: The Other Texts of the *Beowulf* Manuscript." My thanks also to Dana Oswald for generously sharing portions of her dissertation with me while she was still writing it.

1. Michel de Certeau, *The Possession at Loudon*, trans. Michael B. Smith (Chicago: University of Chicago Press, 1972), 227.

2. Certeau, *The Possession at Loudon*, 1.

3. Elizabeth Grosz, *Volatile Bodies: Toward a Corporeal Feminism* (Bloomington: Indiana University Press, 1994), 203.

4. William Ian Miller, *The Anatomy of Disgust* (Cambridge, MA: Harvard University Press, 1997), 204.

5. Dominick LaCapra, *History and Memory after Auschwitz* (Ithaca: Cornell University Press, 1998), 38.

6. LaCapra, *History and Memory After Auschwitz*, 29n19; see also Saul Friedlander, *Memory, History, and the Extermination of the Jews* (Bloomington: Indiana University Press, 1993), 109–15.

7. Certeau, *The Possession at Loudon*, 1.

8. Paul Strohm, *Theory and the Premodern Text* (Minneapolis: University of Minnesota Press, 2000), 93.

9. Andy Orchard, *Pride and Prodigies: Studies in the Monsters of the Beowulf-Manuscript* (Toronto: Toronto University Press, 1995), sec. 27, p. 200. Citations of the Old English and Latin *Wonders*, the Old English *Letter of Alexander to Aristotle* (contained in the Vitellius A.xv manuscript), as well as to the *Liber Monstrorum*, will be to Orchard's editions of these texts (included as appendices in *Pride and Prodigies*), parenthetically, by section and page numbers. All translations, unless otherwise noted, are mine.

10. Jeffrey Jerome Cohen, *Of Giants: Sex, Monsters, and the Middle Ages* (Minneapolis: University of Minnesota Press, 1999), 46 and 49.

11. W.G. Sebald, "An Attempt at Resitution," trans. Anthea Bell, *The New Yorker*, December 20 and 27, 2004: 112 [110–14].

12. Jeffrey Jerome Cohen, *Medieval Identity Machines* (Minneapolis: University of Minnesota, 2003), 9.

13. "Performing the Prioress: 'Conscience' and Responsibility in Studies of Chaucer's Prioress's Tale," *Texas Studies in Language and Literature* 44.1 (Spring 2002): 69 [66–91].

14. Calabrese, "Performing the Prioress," 71.

15. Françoise Meltzer, "Future? What Future?" *Critical Inquiry* 30 (2004): 469 [468–71].

16. For a full accounting and analysis of the details of the Gujarat genocide and its aftermath, see International Initiative for Justice-Gujarat (IIJ), *Threatened Existence: A Feminist Analysis of the Genocide in Gujarat*, December 2003, available at http://www.onlinevolunteers.org/gujarat/reports/iijg/2003/ (hereafter referred to as *Threatened Existence*); Smita Narula, *"We Have No Orders to Save You": State Participation and Complicity in Communal Violence in Gujarat*, *Human Rights Watch Reports* 14.3(C) (April 2002): 1–68, available at http://www.hrw.org/reports/2002/india/ (hereafter referred to as

We Have No Orders); and Siddharth Varadarajan, ed., *Gujarat: The Making of a Tragedy* (New Delhi, India: Penguin Books, 2002).

17. For a full accounting of the Ghodra incident, see Jyoti Punwani, "The Carnage at Ghodra," in *Gujarat: The Making of a Tragedy*, ed. Varadarajan, 45–74. See also Martha Nussbaum, *The Clash Within: Democracy, Religious Violence, and India's Future* (Cambridge, MA: Harvard University Press, 2007), 33–36.

18. On this point, see Siddharth Varadarajan, "Chronicle of a Tragedy Foretold," in *Gujarat: The Making of a Tragedy*, ed. Varadarajan, 5–10 [3–41].

19. On this point, see Nandini Sundar, "A License to Kill: Patterns of Violence in Gujarat," in *Gujarat: The Making of a Tragedy*, ed. Varadarajan, 75–134.

20. Martha Nussbaum, "Body of the Nation: Why Women Were Mutilated in Gujarat," *The Boston Review* 29.3 (2004), <http://www.bostonreview.net/BR29.3/Nussbaum.html> accessed on October 11, 2004. See also Martha Nussbaum, "Genocide in Gujarat: The International Community Looks Away," *Dissent* (Summer 2003): 61–69.

21. Testimony of Javed Hussain, fourteen-year-old survivor of the Gujarat massacre; quoted in "Narratives from the Killing Fields," in *Gujarat: The Making of a Tragedy*, ed. Varadarajan, 138 [135–76].

22. *Threatened Existence*, 8.

23. Flavia Agnes, "Affidavit," in *Of Lofty Claims and Muffled Voices*, ed. Flavia Agnes (Bombay, India: Majlis, 2002), 69.

24. Tanika Sarkar, "Semiotics of Terror: Muslim Women and Children in Hindu Rashtra," *Economic and Political Weekly*, July 13, 2002: 2872–76; quoted in *Threatened Existence*, 26.

25. Nussabaum, "Body of the Nation."

26. Nussbaum, *Hiding from Humanity*, 112.

27. Anne McClintock, "'No Longer in a Future Heaven': Gender, Race, and Nationalism," in *Dangerous Liaisons: Gender, Nation, and Postcolonial Perspectives*, ed. Anne McClintock, Aamir Mufti, and Ella Shohat (Minneapolis: University Press, 1997), 90 [89–112]. See also Nira Yuval-Davis and Floya Anthias, eds., *Women-Nation-State* (London: Macmillan, 1989), and Anne McClintock, *Imperial Leather: Race, Gender, and Sexuality in the Colonial Contest* (New York: Routledge, 1995).

28. Sarkar, "Semiotics of Terror"; quoted in Nussbaum, "Body of the Nation."

29. Quoted in *Threatened Existence*, 8.

30. On the Hindu right's fascist historicizing, see *Threatened Existence*, 17–24.

31. See Gyan Prakash, "Postcolonial Criticism and Indian Historiography," in McClintock et al., *Dangerous Liaisons*, 491–500, where he writes that "[h]istory and colonialism arose together in India. As India was introduced to history, it was also stripped of a meaningful past; it became a historyless society brought into the age of History" (499).

32. E.J. Hobsbawm, *Nations and Nationality Since 1780: Programme, Myth, Reality* (Cambridge: Cambridge University Press, 1990), 9. I am well aware of the extensive work undertaken in medieval studies to revise

Hobsbawm's idea of the nation-state as exclusively modern; on this point, see especially Jeffrey Jerome Cohen, "Introduction: Midcolonial," in *The Postcolonial Middle Ages*, ed. Jeffrey Jerome Cohen (New York: St. Martin's Press, 2000), 1–17; Kathleen Davis, "National Writing in the Ninth Century: A Reminder for Postcolonial Thinking about the Nation," *Journal of Medieval and Early Modern Studies* 28 (1998): 611–37; Bruce Holsinger, "Medieval Studies, Postcolonial Studies and the Genealogies of Critique," *Speculum* 77 (2002): 1195–1227; and Ananya Jahanara Kabir and Deanne Williams, "Introduction: A Return to Wonder," in *Postcolonial Approaches to the European Middle Ages: Translating Cultures*, ed. Ananya Jahanara Kabir and Deanne Williams (Cambridge, UK: Cambridge University Press, 2005), 1–21.

33. The full quotation is, "Place is the beginning of our existence, just as a father" (Roger Bacon, *The Opus Majus of Roger Bacon*, trans. Robert Belle Burke [New York, 1962] 159).

34. *The Wonders of the East* survives in three richly illustrated copies in medieval English manuscripts: in Old English in British Library, Cotton Vitellius A.xv (fols. 98v–106v), dating to the late tenth century, in Old English with facing Latin in British Library, Cotton Tiberius B.v (fols. 78v–87r), dating to the eleventh century, and in Latin in Oxford, Bodleian Library (fols. 36r–48r), from the twelfth century. According to Andy Orchard, the Anglo-Saxon versions of the *Wonders* "derive ultimately from a text represented in mainly continental manuscripts in many different forms, almost all of which share a basic epistolary framework, in which either a character variously named Feramen, Feramus, or Fermes writes to the emperor Hadrian (A.D. 117–38), or a figure called Premo, Premonis, Perimenis, or Parmoenis writes to Hadrian's predecessor, the Emperor Trajan (A.D. 98–116), to report on the many marvels he has witnessed on his travels" (*Pride and Prodigies*, 22–23).

35. Mary Campbell, *The Witness and the Other World: Exotic European Travel Writing, 400–1600* (Ithaca: Cornell University Press, 1988), 82.

36. Susan Kim, "The Donestre and the Person of Both Sexes," in *Naked Before God: Uncovering the Body in Anglo-Saxon England*, ed. Benjamin C. Withers and Jonathan Wilcox (Morgantown: West Virginia University Press, 2003), 165 [162–80].

37. Asa Simon Mittman, *Maps and Monsters in Medieval England* (New York and London: Routledge, 2006), 80.

38. Susan Stewart, *On Longing: Narratives of the Miniature, the Gigantic, the Souvenir, the Collection* (Durham and London: Duke University Press, 1993), 151 and 152.

39. Cohen, *Of Giants*, 84.

40. Nicholas Howe, "Historicist Approaches," in *Reading Old English Texts*, ed. Katherine O'Brien O'Keeffe (Cambridge, UK: Cambridge University Press, 1997), 93 [79–100]. See also Martin Irvine, *The Making of Textual Culture: 'Grammatica' and Literary Theory, 350–1100* (Cambridge, UK: Cambridge University Press, 1994), esp. 272–460.

41. On this point, see Mittman, *Maps and Monsters in Medieval England*, 39–59; Kathy Lavezzo, *Angels on the Edge of the World: Geography, Literature, and English Community* (Ithaca: Cornell University Press, 2006), 27–31; and Martin K. Foys, "The Virtual Reality of the Anglo-Saxon *Mappamundi*," *Literature Compass* 1 (2003): n.p. [online journal]; available at <http://www.literaturecompass.com>.

42. Susan M. Kim, "Man-Eating Monsters and Ants as Big as Dogs: The Alienated Language of the Cotton Vitellius A.xv *Wonders of the East*," in *Animals and the Symbolic in Medieval Art and Literature*, ed. L.A.J.R. Houwen (Groningen: Egbert Forsten, 1997), 40 [38–51].

43. Nicholas Howe, "Historicist Approaches," 95.

44. Brian McFadden, "The Social Context of Narrative Disruption in *The Letter of Alexander to Aristotle*," *Anglo-Saxon England* 30 (2001): 91 [91–114].

45. Cohen, *Of Giants*, 59.

46. The black cannibals, with long legs and feet [sec. 13] might be considered another, albeit minor, instance of negative approbation on the author's part since their name, *hostes*, means "enemy."

47. Jeffrey Jerome Cohen, "Monster Culture (Seven Theses)," in *Monster Theory: Reading Culture*, ed. Jeffrey Jerome Cohen (Minneapolis: University of Minnesota Press, 1996), 6 [3–25].

48. The Latin text of the Tiberius and Bodleian manuscripts indicates *obscentitate* [obscenity], where the Old English translator has *mycelnesse* and *micelnesse*, respectively [giant-ness]. In his edition, E.V. Gordon emended this to *unclennesse* ("Old English Studies," *The Year's Work in Old English Studies* 5 [1924]: 66–72), an emendation Orchard follows in his edition. Although it may well be true that the compiler of the Old English *Wonders* made a mistake in copying *unclennesse*, I would argue that *micelnesse* is an apt substitute for the description of women who are thirteen feet tall, and we do not lose the meaning of their "obscene" bodies since the Old English translation still retains the phrase "æwisce on lichoman 7 unweorðe" [shameful and unworthy in (their) bodies].

49. Janet M. Bately, ed., *The Old English Orosius*, EETS s.s. 6 (London: Oxford University Press, 1980), 66.7.

50. See Ann Knock, "*Wonders of the East*: A Synoptic Edition of the *Letter of Pharasmenes* and the Old English and Old Picard Translations," Ph.D. dissertation, University of London, 1982, 749–62.

51. Orchard, *Pride and Prodigies*, 180.

52. Grosz, *Volatile Bodies*, 203.

53. Kathryn Powell, "The Anglo-Saxon Imaginary of the East: A Psychoanalytic Exploration of the Image of the East in Old English Literature," Ph.D. dissertation, University of Notre Dame, 2001, 151.

54. Dana Oswald, "Indecent Bodies: Gender and the Monstrous in Medieval English Literature," Ph.D. dissertation, Ohio State University, 2005.

55. Orchard, *Pride and Prodigies*, sec. 27, p. 200. This is borne out in the Latin version of the *Wonders* text found in the Tiberius and Bodleian

manuscripts, where we find *in lumbis caudas boum*. It is further significant that, in classical Latin, *caudas* can often stand in for "penis."

56. Oswald, "Indecent Bodies."

57. Julia Kristeva, *Powers of Horror: An Essay on Abjection*, trans. Leon S. Roudiez (New York: Columbia University Press, 1982), 15.

58. Kristeva, *Powers of Horror*, 53.

59. Rositzke, Harry August, ed., *The C-Text of the Old English Chronicles* (Bochum-Langendreer: Heinrich Pöppinghaus, 1940), 55–56. According to Simon Keynes, Æthelred's order was likely not directed against the Danes who were already well established for over a hundred years in the Danelaw and therefore were fully assimilated, but rather was probably "directed against the Danes who had recently settled in various parts of England, whether as traders, as mercenaries, or even simply as paid-off and provisioned members of the armies that had been ravaging the kingdom" (*The Diplomas of King Æthelred the Unready, 978–1016: A Study in Their Use as Historical Evidence* [Cambridge, UK: Cambridge University Press, 1980] 204).

60. Dorothy Whitelock, ed., *English Historical Documents I, c. 500–1042*, 2nd ed. (New York: Oxford University Press, 1979), 591.

61. Powell, "The Anglo-Saxon Imaginary of the East," 157.

62. Powell, "The Anglo-Saxon Imaginary of the East," 160.

63. Kristeva, *Strangers to Ourselves*, trans. Leon S. Roudiez (New York: Columbia University Press, 1991), 182.

64. Leo Bersani and Ulysse Dutoit, *Forms of Being: Cinema, Aesthetics, Subjectivity* (London: British Film Institute, 2004), 126–27.

65. Bersani and Dutoit, *Forms of Being*, 127.

66. Kristeva, *Strangers to Ourselves*, 3.

67. Bersani and Dutoit, *Forms of Being*, 175–76, 177.

CONTRIBUTORS

Suzanne Conklin Akbari is Associate Professor of English and Medieval Studies at the University of Toronto. She has published a book on optics and allegory, titled *Seeing Through the Veil* (2004), and recently completed the manuscript of *Idols in the East: European Representations of Islam and the Orient, 1100–1450*. Akbari has also coedited the forthcoming *Marco Polo and the Encounter of East and West*, and is at work on another collection titled *The Persistence of Philology: Rethinking the Arabic Role in Medieval Literary History*.

Kathleen Biddick is Professor of History at Temple University, Philadelphia. Her most recent book is *The Typological Imaginary: Circumcision, Technology, History* published by the University of Pennsylvania Press. Her current research is devoted to the question of the political theology of the archive.

Heather Blurton is a lecturer in the Department of English and Centre for Medieval Studies at the University of York. Her book, *Cannibalism in High Medieval English Literature*, also appears in the New Middle Ages series.

Jeffrey Jerome Cohen is Professor and Chair of the Department of English of the George Washington University. His previous books include *Hybridity, Identity and Monstrosity in Medieval Britain: On Difficult Middles*; *Medieval Identity Machines*; and *Of Giants: Sex, Monsters, and the Middle Ages*. He is the editor of the collections *Thinking the Limits of the Body*; *The Postcolonial Middle Ages*; *Becoming Male in the Middle Ages*; and *Monster Theory: Reading Culture*. His work has also appeared in *Exemplaria*, *Speculum*, and the *Journal of Medieval and Early Modern Studies*.

John M. Ganim is Professor of English at the University of California, Riverside. His most recent book is *Medievalism and Orientalism: Three Essays on Literature, Architecture and Cultural Identity* published in 2005 by Palgrave. He has served as President of the New Chaucer Society from 2006–2008.

Eileen A. Joy is Assistant Professor and Director of Graduate Studies in English at Southern Illinois University Edwardsville. She is the coeditor of *The Postmodern Beowulf: A Critical Casebook* and *Cultural Studies of the Modern Middle Ages*, as well as the author of numerous articles on Old English literature, ethical philosophy, and cultural studies.

Randy P. Schiff is an Assistant Professor in the English Department at SUNY Buffalo. He has published an essay on anti-feudalism in Kurosawa, as well as encyclopedia articles on Anglo-Scottish conflict and on the Pre-Raphaelites, and is currently at work on a manuscript, *Revivalist Fantasy: Alliteration and Opposition, Medieval and Medievalist*.

Katherine H. Terrell is Assistant Professor of English at Hamilton College. She has published essays on Chaucer and the *Pearl*-poet, and is currently working on a book exploring the continuities between poetry and chronicle in the creation of medieval Scottish identity.

David Townsend is Professor of Medieval Studies and English at the University of Toronto. His verse translation of the *Alexandreis* of Walter of Châtillon was reissued by Broadview in 2007. His edition of a fourteenth-century commentary on the *Alexandreis* is forthcoming in the Toronto Medieval Latin Texts, of which series he serves as a general editor. He has published numerous readings of Medieval Latin texts that bring together close philological analysis with categories borrowed from queer and postcolonial theory.

Jon Kenneth Williams is a doctoral student in the Department of English and Comparative Literature at Columbia University.

Michael Wenthe was trained in medieval literature at Duke, Harvard, Oxford, and Yale. His primary research interest involves the staging of othering and difference as expressed in the polyglot, international literature of King Arthur, and his current book project has the working title *Arthurian Outsiders: The Dynamic of Difference in the Matter of Britain*. He is an Assistant Professor in the Department of Literature at American University.

INDEX